SURRENDER AND TRUST

A DEVOTIONAL JOURNEY
BOOK ONE

SURRENDER AND TRUST

A DEVOTIONAL JOURNEY
BOOK ONE

By DAVID THURMAN
with Pastor Daniel Martin

Printed by KDP Publishing, an Amazon.com company

Available on Amazon.com and other online stores

ISBN-13: 978-0-9990492-4-2

THE CALL Logo and cover contribution by Mary Thurman

Author's Note: Although a few illustrations may be allegorical, most of the stories in this book are true. Pseudonyms have been used for some persons in order to protect their privacy.

DEDICATION

Love never fails (1 Cor. 13:8)

TABLE OF CONTENTS

SECTION I – FAITH, HOPE, AND LOVE

SECTION II - SURRENDER

PRELIMINARY MATTERS FOR YOUR DEVOTIONAL JOURNEY

(Please read this instructional section before you begin the devotions)

This devotional book may not be for you. This devotional is not a "5 minutes a day for a lift" type devotional. This devotional is not a "shot of encouragement," "feel better about yourself," and "brighten your day" type devotional. This devotional is a spend time to "dig deeply," "draw closer," "pursue holiness," and "walk the way of the Cross" type devotional. This devotional points toward fullness and spiritual maturity.

Use of this devotional book can change your life. This book can't change your life. But the Holy Spirit working in you and around you as you journey through this devotional book can transform your existence. This book is a tool for spiritual growth.

This devotional has a specific purpose. It is written for young men and women who are serious about their faith, are considering full-time ministry, and who have a strong desire for a deeper walk with the Lord. In other words, this devotional is written for believers who are willing to make a commitment of time, service, and sacrifice to grow in the Lord and to pursue their destiny in Him.

For years, my coworkers and I have been developing a ministry training program for young people in the form of a residency. The residency programs offer instruction and ministry training while the residents seek God about His call and purpose for their lives. As part of the residency, we ask the residents to engage in a meaningful personal devotion each day. This devotional is written for use by the residents in their devotions.

One thing that we tell the residents is that you will get out of the residency what you put into it. This book can help you grow in the Lord and can open the door to a richer and deeper walk with the Lord. I strongly encourage you to step into it. But this devotional book is only a tool. The benefit you receive from the tool depends on how well you use it. This book will not mean much to you unless you are committed to participate in its devotions wholeheartedly and you engage in them meaningfully.

A. EXPECTATIONS

For many years, I had a "stop and go" devotional life. Occasionally, a sermon, a seminar, or a new methodology inspired me to set aside a quiet time, a prayer time, or a personal meditation time. The inspiration lasted a week or a month, but it fizzled. So my pattern was start and stop…start and stop…start and stop.

My expectations played a major role in this erratic pattern. My inspiration to start daily devotions came from strong encouragement that, during the devotional time, I would experience the thrill of a Holy Spirit unction, a deep movement of my soul, or brilliance from the illumination in my heart. Mind you, these things happen. But well intentioned as my commitment may have been, my expectation was based on what a devotional time would do for me. My expectation was fundamentally selfish.

The only expectation for devotional time is the Lord and only the Lord. If that means that I praise and worship the Lord for weeks but don't feel any great delight, so be it. I have worshipped the Lord. If that means that I wait for an hour each morning for 30 days and I sense nothing, so be it. I have waited for the Lord. The Lord knows what is best for each of us and He will give each of us what we need in His time. The name of this book is *Surrender and Trust*. I can trust my devotional time to Him as I surrender it to Him.

Each person will have different experiences. The Lord may meet you at the threshold of your devotions in a powerful and moving way. But even if you don't have that experience, I still submit one key expectation. If you commit meaningful time to the Lord each day and seek Him, it will bear fruit. It may be after a week, a month, or even three months, but one day a realization will hit you – a realization that says *"My heart has changed!"* If you present yourself to God each day to spend time with Him and to commune with Him, He will do a work in your heart. It may be subtle or it may be intense, but He will respond to your faithfulness.

B. <u>REASONS</u>

The reasons for a daily personal devotional time are so numerous, they cannot all be listed. But here are a few compelling reasons for devotions:

1. <u>Intimacy</u>. In life, we enter into intimacy through cultivated relationship. I get to know you; we spend time together; we share our experiences, our thoughts, and our history; we do things together; and we have disagreements and resolve them. As we do these things, our relationship moves to deeper and deeper levels until it reaches a point of intimacy. There is an intentionality to it.

A daily devotional time cultivates my relationship with the Lord. Through faithfulness in devotion, I develop depth of relationship unto intimacy.

2. <u>Heart Monitor</u>. My heart is not static. As I go through each day, my heart moves closer to the Lord and my heart moves further away from Him. A daily devotional time monitors the state of my heart each day and helps to adjust my heart to the right place to start the day. It is a form of "attitude adjustment."

A mature Christian has an awareness of God in his daily living. This awareness grows as the thoughts and intents of my heart are reviewed often.

3. Transformation. God's plan is that I change, grow, and mature unto fullness in Him. Through my devotional time, God changes me.

During my time with God, He shows me sin, shame, dysfunctions, and other challenges in my life. I don't know they exist until I take time to seek Him and to expose myself to Him. He then lovingly helps me to address them and to grow.

God also shows me gifts and strengths that He has given me. He helps me to apply them in my life and in the lives of others. Through devotion, God reveals myself to me.

4. Illumination and Revelation. In my devotional time, God illuminates scripture to my heart. He makes a path from my head to my heart through which I don't just know scripture but it becomes a part of me. God instills wisdom inside of me.

God also gives me guidance which is direction from God that is specific to me or to others around me. In devotions, I seek God for His will and He answers in ways that I otherwise miss if I were not spending the time with Him.

5. Worship. There are many other reasons for devotions – peace, joy, encouragement, conviction, repentance, discipline, resource, seeking, waiting, knowledge, and creativity. But my existence is wrapped up in God. Devotions are fundamentally about Him and not about myself.

Worship occurs when I acknowledge God and Who He is. A devotional time takes my attention off of myself and places it on God. Through devotion, I place my attention on God and give Him the glory, honor, and praise which are due to Him.

See *Time With God* which follows this section for more reasons for a devotional life.

I. THREE MAJOR KEYS

As you enter into this journey, there are three major keys that facilitate the journey and enhance the impact of the journey. Please attend to these keys before you begin the journey because they will prove to be immensely helpful to you as you enter in.

A. TIME. The first key is to reserve time each day for your devotion. To reserve time, you need to rework your schedule and routine. Devotional time needs to be a priority! The primary devotion in devotions is the devotion of time.

Many of the devotions in this book incorporate the personal devotions of Pastor Daniel Martin, who is a pastor in Selma, Alabama. In 2011, God put it on Pastor Martin's heart to set aside an hour each day for prayer, seeking, and worship. As you read Pastor Martin's devotions, you realize the incredible impact on his life. Please be sure to read *My Story of an Hour With God* by Pastor Martin which follows this section.

The recommended time for daily devotions is an hour a day. But that can be goal if you are starting a devotional life. You can build toward it. A strong recommendation though is a <u>minimum</u> of 30 minutes a day. If you treat this devotional book as a "5 minute boost" then you will get 5 minutes of value from it. In fact, if you only have 5 minutes a day for devotions, there are many other devotional books that may be more valuable to you than this book as other books are written for that purpose. This devotional book is written for a more substantial devotional time.

B. COMPANION. The Biblical mandate for a spiritual journey is to take a companion – a coworker. A companion provides direction, accountability, protection, and encouragement. God did not intend for us to journey alone. In the kingdom of God, persons who function alone ("lone wolves") are actually vulnerable sheep and are prime targets for slaughter.

Going on this devotional journey with a similarly committed companion is the second key to this journey and it is a <u>strong</u> recommendation. Each person has individual devotional time each day, then meets with the companion regularly (recommendation: weekly if possible) to discuss the devotions, thoughts and experiences, issues, and insights, and to pray together.

As part of The Call ministry residency, each resident is assigned a mentor who serves as a guide, a teacher, a resource, and a coworker. If you do not have a mentor (or a spiritual director or guide) who can journey alongside you, find a friend or a peer whom you trust to do it. Both persons will benefit from the journey together. Accountability relationships are vital in the Christian walk and they will be discussed later in this book.

It is also possible to go through this journey together with a small group. Because intimacy and vulnerability are encouraged though, the group needs to be close, trustworthy, and accountable to one another. An atmosphere of freedom, grace, and acceptance is essential.

C. JOURNAL. The third key to this devotional journey is to keep a daily journal of your devotional time. A journal assists in defining thoughts, recording experiences, and remembering important principles and applications. A regular review of the journal is a good reminder of things I have learned, seen, and applied.

This book has some places for notes and for thoughts. But these places are not intended to serve as a journal. My primary recommendation is to maintain a computer journal in a word processing file. A computer journal is in one place and it can be easily revised, expanded, or printed.

The personal devotions of Pastor Martin were written on a computer. Pastor Martin revisited his devotions regularly as a personal reminder to himself and to add to them. He reviewed his devotions monthly, and then often revisited them a year later. Many times he added to them. Sometimes he wrote summaries of a week or a month to remind himself to practice their applications. If the Lord was dealing with him in a certain area of his life, he came back to the same journal entry day after day. Pastor Martin's wonderful devotions are available to us today because he faithfully kept a journal of them on his computer.

Some people prefer to write rather than to type. That also is fine. But please keep a daily journal whether it is in digital form or in written form.

II. THE DAILY DEVOTIONAL TRACK

A. PREPARATION. The manner in which you approach devotional time each day is important. Suggested steps for preparation are:

1. Eliminate Distractions. Find a place of privacy and quiet for your time with God. You are alone with Him. Turn off cell phones, televisions, or other devices that may serve as distractions. Your goal is *uninterrupted* time with God.

2. Submission. Take steps to submit your heart to God. You are entering His Presence. One way to aid submission is a brief time of worship. Another way to submit is simply to focus on God and to love Him. Exalt Him by acknowledging Who He is or by recalling on one or more of His attributes. A third way is by physical expression such as bowing before Him.

3. Be organic. One purpose of devotional time is to cultivate intimacy with God. If you have something pressing on your heart – such as a burden or a joy - take it straight to God. God may have business that He wants to do straightaway. Your emotions can be an impetus for intimacy, or they can be a harmful distraction. Use discernment, but have freedom to go straight to God. Turn your heart toward God.

If the Lord puts a sin or offense on your heart, confess it to Him, repent, and receive forgiveness. Endeavor to tear down any walls in your heart that may hinder your time with God. Seek His presence with grace and joy.

B. HEADINGS. Each devotion has a heading which shows the section, the week and day, and the topic of the week. *Surrender and Trust* at the time of publication has four major sections of 13 weeks each (52 weeks total). The sections are:

BOOK ONE

Section I – Faith, Hope, and Love

Section II – Surrender

BOOK TWO

Section III – Trust

Section IV – Power and Glory

Each week has a different topic that is covered. The topic for the week is shown in the heading.

Please note that the date in the heading of each devotion is blank. The date is blank so that the reader can begin the devotional journey at any point in the year. Some devotional books start with January 1, but our residency programs begin at different times of the year. So your journey can begin when you are ready.

Please write the date of each daily devotion in this blank when you do the devotion.

C. SCRIPTURE. Below the heading of each devotion is the scripture for the day. Every person reads scripture differently, but the primary goal is to incorporate the scripture in such a way that it becomes reality in your heart and in your life.

Please read the scripture carefully and slowly. Some people like to read the scripture quickly, and then go back and read it slowly. That is fine. Other people like to read repetitively – reading the scripture multiple times to allow it to sink in. The manner in which you read scripture is fine as long as you allow time for the Holy Spirit to speak through the scripture or to highlight certain portions of it to you.

Note your feelings as you read the scripture. Sometimes I am drawn toward the scripture in a positive way. Other times I don't feel good about what the scripture says. Attraction or repulsion toward scripture is important for discernment. It may say something about my heart or about my thought process. Try to discern the reason for these movements if they occur.

Other times you may be struck by, or drawn toward, a certain theme, phrase, or even a word in the scripture. If that occurs, take time to dwell on it. Allow the Holy Spirit to quicken that portion to you and to illuminate it divinely to your heart.

D. THEME/ILLUSTRATION. In most devotions, a one line theme will appear below the scripture passage followed by an illustration (in bold) such as a story, a quote, or most often, a personal devotion of Pastor Martin. Pay attention to the theme and illustration as they provide guidance for the devotion. But you are not bound by them. If the Holy Spirit prompts you to focus on a different theme or aspect from the scripture, that is fine.

E. APPLICATION. The body of the devotion is the application. The application is one or more points about the theme for the day. Carefully consider these points as you read them.

F. MEDITATION. The end of the devotion is a suggested meditation. The focus and method of the meditation will vary. Setting aside a block of time (at least 10-15 minutes) each day for the meditation is recommended. Use the meditation for a time of quiet and of listening to the Holy Spirit.

Then be sure to write in your journal thoughts, insights, questions, movements, or applications that you received during the devotion. Although your feelings are not your guidepost, your feelings can be instructive so record your feelings during the devotion.

G. REVIEW. Every seventh day is a review day. This day is a chance to go back over the past week and review what the Lord has been doing over the course of the week. Keeping your journal faithfully is very important for this review. Take time to review your journal entries over the past week and note any prominent themes, patterns, or applications. The seventh day affords the opportunity to explore an area over the past week in more detail.

H. <u>FREEDOM</u>. The Lord works in each person differently because each person is uniquely and wondrously created. So exercise freedom in doing these devotions. You are free to explore areas or themes related to a devotion as the Holy Spirit may move you.

One important freedom is that you can stay on the same devotion for more than one day – especially if you sense changes are being made in your heart, your life, your lifestyle, or your disciplines. If you want to take time to explore the devotion topic and its application more thoroughly, then spend two or three days on it. Because the devotional dates are blank, you can pick up the next devotion when you have explored the prior devotion fully. Book One and Book Two contain a total of 365 devotions. But take the time you need to absorb the devotion. You are *in no way* limited to a year to complete this devotional.

But there is a danger to freedom. Let me encourage you not to use freedom as an excuse to neglect your daily devotional time or to stop your personal devotions. Devotional time is vital to your journey with the Lord. Be faithful and consistent in it.

(For more tips on devotional time, see *Ten Tips for Devotional Time* below.)

III. FINAL WORD

The final word is to give yourself grace in growing in your devotional life. During this journey over time, you will experience ups and downs. You will have moments of inspiration and of joy. At other times, you may feel nothing or may get discouraged. Persevere!

Also, my mind wanders. I have been doing devotions for many years, and my mind still wanders. If your mind wanders during your devotional time, it is okay. Do not beat yourself up over it. When you catch it, simply bring yourself back to the devotion. Allow yourself to come back and to enter in. If you can pick up where you left off, then do so. If you need to start the devotion over, then do that. Give yourself grace in the devotional discipline. The Lord knows your heart in it.

Further, don't allow the devotion to minister condemnation to you. If the Holy Spirit convicts your heart, then be convicted and address the conviction appropriately with repentance and a commitment to change. But the purpose of this journey is to avail yourself of grace. God gives grace – abundant grace. Give yourself grace as well.

Let's begin and dig in!

TIME WITH GOD

Time with God daily is necessary for me to:

1. Discern the movements of my heart.
2. Increase in my knowledge of Him.
3. Live daily in the presence of the Lord.
4. Hear His word for the season of my life.
5. Correct my fluctuating attitudes and emotions.
6. Yield myself fully to Him.
7. Bring me back into right standing before Him.
8. Find direction and purpose for my life.
9. Reveal my own heart to yourself.
10. Be instructed in God's ways.
11. Renew my mind.
12. Reorient me to God and to His thoughts.
13. Walk with God as the king of my heart.
14. Allow God's love to infuse me so I can likewise love other people.
15. Sense the times that the Holy Spirit gives me a gentle nudge instead of using the baseball bat that I normally require.[1]

---

[1] Unless otherwise attributed, stories and material are by the author.

TEN TIPS FOR DEVOTIONAL TIME

1. Be honest with yourself and with God. God knows the thoughts and intentions of your heart anyway so be as honest with God and with yourself as you can. Don't try to "hide" from God.

2. Eliminate all distractions during devotional time. No TV; cell phone and computer off; be alone in a place of quiet.

3. If your mind wanders during your devotional time, don't beat yourself up. Receive grace and just come back to where you were in your devotion.

4. You may need to slow down your mind or emotions to enter into the devotional time. You can use imagery or relaxation exercises to take your mind off of worldly matters.

5. Don't focus on time. Allow the devotion to flow naturally. Sometimes most of the devotional time is preparation of your heart. Other times it is spent on the scripture. Other times it is worship and meditation. Allow yourself to be led by the Holy Spirit in your time.

6. Reference the devotional instructions above often for guidance.

7. Give your devotional life time to develop. If you feel lost or overwhelmed, then take comfort in the normalcy of that. Give yourself time to grow in your devotional life.

8. Ask for revelation of the root cause of sin or problems in your life. Part of surrender is vulnerability. Be prepared to be exposed or even torn apart as the Holy Spirit works in your heart to address issues, to heal your heart, and to pour Himself into it.

9. Just listening. Abide in His presence and listen. God moves all around us. He is always working in our lives. We need to develop sensitivity to those movements. There are interior movements (such as whispers to our mind or a tug on our heart) and exterior movements (such as circumstances of our life). We need quiet reflection and patient alertness to detect God's movements. Pay attention to the movements of your heart and your mind. Important things are often soft and gentle. Jesus is gentle with us and He is patient.

10. Grace, grace, and more grace.

MY STORY OF AN HOUR WITH GOD
By Pastor Daniel Martin

I was plodding along in my ministry and with my walk with God - treading water, trying to gain traction in my walk with Him, having spurts of success, but mainly on a roller coaster ride with more dips than highs.

Then November 2011...

I was listening to the radio in my car, when I heard that the Church of Egypt was calling for the church around the world to fast for them the 40 days before the New Year. They realized that they were probably going to be free of their current oppressive dictator in 2012 in what came to be known as "Arab Spring." But they were fearful that they would be trading one tyrant for another worse tyrant from the Muslim Brotherhood—which is what eventually happened.

I was slightly concerned about their plight, enough to consider fasting. But in my considerations, I immediately realized, the 40 days before the New Year included Thanksgiving and Christmas meals, gatherings, etc. (Please forgive my lack of depth here!)

But I decided I would do something. I graciously volunteered to "fast" several (5-10?) small things. I don't remember them all, but chocolate was one of them (I love chocolate).

The day before the fast began I felt a "nudge" from God - "Why don't You fast the first hour of every day during the 40 days to Me—give Me the first hour of every day?"

"But God, I am already doing early things (two 6 AM prayer meetings each week, etc.), and that would mean getting up even earlier than I already am!"

Being the gracious, obedient (ahem!) child of God that I am, I told Him that I was not going to promise to give Him the first hour all 40 days, but that I would begin doing it and see how it turned out.

Our God is a God of Great Grace!

The night before the 40 days began, I set out my clothes in the kitchen so I would not disturb my wife too much with my early rising. My alarm went off, I got out of bed and walked to the kitchen.

I dressed and began walking back to my study and...

On the way, the only way I know to describe it...God Met Me! His Presence was so real! His Joy, Love, Peace, Grace so flooded me!

I spent an hour basking in that Presence, typing my love for Him, playing/singing songs of praise, reading scriptures He brought to mind enjoying Him!

The hour flew by before I knew it.

GLORY!

The next day - the same.

The next day - the same.

Every day for 40 days.

At the end of the 40th day, I asked God, "Will You meet with me? Can we do this another 40 days?"

I felt a "Yes!" And He did. I did.

At the end of that 40 days, I told God, "Let's just forget the 40 days. Let's just meet every day until You take me home to be with You."

That was 8+ years ago, and this morning was even more alive than that first one. He is Here!

There have been many changes in my life as a result of it, some which I am sure I am not aware of. He, His Presence, His Life, His dealing with me in my life, His cleansing, His empowering, His nearness have all transformed me.

I cannot express the Delight, Thrill, Ecstasy, and Glory which are in my life now that I knew nothing of before November, 2011. There are mornings of great joy, delight, peace, and grace!

There are also mornings of Glory, when He sets His plow in my life deeper than ever, turning over soil, exposing roots, rocks, hardness, etc., in my life which have to go. There are mornings when I later realize that He has been planting seeds in my life which later spring up into Glorious Fruitfulness!

He is using this hour in so many ways, most of which I probably have no awareness.

He took me through the death of my wife in the summer of 2016 with a grace which I never knew existed, a grace which in her words "cocooned us together" and kept us alive and overflowing with Joy and Confidence that He was working All things together for our good throughout the process.

Then in the summer of 2017, He led me to get out my 12' x 6' cross and again walk every street of my city (Selma, Alabama) praying over every home, going to everyone I saw - all with No Fear, no Dread, with great delight, joy, and freedom to say, do whatever I felt He was leading. All Him!! All flowing from Time With Him!! Time He gave me, then asked for 1/24th of it back each day.

The best investment I have ever made.

Time is an investment. It is exactly like money.

We all have 24 hours every day.

No one, no matter their position, no matter their other possessions has more than 24 hours in one day. No one has less than 24.

And we All spend All of them every day. We are very unaware of spending them, but we do spend them All every day. We choose how we spend them.

Too much of the time we spend them mindlessly, with no thought about what we are purchasing with them. Many of our purchases are empty at best; evil at worst.

Let's consciously Choose to make Life expenditures with our hours.

Ps. 4:2 NEB "...how long will you...set your heart of trifles and run after lies?"

Deut. 30:19 NKJV "...I have set before you life and death, blessing and cursing; therefore Choose Life, that both you and your descendants may live."

I recommend Him to you.

I highly recommend TIME with Him to you.   *-Pastor Daniel Martin, 6/8/20*

(For more information go to **www.surrenderandtrust.net**)

SECTION I – FAITH, HOPE, AND LOVE

Week One: Attributes of Love

Week Two: Love - Flow and Blockage

Week Three: Growth in Love

Week Four: Faith – Pleasing God

Week Five: Faith – Endurance

Week Six: Faith and Hope – Rebirth

Week Seven: Hope Builders

Week Eight: Love and Hope

Week Nine: Demonstrations of God's Love

Week Ten: Receiving Love – Hindrances

Week Eleven: Journey – Faith, Hope, and Love

Week Twelve: Overcoming With Joy

Week Thirteen: Practicum - Loving God

STOP!

Please read instructions
in Preliminary Matters
before you begin these
devotions. The guide-
lines are important!

NOTES:_____

_____

_____

_____

_____

_____

_____

_____

_____

_____

_____

_____

_____

_____

_____

SECTION I – FAITH, HOPE, AND LOVE: WEEK ONE

> For this reason I bow my knees before the Father, from whom every family in heaven and on earth is named, that according to the riches of his glory he may grant you to be strengthened with power through his Spirit in your inner being, so that Christ may dwell in your hearts through faith—that you, being rooted and grounded in love, may have strength to comprehend with all the saints what is the breadth and length and height and depth, and to know the love of Christ that surpasses knowledge, that you may be filled with all the fullness of God. **Eph 3:14-19**

Love is our destination.

O, Your sweetness and Your love mean so much to me! Your agape love, where You show me the worth and value I have in Your eyesight are so rich to me! Come and show me all You are, O my God!! I love You and want You, need You and treasure You more and more. O, anoint me to treasure You, to value You more and more highly every day!! I need more and more growth in this.

One of the things I have experienced in these hours with You, is that <u>the more I love You, treasure You, value You—the more treasured, valued, loved and cared for I feel</u>. O Your ways are so good, so high, so much better than mine ever could be. Help me to seek Your ways, O my God!!   -Pastor Daniel Martin, 8/15/13

Love is the culmination of our journey on this earth. The experiences we have – the joys, the trials, the relationships, the sufferings, the achievements, the failures, the challenges – all of our experiences are designed to draw us into His perfect love. Joy, happiness, delight, pleasure, fellowship, victory – He knows. Grief, loss, pain, stress, anxiety, separation, failure – He knows.

Every (apparently) good thing that happens to us, directs us to God's love. Every (apparently) bad thing that happens to us, directs us to His love.

So we start with this devotional track with love so that we are mindful where we are headed.

Meditation: Read the scripture passage above slowly and let the words wash over you. Then repeat. Acknowledge to God the ways in which you experience His love on a daily basis. Then write them down in your journal.

☩   ☩   ☩   ☩   ☩   ☩   ☩

> Love is patient and kind; love does not envy or boast; it is not arrogant or rude. It does not insist on its own way; it is not irritable or resentful; it does not rejoice at wrongdoing, but rejoices with the truth. Love bears all things, believes all things, hopes all things, endures all things. Love never ends. **1 Cor 13:4-8a**

How do you define love?

My father passed away earlier this year.[2] He lived to a ripe, old age. Looking back, my father and I had one conversation I will never forget.

My father had many interests, but his vocation was a college professor. My father loved to impart his knowledge. In his own words, it "floated his boat." So his primary means of communication was the lecture – not, mind you, the short, concise version. My father's lectures lasted a minimum of 45 minutes, and if the lecture lasted less than an hour, you counted yourself fortunate. My father engaged in streaming long before streaming was a thing.

Interest in the topic was not germane. If you were interested in the topic of the lecture, you heard a thoughtful and profound discourse that vetted the subject thoroughly. If you were NOT interested in the topic of the lecture, you heard a thoughtful but profoundly boring discourse that vetted your patience thoroughly. But once the lecture began, it was going to be delivered in its entirety, preferably uninterrupted. The level of interest did not matter.

So we children learned at an early age to avoid words or actions that would trigger a lecture. My father steadfastly prowled the landscape, looking for occasions to lecture. His children just as steadfastly avoided interactions or situations that smelled like a lecture. And the first rule of lecture avoidance was: Never ask Daddy a question.

But a few years ago, I was curious. I had ideas, but I did not have a good understanding. I had read about it, thought about it, and tried to practice it. But I just didn't seem to get it. So I decided to turn to the one person that must have knowledge to share about the topic. It was a brave decision. But I decided to ask the question despite the torrent of words that would surely follow.

So I turned to my father and asked "Daddy, what is love? How do you define love?"

My father paused for a minute. Then he turned to me and said "You know what? I am not sure I can answer that question. I don't think I can really define love."

---

[2] Unless attributed otherwise, the stories and illustrations in this devotion are by the author.

And that was it. No thoughts; no musings; no historical references; no educated speculations; no special knowledge; no commentary. NO LECTURE! It was the rare occasion that my father was speechless. I was stunned.

Love is difficult to define.[3] Its stature as the highest virtue and as the greatest commandment seems to elevate love above the limitations of language. For me, love is embodied more meaningfully than it is defined. But Paul does list some attributes of love.

- Love is patient.
- Love is kind.
- Love does not envy.
- Love does not boast.
- Love is not arrogant.
- Love is not rude.
- Love does not insist on its own way.
- Love is not irritable.
- Love is not resentful.
- Love does not rejoice at wrongdoing.
- Love rejoices with the truth.
- Love bears all things.
- Love believes all things.
- Love hopes all things.
- Love endures all things.
- Love never ends.

Meditation: Read the attributes of love slowly. Note carefully what comes to mind when you read the list.

Read the attributes of love again. Note carefully how you feel when you read the list. Write down how you feel.

Finally, read the list a third time, but as you read the list, think of God and how He embodies these attributes of love. Consider the fullness of the love of God. Give thanks to God for His love toward you.

---

[3] One definition: Love is "willing the good of the other as other." Bishop Barron, *What is Love?* (2007) (Cf. Thomas Aquinas)

NOTES:_____

_____

_____

_____

_____

_____

_____

_____

_____

_____

_____

_____

_____

_____

_____

_____

_____

_____

So, as those who have been chosen of God, holy and beloved, put on a heart of compassion, kindness, humility, gentleness and patience; bearing with one another, and forgiving each other, whoever has a complaint against anyone; just as the Lord forgave you, so also should you. Beyond above all these things put on love, which is the perfect bond of unity. **Col 3:12-14 (NASB)**

Put on love.

My maternal grandfather and grandmother (Papa and Meme) were godly people. But they realized that often love doesn't just happen. Many forms of love require will and work. There is an intentionality to it.

My grandparents decided to read 1 Corinthians 13 every morning at the breakfast table. They read it aloud as a reminder of the heart with which they wanted to start that day. And it was an encouragement of how they wanted to live that day.

The daily reading of the "love chapter" continued for a long time. For many years, when I came to visit my grandparents, we read 1 Corinthians 13 together every morning.

Put on love. Paul uses an analogy of clothing. Love is put on like a garment. That is what my grandparents were trying to do every morning. They put on their clothes and came to the breakfast table. Then they put on love as their spiritual attire.

Meditation: How can you put on love as your spiritual clothing today? Look at the list of the attributes of love from Day 2. Pick one attribute that stands out to you. It may be an attribute that is a strength. Or it may be an attribute that is a weakness. Ask God – the embodiment of Love - to help you walk in that attribute today. Then go and do it.

Remember to journal as you do your devotions. A journal will help to affirm and to imprint the things that the Lord shows you on your devotional journey.

> So, as those who have been chosen of God, holy and beloved, put on a heart of compassion, kindness, humility, gentleness and patience; bearing with one another, and forgiving each other, whoever has a complaint against anyone; just as the Lord forgave you, so also should you. Beyond above all these things put on love, which is the perfect bond of unity. **Col 3:12-14 (NASB)**

COMKINHUMGENPA.

For many years, we had a weekly meeting for young men who lived in inner city Charlotte. We called it Boyz Club. Most of the young men were refugees from foreign countries. They and their families had suffered threats, danger, death, and displacement due to civil war, racial strife, and in some cases, genocide. Post traumatic stress disorder (PTSD) was not an unusual condition.

COM-KIN-HUM-GEN-PA was our Boyz Club motto. It was shorthand for compassion, kindness, humility, gentleness, and patience. COMKINHUMGENPA was a value that we wanted to practice at Boyz Club. We each wanted to be treated with COMKINHUMGENPA, so we encouraged one another to practice it in our words, our attitudes, and our actions toward one another.

And if you were a member of Boyz Club and you felt another member was not treating you with the right attitude, you had the right to turn to the other member and say "Hey! COMKINHUMGENPA!"

Paul encourages us to put on love above all. But there is more. Paul tells us that love does something. Love binds everything together in perfect harmony. From the context, "everything" includes **COMKINHUMGENPA**.

Love is like a glue that binds together the other virtues and makes them effective.

Meditation: Focus on **COMKINHUMGENPA** - compassion, kindness, gentleness, humility, and patience. Consider how Jesus manifested each of these attributes fully. Think of events or occasions where Jesus lived out these virtues.

Use your meditation as a basis for praise, blessing, and adoration for the goodness of God.

☩   ☩   ☩   ☩   ☩   ☩   ☩

NOTES:_____

_____

_____

_____

_____

_____

_____

_____

_____

_____

_____

_____

_____

_____

_____

_____

_____

_____

> "For the LORD sees not as man sees: man looks on the outward appearance, but the LORD looks on the heart." **1 Sam 16:7b**

Love is kind.

O God, help me to grow in Godly sorrow in every detail of my life that misses the marks You have set for my life, and help me to deal with those missings in great detail, thoroughly! Help me to confess (out loud, if possible) each one of them. Alert me to do this <u>hourly</u>, reviewing the previous hour of missing the marks (both of omission and commission), so that I can rise above them, put them to death, etc.

Help me to see the ROOT causes of missing the mark, the deep things like MOTIVES which persist in hanging around, even sometimes causing the right things I do to be for the wrong motives/reasons and leaving me with another round of bondage to fear of man, etc. O God, I want to be clear and cleaned in "the innermost being...in the hidden parts" of my life that I don't see! Come and change me and change me and change me!

This child/sheep needs so much improvement!

Have Your way in my life, O God and King!!   -Pastor Daniel Martin, 12/28/14

Our motivation makes all the difference in the world.

Over my years of ministry, I learned that people know the motivation for your actions. People know when they are being loved. They understand whether the act of service is offered out of love for them, or from a more selfish motive. I must confess that the times that I had a selfish motivation demonstrated this fact. I realized that they saw my masquerade.

As a parent, I realized the same thing about my children. My children knew whether my actions toward them arose out of love for them, or out of my own pride or selfishness.

It is a beautiful thing to be loved. And it is an awful thing to be an object for the pride or selfishness of another.

Here is a key: To God, the heart with which you do something is just as important as the activity itself. He desires that our words and actions be motivated from a heart of love. After all, everything that He does arises out of love. He Himself is love.

Meditation: When you talk with your friends, what is your motivation? Are you loving them at that moment? How about your coworkers? Or the stranger at the grocery store?

Today, as you interact with people, try to love them. Allow your words and actions toward them to arise out of the love you have for them.

If I speak in the tongues of men and of angels, but have not love, I am a noisy gong or a clanging cymbal. And if I have prophetic powers, and understand all mysteries and all knowledge, and if I have all faith, so as to remove mountains, but have not love, I am nothing. If I give away all I have, and if I deliver up my body to be burned, but have not love, I gain nothing. **1 Cor 13:1-3**

Love is the glue which binds all together.

O the glory of Your PRESENCE!

This child/sheep needs You, Your Presence, and Your LAD (Love, Acceptance and Desire)!

Your Love:

O the glory of the value and worth (VW)! You see me as having, the VW I have because You place it on me, give me the VW, bestow it on me, and stay with me, working with me Until I accept it and thrive on it! O the wonder of the value and worth (agape love) that You have given to me! It really does Lift me out of

Stormy waves	**Corruption**
Deep depression	**Stains of sin (deeply stained within)**
Bad habits	**Fears**
Instability	**Bitterness**
Unforgiveness	**Worries**
Inferiorities	**Weaknesses**
Hopelessness	-Pastor Daniel Martin, 12/27/14

Without love, other virtues have little value. In fact, the correct word is meaningless. Love brings meaning to our words and our actions. Love brings meaning to our lives.

Meditation: Today, you are just going to be quiet before the Lord, and to be sensitive to His movements in your heart. This exercise can be difficult because we are accustomed to the use of our mind, of our senses, and of our emotions.

Try to eliminate outside stimulations or distractions. Try to empty your mind of thoughts. Ask the Holy Spirit to come and guide your heart and mind. Then, sit quietly before the Lord for as long as you are able. If you need a focus, then focus on His love for you. Write in your journal anything that you hear or sense.

Review: Today is a review day. Go back and read your journal notes from this week. What is the Lord showing you? What is He calling you to change? Are there steps that you can take to implement those changes?

- Love is patient.
- Love is kind.
- Love does not envy.
- Love does not boast.
- Love is not arrogant.
- Love is not rude.
- Love does not insist on its own way.
- Love is not irritable.
- Love is not resentful.
- Love does not rejoice at wrongdoing.
- Love rejoices with the truth.
- Love bears all things.
- Love believes all things.
- Love hopes all things.
- Love endures all things.
- Love never ends.

> **Meditation:** Read the attributes of love above. Ask God to show you how God fully embodies these attributes of love.
>
> What response does your heart make to His love? What are you going to do in response to His love?

Please, please meet regularly with someone about your devotions. There is great benefit in reviewing your experience with a person that you trust!

SECTION I – FAITH, HOPE, AND LOVE: WEEK TWO

I.Week Two, Day 1 (Date:)   **LOVE – FLOW AND BLOCKAGE**

> The grace of the Lord Jesus Christ and the love of God and the fellowship of the Holy Spirit be with you all. **2 Cor 13:14**

Love is a Presence.

Let this Love, Grace, and Fellowship flow into my life in a steady stream all day today!

This child/sheep needs more and more of these Life-giving STREAMS!! Come and quench this thirsting of my soul with them! As I typed those words I also realized that -

I need Deeper Thirst in my soul, thirst that is satisfied with the flow, but that also increases with the flow instead of thinking it has enough!

Satisfies, but at the same time creates longing for more!!

O give me this glorious thirst!   -Pastor Daniel Martin, 9/10/14

God is love. God is the Source of love.

We abide in His love. Abide. Allow His love to flow through you, in you, and around you. Invite it and yield to it. Then abide in it.

Meditation: The Bible speaks of a spiritual flow - "rivers of living water" (Jn. 7:38); "anointing" (I Jn. 2:27); and "a spring of water welling up to eternal life" (Jn. 4:14). Pastor Martin speaks of "life-giving streams." How does this flow relate to love? How can you receive this flow and abide in it?

✝   ✝   ✝   ✝   ✝   ✝   ✝

> Requesting and seeking the Presence of the Holy Spirit during devotions is a beneficial practice. His Presence envelopes us in His love and He changes our hearts! Make it a regular practice.

> As the Father has loved me, so have I loved you. Abide in my love. If you keep my commandments, you will abide in my love, just as I have kept my Father's commandments and abide in his love. These things I have spoken to you, that my joy may be in you, and that your joy may be full. **John 15:9-11**

Love does not rejoice in wrongdoing.

My mother-in-law, Nana, grew up on a farm in the mountains and returned to live on that farm when she retired. The sink in her kitchen had a disposal, but when she had a large pile of food scraps, she took them to the back yard and threw them over the fence for the farm animals.

Late in her life, Nana developed Alzheimer's. She still functioned in her home for a long time, but suffered increasing dementia.

One day, the commode in the main bathroom backed up. It wouldn't flush, and no amount of plunging could unplug it.

They called a plumbing company who put "snake line" down the commode to try to unplug the pipe. What the plumber discovered is that someone had flushed a bunch of cantaloupe rinds down the commode. Apparently, Nana had confused the disposal, the commode, and the backyard fence, and had dumped her food scraps into the commode. The drainage pipe was completely blocked.

"If you keep my commandments, you will abide in My love." That statement can be received in a legalistic way. "You <u>must</u> obey My commandments in order to abide in my love." True enough. But compulsion is a harsh motivator, and sets us up for failure.

"If you keep my commandments, you will abide in My love, just as I have kept My Father's commandments and abide in His love." There is a more organic way to view it: Sin in our lives hinders the flow of love - just as cantaloupe rinds block the flow of a drainage pipe.

Sin hinders our ability to receive His love. And it has a tainting and a corrupting influence for the love that we do receive.

Sin also hinders our ability to walk in love and to show it to others. Our selfishness hampers our kindness, care, and patience. Sin impacts our ability to love.

Meditation: O God, come and show me Your ways, show me how You want me to be, what You want to do in my life. Come and deliver me from all the stuff of the enemy, from every devastating thing that causes this "hose" to be clogged and unable to have the full flow of Your Spirit, life, love, and salvation flow from it!

I need You more! Come and show me Your ways!

Help me to have the needed urgency, the desperation for Your leading, cleansing, purifying, and empowering grace flowing to me and out through me into this broken world around me! Give me what You are looking for in me!

And then give me the simple rest that comes from trusting You, relying on You, depending on You taking care of things as I just yield myself to You as a simple hose for You to flow through!! — Pastor Daniel Martin, 1/30/14

✝ ✝ ✝ ✝ ✝ ✝ ✝

NOTES:_____

_____

_____

_____

_____

_____

_____

_____

_____

_____

_____

Beware lest there be among you a man or woman or clan or tribe whose heart is turning away today from the LORD our God to go and serve the gods of those nations. Beware lest there be among you a root bearing poisonous and bitter fruit, one who, when he hears the words of this sworn covenant, blesses himself in his heart, saying, 'I shall be safe, though I walk in the stubbornness of my heart.' This will lead to the sweeping away of moist and dry alike.   **Deut 29:18-19**

Eradication.

I have English ivy in my backyard. A horticultural friend tells me that English ivy is an invasive specie. English ivy is not native to North Carolina, and it spreads like wildfire.

English ivy is hard to get rid of. If I mow over a patch of English ivy or cut it with a weed eater, that patch looks good for a week or two. Then the English ivy comes back. I have only dealt with the plant on the surface, not with the roots.

The only way to eradicate English ivy is to pull it up by the roots. This process is hard, because English ivy is a vine, and every foot or two, the vine has put roots into the ground. When you pull out a patch of English ivy, it seems like all the vines are connected in an intricate network of well rooted plants.

The sins that we have in our lives are manifested in many ways – such as bad thoughts, disordered desires, dysfunctions, or addictions. These manifestations are what we see on the surface.

So we resist the sin and fight against it.

But beneath the surface is a root cause. The root cause (or causes) motivates us to sin in ways that we don't want or even abhor. But if we want for the sin to go away and not to keep coming back, we must pull it up by its roots. Eradication.

One difficulty is that a root cause is often hidden. It may not have an apparent connection to the sin itself. For example, lust may be rooted in pride; greed may be rooted in insecurity; or jealousy may be rooted in low self esteem. But the root bears "poisonous and bitter fruit."

We need the help of God not only to fight the sin on the surface, but also to pull it out by its roots.

Meditation: Come before God and confess the sins to Him that He brings to mind. Ask Him for help. Ask Him to identify the root of the sins. Ask Him to help you pull out those roots. Write in your journal what God shows you regarding the roots of sins.

> Search me, O God, and know my heart: try me, and know my thoughts:
>
> And see if there be any wicked way in me, and lead me in the way everlasting. **Psa 139:23-24** (KJV)

Search my heart, O God.

O the blessed glory, delight, thrill, and wonder there is in the transformation process as You take me from where I am in every room of my life, begin to clean house, and fill the empty rooms with Your furniture and accessories!

What glory there is in my life as one by one You take what is ugly, smelly, rotten, destructive, and demeaning out, and replace it with the truth, the glory, the beauty, wonder, honor, and true wealth of all You are!

O the glory of "higher ground" that You are continually calling me to. Thank You for the glory of Your sanctification and the process of it!

Thank You for the transformation of taking me from walking in my human, frail, prideful, and warped ways into the life, peace, fulfillment, and truth that comes from walking in Your ways!

O God, come and transform me and transform me and transform me!! I want to be transformed, conformed, formed, and changed into all You want me to be! O the glory of the wonder of Your ways! You are so GOOD!! What an awesome God You are!! I love You, O my God.

Change me through the entrance of Your Word, from darkness to light! The entrance of Your Word brings light. O cause me to come to know YOUR will for my life—long term and short term.

Let me know Your will for me for the remainder of this hour, for this day, for the near future, for the things way out there, which I need to be preparing for now!

Lord, prepare me to be a sanctuary...   -Pastor Daniel Martin, 1/20/14

Search my heart, O God. For many years, I regularly ask the Holy Spirit to go through the rooms of my heart. My heart has many rooms. Some of them are open and well lit. I want people to see them.

But other rooms are hidden and carefully walled off. They may even be sealed to exclude outsiders.

Some rooms of our heart are closed by shame. We are ashamed of the thoughts and memories they hold, so we close them off.

Some rooms are sealed by pain. We have been wounded deeply and have formed a hard barrier to prevent further pain.

Some rooms are guarded by pride. These rooms belong to us for our personal use and we don't allow anyone else to enter.

When I ask God to go through the rooms of my heart, He shows me hidden rooms. It is as if His light shines in places of deep darkness. So I ask Him to bring His light to explore my heart.

Every time I do it, He shows me a new room. Or He shows me a hidden room that He found before, but the room is still walled off. I still try to hide it from Him. I ask Him to help me open the room to His light and His love.

Meditation: Ask God to search the rooms of your heart. Open your heart to the Lord. Allow Him to go from room to room. Take time for inspection of each area. Expose any hidden closets. Note in your journal what He shows you.

✝   ✝   ✝   ✝   ✝   ✝   ✝

NOTES:_____

_____

_____

_____

_____

_____

_____

_____

_____

_____

> Your hands have made and fashioned me; give me understanding that I may learn your commandments.
>
> Those who fear you shall see me and rejoice, because I have hoped in your word.
>
> I know, O LORD, that your rules are righteous, and that in faithfulness you have afflicted me.
>
> Let your steadfast love comfort me according to your promise to your servant. **Psa 119:73-76**

Let your steadfast love comfort me.

You cannot be satisfied with any temporal good, because you were not created to enjoy these alone. Although you should possess all created good, yet you could not be happy therewith nor blessed; but in God, Who created all things, consists your whole blessedness...All human comfort is vain and brief. Blessed and true is the comfort which is received inwardly from the truth. A devout man bears everywhere with him his own Comforter, Jesus.[4]

God wants His steadfast love to comfort us. His steadfast love is the Source of our comfort.

But when I feel bad about myself or feel down, I often seek comfort in worldly things or even in harmful relationships. When I seek comfort in the wrong places, it can block the flow of God's love in my life. That is so ironic because it is blocking the very source of comfort that God desires to provide for me.

When I learn to seek comfort in God, He helps me untangle the blockages I have created in my attempts to make myself feel better. He is the God of all comfort Who desires to be your Comforter. In fact, the Holy Spirit has a name – the Comforter (John 14:16) (KJV).

> **Meditation:** For what do you seek comfort? What are the wounds, the struggles, or the afflictions for which you need comfort?
>
> Or are there times where you feel bad about yourself or you feel down, and you seek comfort? Write down what the Lord shows you about comfort.
>
> Spend time with the Lord. Ask the Lord to comfort you in these areas through His steadfast love.

---

[4] Thomas a Kempis, *The Imitation of Christ* , pp.126-127 (Moody 1958).

NOTES:_____

_____

_____

_____

_____

_____

_____

_____

_____

_____

_____

_____

_____

_____

_____

_____

_____

_____

_____

> As the Father has loved me, so have I loved you. Abide in my love. If you keep my commandments, you will abide in my love, just as I have kept my Father's commandments and abide in his love. These things I have spoken to you, that my joy may be in you, and that your joy may be full. **John 15:9-11**

My commandments lead you to love.

What a delight and glory it is to be Yours, to know You, to experience Your love and acceptance! You are so good and amazing! What wondrous joy and excitement there is in meeting with You day by day, in having You make Yourself known to me, in You manifesting Yourself to me!! How great and awesome You are!

I just remembered again, <u>the wonder and glory of the last several days, last week especially, how You have so ordered my days, my schedule, my contacts, etc. to flow so powerfully together and make Your glory known to me!</u> What an awesome God You are!! I was stunned some days at how You had my path cross other's paths at just the right time, at the awareness I had of what I needed to say to specific ones, etc. You are so amazing!

Father, take my life today and let it be what YOU want it to me. Do what You want to do in my world through me today.

<u>Come and help me to surrender, submit, yield, and flow with You in every way You design and desire.</u>

Come and have Your Way in me. Show me what You see in the people and situations I encounter today. Let me be Your vessel of honor today!

I want to see Your Kingdom come, Your will be done in my world. I want to see the way You see things.

<u>I want to see You drive back the darkness, the pain, the brokenness, the bondages and slavery that is all around me!</u>

<u>O come and deliver me to deliver the bound around me!</u>

I need to:

- Know Your commands
- Know when I am failing to live by them
- Know when I am deceiving myself about following them
- Obey them
- Love them

- **Delight in them**
- **Glorify You through them**
- **Embrace them tightly**

O Your commands are ways of life! They are so good, life-giving, fulfilling, gracious, and packed with veins of rich ore! –Pastor Daniel Martin, 11/11/14

"If you keep my commandments, you will abide in My love." This statement can be viewed as a hard one: If you don't keep My commandments, you will not abide in My love.

Or it can be viewed organically: Sin blocks the flow of My love.

But it also should be viewed affirmatively: Keeping My commandments will draw you into My love. Everything He does in your life draws you into His love. The things He has spoken - the instructions He has given - those words place you securely in His love. Follow them, and you will abide in His love.

And what He wants us to experience is joy. His words bring joy. They are words of life and words of joy. His commandments bring joy. And not just joy...fullness of joy.

Meditation: Give thanks to Jesus for His instructions and His commandments. Tell Him that you desire to follow them and to abide in His love. Ask Him to help you follow His words unto fullness of joy.

---

‡ ‡ ‡ ‡ ‡ ‡ ‡

NOTES:_____

_____

_____

_____

_____

_____

_____

_____

- Love does not boast.
- Love is not arrogant.
- Love is not rude.
- Love does not insist on its own way.

Love is our destination. Review your journals over the last week. What stands out to you? How is God prompting you to change?

> **Meditation:** Look back over the meditations over the past week. Was there a meditation that you felt you could explore more? Select one of the meditations and go through it again. Explore it further and deeper.

✟   ✟   ✟   ✟   ✟   ✟   ✟

NOTES:_____

_____

_____

_____

_____

_____

_____

_____

_____

_____

I.Week Three, Day 1 (Date:)   **GROWTH IN LOVE**

> Rather, speaking the truth in love, we are to grow up in every way into him who is the head, into Christ, from whom the whole body, joined and held together by every joint with which it is equipped, when each part is working properly, makes the body grow so that it builds itself up in love. **Eph 4:15**

Love grows.

I visited my grandparents (Papa and Meme) often. Throughout my life, I made regular trips to stay with them. So I was able to observe them closely in their later years.

Here is one thing I observed: Papa and Meme continued to grow in love. They grew in love in many ways. Reading the "love chapter" (1 Corinthians 13) every day helped that growth. But they did many other things that cultivated love.

One day, I realized that you are either moving toward love or moving away from it. Our hearts are not static. Your heart is moving toward God or your heart is moving away from Him. You are growing or you are diminishing.

My grandparents encouraged us to continue to grow in love, and they modeled it.

Sometimes growth is a rapid process. Other times growth is a slow, often imperceptible, process. We need awareness of our hearts. Awareness of our hearts helps us to move toward love, and to stop movements away from love.

Awareness of our hearts results from a meaningful devotional time. Awareness increases as we prioritize our time with God. During devotions, we explore our hearts and we ask God to show us where we are. Sometimes, our hearts grow in love as we remain close to the Lord. We are encouraged.

Other times, we realize that our hearts have drifted further from the Lord, and maybe even hardened some. At that point, we can stop that drift and ask the Lord to help us change direction.

Patterns often emerge. I find myself walking closely for a few days. But then bad thoughts or selfish desires creep in and my heart turns away. Consistency occurs from regular correction of the drift of my heart. Our devotions help us to keep growing up in love.

Meditation: Ask God where you are. Have you been growing in love? What things encourage that growth? What things hamper that growth? Write in your journal that things God shows you about growth. Ask God to help you to grow in love.

> Let all that you do be done in love. **1 Cor 16:14**

Everything is done with a view toward love.

Brother Lawrence devoted his life to God and to seeking the love and Presence of God. The Practice of the Presence of God is a short but rich collection of the sayings, teachings, and letters of Brother Lawrence.

Brother Lawrence was assigned kitchen duty for many years. He had a natural aversion to it. But he proceeded to do everything in the kitchen for the love of God. He reported that his kitchen work became easy during the 15 years he did it because he did it for the love of God. Brother Lawrence said:

"We should not become weary of doing little things for the love of God. God regards not the greatness of the work, but the love with which the work is done. We should not be surprised if in the beginning we often fail in our endeavors. In the end we will develop a habit, which will naturally produce acts through us without effort, to our exceeding great delight."[5]

"Let all that you do be done in love." This instruction is simple. It is only 9 words. You can easily memorize it. Yet it may be one of the most difficult instructions in scripture.

Sometimes, when we are doing a religious act or a ministry that we think is important, we may think of God. We may even feel a love for Him. But, speaking for myself, the feeling of love is usually a fleeting one.

A key to growth in love is to practice it. And here is a good way to practice it: In everything you do, do it for the love of God. In everything that you do, tell God you are doing it with love for Him.

Do the large things out of a love for God. Do the small things – especially the small, mundane things - out of a love for God.

Meditation: Think of the things in your life that are drudgery. What are the things you have to do today that are distasteful, but you have to do them? Write them down. The next time you have to do something you don't like, commit to do it out of love for God.

╬   ╬   ╬   ╬   ╬   ╬   ╬

[5] Brother Lawrence, *The Practice of the Presence of God*, p. 124 (Translated by Marshall Davis 2013).

NOTES:_____

_____

_____

_____

_____

_____

_____

_____

_____

_____

_____

_____

_____

_____

_____

_____

_____

_____

_____

> If I speak in the tongues of men and of angels, but have not love, I am a noisy gong or a clanging cymbal. And if I have prophetic powers, and understand all mysteries and all knowledge, and if I have all faith, so as to remove mountains, but have not love, I am nothing. If I give away all I have, and if I deliver up my body to be burned, but have not love, I gain nothing. **1 Cor 13:1-3**

Love is the difference maker.

Our sanctification does not depend on changing what we do, but in doing for God's sake what we normally do for own sake. It is sad to see how many people mistake the means for the end, addicting themselves to religious works, which they perform very imperfectly because of their human or selfish motives.[6]   -Brother Lawrence

Our motivation determines our destiny. If we take out the garbage to please ourselves, it is nothing. In fact, it is worthless. But if we take out the garbage out of a love for the Lord, it glorifies Him. And it pleases Him.

Virtue without love is worthless. Acts of kindness and compassion without love are empty acts.

It may take a long time to learn to do things out of a love for God. But it can be learned. Brother Lawrence calls it a habit, and he encourages us to persevere in developing that habit.

> **Meditation:** Think of the person that rubs you the wrong way. Who is the person that you find distasteful, but you have to interact with that person? The next time you interact with that person, commit to interact out of a love for God. As you speak with that person, tell God that you love Him.

⚜ ⚜ ⚜ ⚜ ⚜ ⚜ ⚜

> The movements of your heart as you engage in devotions are very important. Be sensitive to them and record them. They are precious and instructive!

---

[6] *The Practice of the Presence of God,* p. 23.

> I know, O LORD, that the way of man is not in himself, that it is not in man who walks to direct his steps.
>
> Correct me, O LORD, but in justice; not in your anger, lest you bring me to nothing. **Jer 10:23-24**

God often allows things in our life that we don't like.

<u>It is not in man who walks to direct his own steps</u> (NKJV).

O God, correct me today when I fail to seek You, when I allow little foxes to spoil the vines, when I just go through the motions of living for You, while actually just following the dictates of my flesh, "counting my life dear unto myself."

I need YOU more!!   -Pastor Daniel Martin, 9/3/14

God often allows things in our life that we don't like because we need to experience things that we don't like.

- Love does not insist on its own way.
- Love is not irritable.
- Love is not resentful.

God isn't trolling us. His motivation is not a twisted pleasure, but a love for us. God allows things that we don't like in our life for our own good. Why?

They help us to grow in love. Many circumstances we don't like rub us the wrong way. God is putting His finger on a feature of our selfishness. And we squeal like a stuck pig...because after all, we are pigheaded.

But God is revealing our own willfulness to us. We want our own way. When we don't get it, we become irritable and resentful.

But love does not insist on its own way. Love is not selfish. And when love does not get its own way, it is not irritable or resentful.

Meditation: Who are the people that came to mind in yesterday's meditation? Look back to see. Here is a thought: Maybe God put the person who offends you...who rubs you the wrong way...someone you really don't like, maybe God put that person into your life to help you to grow in unselfishness...to grow in love. Maybe that person is actually a blessing from God.

If God quickens that possibility to you, will it change the way that you view that person? How can it change the way in which you interact with that person?

NOTES:_____

_____

_____

_____

_____

_____

_____

_____

_____

_____

_____

_____

_____

_____

_____

_____

_____

For I know that nothing good dwells in me, that is, in my flesh. For I have the desire to do what is right, but not the ability to carry it out. For I do not do the good I want, but the evil I do not want is what I keep on doing. Now if I do what I do not want, it is no longer I who do it, but sin that dwells within me. So I find it to be a law that when I want to do right, evil lies close at hand. For I delight in the law of God, in my inner being, but I see in my members another law waging war against the law of my mind and making me captive to the law of sin that dwells in my members. Wretched man that I am! Who will deliver me from this body of death? Thanks be to God through Jesus Christ our Lord! So then, I myself serve the law of God with my mind, but with my flesh I serve the law of sin. Rom 7:18-25

Love does not insist on its own way.

St. John of the Cross was a trained theologian who wrote books on Christian meditation and spirituality. He is the author of a number of Christian classics including The Dark Night of the Soul. St. John of the Cross wrote counsels on how to enter a deeper walk with the Lord. Some of these counsels are hard words:

> **Endeavor to be inclined always:**
>
> **Not to the easiest, but to the most difficult;**
>
> **Not to the most delightful, but to the most distasteful;**
>
> **Not to the most gratifying, but to the less pleasant;**
>
> **Not to what means rest for you, but to hard work;**
>
> **Not to the consoling, but to the unconsoling;**
>
> **Not to the most, but to the least;**
>
> **Not to the highest and most precious, but to the lowest and most despised;**
>
> **Not to wanting something, but to wanting nothing.**
>
> **...for Christ, desire to enter into complete nakedness, emptiness, and poverty in everything in the world.[7]**

Our selfishness wages war with God's law – a law that is based on love.

---

[7] St. John of the Cross, *The Ascent of Mount Carmel*, I.13.6 (From *The Collected Works of St. John of the Cross*, Kavanaugh and Rodriguez (ICS Publications 1991)).

These counsels are not only hard, but they seem counterintuitive to the pursuit of happiness in life. But these counsels strike at the heart of selfishness. They are designed to help us grow in unselfishness and in love. And St. John of the Cross tells us that these counsels (and others that accompany them) are profitable and effective.

You should embrace these practices earnestly and try to overcome the repugnance of your will toward them. If you sincerely put them into practice with order and discretion, you will discover in them great delight and consolation.[8]

> **Meditation:** What was your reaction to the counsels of St. John of the Cross? Why did you have that reaction? Write about your reactions in your journal. Are these counsels something that you can put into practice as St. John of the Cross encourages?

✠   ✠   ✠   ✠   ✠   ✠   ✠

NOTES:_____

_____

_____

_____

_____

_____

_____

_____

_____

_____

[8] *The Ascent of Mount Carmel*, I.13.7.

> The steps of a man are established by the LORD, when he delights in his way;
>
> though he fall, he shall not be cast headlong, for the LORD upholds his hand. **Psa 37:23-24**

One step at a time.

At times I need to highlight one word, at other times I need to highlight a different word. For example: Step by step You will lead me.

-STEP BY STEP You will lead me.

This is a process. You will lead me step by step into more and more of the life You have for me.

I actually Need to be way down the road from where I am, but I can get there only step by step. You are satisfied in taking me step by step.

You patiently put up with the progress I am making, even though I need more, simply because You delight in growth and progress.

I thank You for taking me step by step, for being so patient, loving, tender, kind, and understanding—knowing You are dealing with a child/sheep. O Your love, care, mercy, and grace minister so much to me! I need You and Your great love and care in my life!

-Step by step YOU will lead me!

It is all about YOU! YOU do the leading. YOU do the choosing of the steps. YOU decide which area of my life needs change and uplift right now. YOU are the guide in my life. It is not in me to direct my own steps—even the steps of growth.

It is not in man who walks to direct His own steps. The Lord directs the steps of the Godly, And He delights in every detail of their lives! O the glory of those precious words to me, O my God and King!! I love You for Your leading and guiding, directing and working things out in my life.

 I thank You that my Leader has so much love, care, and power for the one He is leading! What an amazing God and Father You are to me!

-Step by step You WILL lead me!

O this one word is so valuable to me, so assuring, so life-giving, so satisfying, so wholesome and enriching! You WILL lead me, take care of me, see me through to the very end, stand by me, etc. It is not a question of If at all! You WILL do it. I can count on it. Your hand of love is on my life.

You have invested tremendously in my life. I am valuable to You. It matters to You that I make it.

You have poured so much into my life that it makes a difference to You, a huge difference, whether or not I am led to where I need to go.

I don't have to see the entire road from where I am to where I need to be, all I need to do is to see the next place I have to put my foot. Then after I have obeyed and placed my foot there, You will show me the next place to put it.

How rich and glorious it is to live with You, letting You lead and guide, depending on Your ability to get me where I need to go!

I can rest in the fact that You WILL lead me! What an awesome and wonderful God, Father, Shepherd, and Guide You are to me! O, I need You so much!!
-Pastor Daniel Martin, 10/12/14

The Father has immense patience. He not only allows - He encourages - us to grow step by step and bit by bit. That growth process includes growth in love.

I need to rest in His patience. He will permit me to see as far down the road as I need to see in order to grow in Him. If my Father is patient with me – holding my hand even when I fall, then I need to be patient with myself.

Meditation: Consider the idea that the Lord normally does not reveal numerous steps I need to take, but shows me only the next step – the next thing to address or the next action to take. Why does He work in that way?

Next, consider the amount of trust His servant must put in Him as He reveals the next step but not many other things that he or she must experience, see, or do? Spend time with God expressing to Him your trust in Him in the process.

Remember to take your time with these devotions. It is fine to spend more than one day on a devotion – step by step is the path. For example, the guidance from St. John of the Cross in Day 5 may take some time to digest. We will come back to many of the themes in this devotional, but take the time you need to put areas we cover into practice.

I.Week Three, Day 7 (Date:)   **GROWTH IN LOVE**

Review the notes from your journal over the past week.

The practice of loving God in all things (Brother Lawrence – Day 2) – loving Him in both the large things and the small things, takes years to learn.

The practice of unselfishness (St. John of the Cross – Day 5) may take a life time to learn.

In His great mercy, God meets us where we are. He doesn't ask us to climb a mountain in a single leap. He asks us to take the next step. And that is our focus - the next step in the direction that He gives to you.

> **Meditation:** Ask the Lord for His direction for you. Ask Him for the next step for growth. Write it down in your journal. Then take that step.

✝   ✝   ✝   ✝   ✝   ✝   ✝

NOTES:_____

_____

_____

_____

_____

_____

_____

_____

_____

_____

_____

I.Week Four, Day 1 (Date:)   **FAITH – PLEASING GOD**

> He who has prepared us for this very thing is God, who has given us the Spirit as a guarantee. So we are always of good courage. We know that while we are at home in the body we are away from the Lord, for we walk by faith, not by sight. Yes, we are of good courage, and we would rather be away from the body and at home with the Lord. So whether we are at home or away, we make it our aim to please him. **2 Cor 5:5-9**

Love is our destination. Faith is the fuel to get us there.

...unfailing love *enfolds* **him who** *trusts* **in the Lord. Psa 32:10b (NEB).**

O God, thank You for the truth that in one sense I am in charge of whether or not unfailing love is enfolding me!

When I put my Trust in You, then Your unfailing love automatically shows up in powerful ways, which results in Life regardless of what the ensuing circumstances are!

How can I be so sure about this? Your Word here is true! It is reliable! It will never fail! Thank You for the picture of Your love ENFOLDING me! Unfailing love enfolding me!

O the Glory and Life of these words!   -Pastor Daniel Martin, 4/30/15

Love and faith work together. Perfect love is our destination. During our journey, we grow in love and we are motivated by love. But faith fuels that journey, because we walk by faith, not by sight.

Our faith keeps us moving forward. We face challenges, hindrances, temptations, losses, and sorrows. Our faith sustains us.

We see blessings, successes, milestones and joys. Our faith maintains us.

We must exercise faith at every juncture in order to journey on the way that the Lord wills, and in order to please Him and to love Him.

Meditation: Consider the connections between faith and love. How much does love lead you to faith? How necessary is faith to help you keep growing in love?

Next, meditate on faith. How easy is it to walk by faith and not by sight? What things in your life hinder your ability to walk by faith?

☦   ☦   ☦   ☦   ☦   ☦   ☦

NOTES:_____

_____

_____

_____

_____

_____

_____

_____

_____

_____

_____

_____

_____

_____

_____

_____

_____

_____

_____

When they found him on the other side of the sea, they said to him, "Rabbi, when did you come here?"

Jesus answered them, "Truly, truly, I say to you, you are seeking me, not because you saw signs, but because you ate your fill of the loaves. Do not work for the food that perishes, but for the food that endures to eternal life, which the Son of Man will give to you. For on him God the Father has set his seal."

Then they said to him, "What must we do, to be doing the works of God?"

Jesus answered them, "This is the work of God, that you believe in him whom he has sent." **John 6:25-29**

Faith during our journey is God's work.

When the Jews talked about "works of God," they had in mind wondrous signs and miracles. *For Jews demand signs* (1 Cor 1:22a).

But Jesus brought them to the essential thing. Belief in Jesus! Faith! Faith is belief in the Unseen that is evidenced by words and by actions of change.

Faith is the thing you pursue. Faith is necessary every step of the way. So you cultivate it; you nurture it; and you encourage it.

Your faith will be tested. But if you maintain it through the trials and tribulations of your life, you will accomplish and fulfill the work of God.

Faith is the greatest work of God.

Meditation: Spend time with the Holy Spirit. Ask Him to build your faith during your time with Him so that you can exercise it during your day.

If your mind wanders during your devotional time, don't let it derail you. That is normal as you learn a new discipline. Don't beat yourself up. Just acknowledge it and enter back into the devotion.

> "I am the Alpha and the Omega, the beginning and the end. To the thirsty I will give from the spring of the water of life without payment." **Rev. 21:6**

I believe in You, O Lord, Maker of the heavens and the earth.

"I shall not be shaken" (Psa. 16:8b).

As I considered these truths, I was reminded of some human "sources" of income that might one day soon fade or disappear. What will be my situation then?

It all depends on Who my SOURCE now is!

If now they are my source, then with their removal, I will be shaken, moved.

But if You are right now my only source (just using them), then when they are no longer providing I am all right, because You will never fade or be removed, and I will not be shaken or moved. O help me to guard against putting my trust on the means You are using to provide for me. They are not the providers, only the tools You are using to provide.

As long as You are my sole Provider, I am all right, even if the tools are removed. You have no difficulty in raising up other tools, or just supernaturally providing! You have done it before so many times in my life, and You are capable of doing it again!

What an awesome God You are!!   –Pastor Daniel Martin, 5/7/14

"I believe in You, O Lord, Maker of the heavens and the earth."

This statement is the first of my core confessions – my "lifelines." When I face a significant challenge, when I feel weak, or when I feel a large amount of stress, I repeat my core confessions. "I believe in You, O Lord, Maker of the heavens and the earth" is the first of my four core confessions.

These "lifelines" did not develop overnight. I suffered a very painful and debilitating illness. For months, I could not function. At times, I felt very close to death. It took two years for me to feel normal again.

During that awful season, when the pain was most excruciating and the darkness seemed to surround me, I needed something to grasp onto. I needed a lifeline. The Lord gave me these lifelines to hold and not to let go.

"I believe in You, O Lord, Maker of the heavens and the earth."

Jesus is the Founder and Perfecter of our faith (Heb. 12:2). He is the Source – the Source of life and the Source of the faith that leads us to eternal life. All of our essence, all that lives and that flows in us, comes from Him.

He is the Spring – the Source of life bubbling out of the ground that quenches our thirst. For those walking in a dry and parched place where sun and heat beat upon them, He offers springs of water to quench their thirst. For those who hunger and thirst for righteousness, those who thirst for the kingdom of God in a barren land, He gives an abundant flow of His Spirit to satisfy the thirsty soul.

Singers and dancers alike say, "All my springs are in you" (Psa. 85:7).

All of my springs are in you!

Meditation: Focus on God as the Source of all things. Think of the many ways in which God is the Source.

Next, focus on thirst. *"To the thirsty I will give from the spring of the water of life…"* How thirsty are you for God? How thirsty is your soul for the flow of life within you?

What do you do on a daily basis to connect with the Source and to draw from it? What are the springs of the water of life given "without payment" (Rev. 21:6)? Seek the Lord for those springs in increasing measure.

✝   ✝   ✝   ✝   ✝   ✝   ✝

NOTES:_____

_____

_____

_____

_____

_____

_____

_____

_____

> And without faith it is impossible to please him, for whoever would draw near to God must believe that he exists and that he rewards those who seek him. **Heb 11:6**

Without faith, it is impossible to please Him.

(Brother) Lawrence said that he had always been governed by love without thought of self. He resolved to make the love of God the goal of all his actions. He had become satisfied that this method was the best path. He was pleased when he could pick up a straw from the ground for the love of God, seeking only Him and nothing else, not even His gifts.[9]

We should examine our motivation often. Faith powers our journey. But our aim is to please Him.

Which brings us back to love. If we love Him, we want to please Him. That is a primary goal of the lover - to please.

The motivation to please God grows as our love for Him grows. But faith is necessary. We must believe that He is, and we must believe that He responds to those who seek Him. Both beliefs require the exercise of faith.

Further, it might be said that the amount that we seek Him is proportional to the amount of our faith.

Meditation: Think of a person that you love dearly, closely, and deeply. How much do you want to please that person? What steps do you take to please that person? To what lengths do you go (or are you willing to go) to please that person? Journal about it.

Now consider the Lord. Spend time loving Him. Then tell Him that you want to please Him. Rest in Him and listen for His response to your heart.

Focus on God during your devotion. We are trying to please Him. Eliminate all outside distractions. Devote your time to Him as you would to a lover.

---

[9] *The Practice of the Presence of God*, p. 13.

NOTES:_____

_____

_____

_____

_____

_____

_____

_____

_____

_____

_____

_____

_____

_____

_____

_____

_____

_____

> "And he who sent me is with me. He has not left me alone, for I always do the things that are pleasing to him." **John 8:29**

"I always do the things that are pleasing to Him."

As I have lived my life seeing worth in worthless things and as this has been embedded in me in powerful, strong ways, help me to now be changed, renewed and come alive, really alive with the power of Your Word, seeing worth and value in Your Word and Ways!

Show me where I am needing changes in this, and draw me more and more into all You are! O, I want to <u>honor, magnify, glorify, delight, and bring You praise</u> **in the earth.**

Deliver me from all that is contrary to You and Your nature, to Your holiness!

O, I want purity and holiness in all my actions, motives, thoughts, and meditations! I need You more!   -Pastor Daniel Martin, 4/21/15

"I always do the things that are pleasing to Him."

This statement is astounding. It certainly left its hearers stunned.

Always - not sometimes, not occasionally, not just when I think about it – but always I do what is pleasing to Him.

That is part of the change that arises from faith. When we have faith and we exercise our faith, we want to please Him always. So we begin to learn how to please Him and to take steps to please Him.

And the fruit of that pleasure is He does not leave me alone. The pleasing is reciprocated with Presence. That is a secret that Brother Lawrence seemed to know. He focused on loving and pleasing God, and sensed His Presence and love for the rest of his days.

Meditation: Meditate on the connection between pleasing and presence. When you please the person that you love, what are you communicating to them? How does pleasing that person solicit that person's presence?

Tell God that you want to please him and that you desire His Presence. Then allow time for His Presence and His love.

✠   ✠   ✠   ✠   ✠   ✠   ✠

> For I know that nothing good dwells in me, that is, in my flesh. For I have the desire to do what is right, but not the ability to carry it out. For I do not do the good I want, but the evil I do not want is what I keep on doing. Now if I do what I do not want, it is no longer I who do it, but sin that dwells within me. So I find it to be a law that when I want to do right, evil lies close at hand. For I delight in the law of God, in my inner being, but I see in my members another law waging war against the law of my mind and making me captive to the law of sin that dwells in my members. Wretched man that I am! Who will deliver me from this body of death? Thanks be to God through Jesus Christ our Lord! So then, I myself serve the law of God with my mind, but with my flesh I serve the law of sin.
>
> There is therefore now no condemnation for those who are in Christ Jesus. For the law of the Spirit of life has set you free in Christ Jesus from the law of sin and death. **Rom 7:18-8:2**

You are accepted by God.

O the glory of Your Presence!

This child/sheep needs You, Your Presence, and Your LAD (Love, Acceptance, and Desire)!

Your ACCEPTANCE:

What an absolute marvel this one is! That You would even accept me into Your Presence at a great distance would be something almost unbelievable-but that You would want me in Your Presence always, that You would want me near to You, that You would even want to be in me, then want me to be in You is staggering!

And this is at all times!

Your acceptance successfully (as I take it in):

- **Heals my wounds**
- **Feeds my deepest emotional needs**
- **Sets me free from the junk of my flesh (as I let it override them)**
- **Gives me deep peace**
- **Allows me to walk gracefully, poised, and at ease through tough times**
- **Gives me needed patience when I don't understand You, Your ways, Your timing**
- **Gives me joy for the journey**   -Pastor Daniel Martin, 12/27/14

It is as if Paul is saying "Yes, it is a struggle to fulfill my desire to please Him. But don't be overwhelmed and don't be condemned. Christ has accepted us and set us free!" You are accepted by God.

The law condemns. The Spirit ministers life and grace. Our destiny is love and life, not condemnation and death.

Meditation: Today is a day of quiet listening before the Lord. Be quiet before the Lord, but also be sensitive to movements or direction from the Holy Spirit.

Try to eliminate outside stimulations or distractions. Try to empty your mind of thoughts. Ask the Holy Spirit to come and to direct your heart and mind. Then, sit quietly before the Lord for as long as you can. Be sensitive to a nudge or leading of His Spirit. Write down any nudges or leadings.

NOTES:_____

_____

_____

_____

_____

_____

_____

_____

_____

_____

_____

_____

> For in Christ Jesus neither circumcision nor uncircumcision counts for anything, but only faith working through love. **Gal 5:6**

Today is a review day. Review your journal notes for this week. Focus on faith, love, and pleasing God.

- Love bears all things.
- *Love believes all things.*
- Love hopes all things.
- Love endures all things.
- Love never ends.

Meditation: What is the connection between faith and love? What does it mean when it says "Love believes all things"?

Meditate on pleasing God. Is there a correlation between "faith working through love" and pleasing God?

Remember to journal about your devotional time – even if you make notes and go back and journal from the notes later. It is beneficial to review your journal regularly. Pastor Martin often reviewed his prayer journal at the end of every month. We have finished the first four weeks of this devotion. This might be a good time to take some extra time and to review your journal notes.

For you had compassion on those in prison, and you joyfully accepted the plundering of your property, since you knew that you yourselves had a better possession and an abiding one.

Therefore do not throw away your confidence, which has a great reward. For you have need of endurance, so that when you have done the will of God you may receive what is promised.

For, "Yet a little while, and the coming one will come and will not delay; but my righteous one shall live by faith, and if he shrinks back, my soul has no pleasure in him." But we are not of those who shrink back and are destroyed, but of those who have faith and preserve their souls. **Heb 10:34-39**

It is a marathon, not a sprint.

I will seek You in the morning!

How blessed I am that You called me to this over 2 ½ years ago, and have met me every morning, have anointed me every morning, have blessed me with this hour every morning since!

Thank You for the richness, revelations, wisdom, understanding, desires, love, acceptance, and life that You have given me and blessed me with through this!

O let it increase and increase in my life! The most recent issue in it has been the matter of seeking you, and You are growing me in it, despite my seeming lack of success in actually reaching You, knowing You more through waiting on You.

But the truth is, that I don't need to grow weary in well doing. I just need to simply continue even when it seems like I am making no progress. A car must first go one mile per hour before it can go sixty! If all I am capable of it less than one, then let me go that part of one that I can, knowing that You will enable, equip, and empower me to go the sixty down the road in due time—IF I faint not.

So I will stop right now and spend some minutes just trying to get quiet before You, get through to You and whatever You are wanting to share with me. I want to hear Your voice, to break through into there be deeper, clearer communications with You!!
        -Pastor Daniel Martin, 7/18/14

"You have need of endurance." "My righteous one shall live by faith."

Love is the destination. Faith is the fuel for our journey there. But the journey is long and often difficult.

"You joyfully accepted the plundering of your property." I haven't heard many sermons preached on this scripture. Faith was needed for those believers to endure this persecution and pillage.

Endurance and perseverance are only possible through faith. Faith keeps me going even when it seems like I am making no progress. Faith leads me to go one mile per hour from zero so that I can be enabled, equipped, and empowered to go sixty miles per hour when the time comes.

> **Meditation:** Think back over your life and identify the key events that shaped your faith. How did you view those events at the time that they happened? Write about those events in your journal.
>
> How do you view those events now? For the events that were challenges or were difficult, do you see the Hand of God at work in them now?

☩   ☩   ☩   ☩   ☩   ☩   ☩

NOTES:_____

_____

_____

_____

_____

_____

_____

_____

_____

_____

_____

_____

> Not that I am speaking of being in need, for I have learned in whatever situation I am to be content. I know how to be brought low, and I know how to abound. In any and every circumstance, I have learned the secret of facing plenty and hunger, abundance and need. I can do all things through him who strengthens me. **Phil 4:11-13**

I trust You, O my God, at all times and in all places.

I can do all things through him who strengthens me (Phil 4:13).

For many years, when I read this verse, I thought of amazing feats – the miraculous, the magical, and the impossible. ALL things...doesn't all things mean ALL things? I can do ALL things!

But the magical isn't necessarily the context of Paul's declaration. In the prior two verses, Paul talks about the diversity of circumstances he has faced and endured – plenty and hunger, abundance and need.

Paul has learned the secret. He has learned to be content in whatever situation. He can do all things through Christ. "Do all things" means, at least in part, that he can face any circumstance which God allows. God will give him the strength to face it.

Paul has learned to trust God – at all times and in all places.

"I trust You, O my God, at all times and in all places." This statement is my second core confession – my second lifeline.

Meditation: Pray the following prayer three times slowly: "I trust You, O my God, at all times and in all places. I trust you in any situation and especially in my situation for today. You are a good God at all times and in all places. I trust in Your Goodness, O my God. Amen."

When you prayed that prayer, did you feel any resistance to it? Why?

When you prayed that prayer, did you feel any encouragement from it? Why?

Spend the rest of your devotional time figuratively giving your heart to God and allowing Him to have full control of it.

Lifelines:

I believe in You, O Lord, Maker of the heavens and the earth.

I trust You, O my God, at all times and in all places.

> And the LORD said to Satan, "Have you considered my servant Job, that there is none like him on the earth, a blameless and upright man, who fears God and turns away from evil? He still holds fast his integrity, although you incited me against him to destroy him without reason." Then Satan answered the LORD and said, "Skin for skin! All that a man has he will give for his life. But stretch out your hand and touch his bone and his flesh, and he will curse you to your face."
>
> And the LORD said to Satan, "Behold, he is in your hand; only spare his life." **Job 2:3-6**

What happened to Job, the servant of the Lord?

Satan issued a challenge. The challenge struck at the core of the relationship between God and man. The challenge essentially said:

> There is no such thing as faith in God. Man only pretends to believe in God. Man is motivated by self interest. If you remove that self interest, then so-called faith will disappear. Faith – the means that supposedly connects man to God – is not real.

So Satan removed everything that pleased Job in the most painful and grievous ways. And what did Satan find in Job? What was left? Real faith!

For I know that my Redeemer lives, and at the last he will stand upon the earth (Job 19:25).

Job had the faith to persevere through his tribulations…faith for both earth and heaven to see.

Meditation: Consider a time that you wondered whether you would make it. It can be a challenge, a loss, or a stumble that you had. How did you survive? What role did your faith play in surviving that circumstance? Write about that time in your journal.

One of Job's burdens is that he did not have faithful friends to walk through his test with him. Don't let that happen to you! Please meet regularly with your mentor or friend to discuss these devotions and to pray together.

NOTES:_____

_____

_____

_____

_____

_____

_____

_____

_____

_____

_____

_____

_____

_____

_____

_____

_____

_____

> "Simon, Simon, behold, Satan demanded to have you, that he might sift you like wheat, but I have prayed for you that your faith may not fail. And when you have turned again, strengthen your brothers." Luke 22:31-32

What does it mean to be sifted like wheat?

Sometimes we are sifted like wheat. And God allows it.

Sifting wheat removes everything extraneous – rocks, dirt, straw, and chaff. Sifting removes everything except the kernel – the thing of value.

God allowed this sifting for His purposes in Peter's life. But Jesus prayed that the essential thing would remain – Peter's faith.

Yes, Peter lied, denied, and betrayed. He acted wickedly. He sinned. But his faith remained. Peter's faith survived the sifting.

There may be many reasons that God allows His beloved to be sifted. Maybe one reason is for His child to realize that, in the midst of the maelstrom, His child still has faith.

Meditation: Has there been a time in your life that you felt that faith was all that you had? If so, what were the circumstances that brought you to that realization? As you review that time, what are the things for which you can be thankful? Record your thoughts in your journal.

⸬   ⸬   ⸬   ⸬   ⸬   ⸬   ⸬

As you engage in devotions, be sensitive to movements around you and in you. The movements of the Holy Spirit can be strong or subtle. But they run deep. Pay attention to what occurs so you can respond appropriately to God's work and direction.

> Then when Judas, his betrayer, saw that Jesus was condemned, he changed his mind and brought back the thirty pieces of silver to the chief priests and the elders, saying, "I have sinned by betraying innocent blood." They said, "What is that to us? See to it yourself." And throwing down the pieces of silver into the temple, he departed, and he went and hanged himself.   **Matt 27:3-5**

Was Judas Iscariot braver than Peter?

Peter denied Jesus and betrayed their friendship. Judas also betrayed Jesus. But when Judas realized what had occurred, he went back and confronted the chief priests and elders. He told them of his mistake. He even returned the rewards of his betrayal. Do you think Judas considered what they would think of him or, perhaps worse, what they might do to him?

Despite this brave act, Judas' reaction was different than Peter's. He hung himself.

> **Meditation:** Why did Judas react differently than Peter? What caused Judas to hang himself while Peter endured and became a great man of God?

✝ ✝ ✝ ✝ ✝ ✝ ✝

NOTES:_____

_____

_____

_____

_____

_____

_____

> For he was crucified in weakness, but lives by the power of God. For we also are weak in him, but in dealing with you we will live with him by the power of God. Examine yourselves, to see whether you are in the faith. Test yourselves. Or do you not realize this about yourselves, that Jesus Christ is in you?—unless indeed you fail to meet the test! **2 Cor 13:4-5**

Examine yourselves!

Spiritual MRI's.

Put me on trial, Lord, and cross-examine me. Test my motives and my heart.

I at first recoiled from this—but <u>with the covering of the blood I can endure a spiritual MRI.</u> Whatever You find wrong, the "MRI" didn't create it—only exposed it. Exposed it so it could be corrected and put under the blood. Lord, come and cleanse me, expose to me everything in me that needs changing.

I want to be what pleases and delights You. I want all about me that doesn't please or bless You to be removed. I want to be totally what YOU want me to be. Come and change me, O my God!!   –Pastor Daniel Martin, 1/31/13

Paul tells the Corinthians to examine themselves to see whether they are in the faith.

Paul describes his own weakness and that of his coworker. (2 Corinthians was addressed from both Paul and Timothy.) Yet, in that weakness, Paul says they will live by the power of God.

Pastor Martin asks for a spiritual MRI. Why? So he can please and delight God. And so that whatever does not please and delight God can be removed.

Meditation: Ask God for a spiritual MRI. Ask Him to show you whatever pleases Him. How can you become a child that pleases Him more?

Ask Him to show you whatever does not please Him. How can you remove what does not please Him? Write down what God shows you.

Submit yourself to the Lordship of God.

Review your notes over the past week. Consider the foundations of your faith.

- Love bears all things.
- Love believes all things.
- Love hopes all things.
- *Love endures all things.*
- Love never ends.

> Meditation: "Love endures all things." What does this statement mean? How do faith and love work together to endure all things?
>
> Focus on God and on how God exhibits each of these attributes of love. As you focus on His love, ask Him to help you fulfill each of these attributes.

✝   ✝   ✝   ✝   ✝   ✝   ✝

NOTES:_____

_____

_____

_____

_____

_____

_____

_____

_____

_____

I.Week Six, Day 1 (Date:)   **FAITH AND HOPE – REBIRTH**

> Now faith is the assurance of things hoped for, the conviction of things not seen. For by it the people of old received their commendation. By faith we understand that the universe was created by the word of God, so that what is seen was not made out of things that are visible. **Heb 11:1-3**

Faith is the assurance of things that we hope for.

Were it not for the cross, I would find great difficulty in believing it could be so!

What a horrible gulf my sin made between You and me!

What an amazing grace and love, surrender and devotion to me that caused You to pay so high a price for that gulf to be removed.

But I know the cross happened, and with that I KNOW that the price was paid, which could mean only one thing—

IT'S REAL, IT'S REAL, O I KNOW IT'S REAL!!!

PRAISE GOD, THE DOUBTS ARE SETTLED,

FOR I KNOW, I KNOW, I KNOW, I KNOW, I KNOW IT'S REAL!!

-Pastor Daniel Martin, 10/11/13

Faith arises through hope. Faith is the assurance of things hoped for – a deep and abiding assurance.

First, we hope for something. If only it could be true! But we don't see it with our senses.

Then comes assurance. Although we can't see it, we receive assurance in our hearts that it is true. So we believe it. We know that it is real! We have faith.

Love is our destination, and faith is the fuel to get us there. Hope is an essential ingredient to build faith. Then it bolsters that faith. Hope is like a boost that adds octane to the fuel of faith.

Meditation: Consider things that you hope for in your life. Write them down.

What assurances do you have that they will happen or become true?

That is why it depends on faith, in order that the promise may rest on grace and be guaranteed to all his offspring—not only to the adherent of the law but also to the one who shares the faith of Abraham, who is the father of us all, as it is written, "I have made you the father of many nations"—in the presence of the God in whom he believed, who gives life to the dead and calls into existence the things that do not exist. In hope he believed against hope, that he should become the father of many nations, as he had been told, "So shall your offspring be." He did not weaken in faith when he considered his own body, which was as good as dead (since he was about a hundred years old), or when he considered the barrenness of Sarah's womb. No unbelief made him waver concerning the promise of God, but he grew strong in his faith as he gave glory to God, fully convinced that God was able to do what he had promised. That is why his faith was "counted to him as righteousness." **Rom 4:16-22**

In hope, he believed against hope.

My grandmother (Meme) contracted rheumatic fever as a child. She was severely ill for many months. Weak and bedridden, her family despaired of her life. The little girl's health was declining.

Her mother asked the doctor if there was anything they could do. He made a suggestion but said there was no guarantee it would work. The doctor suggested that the family move from north Texas to the arid climate of south Texas. Maybe the dry, warm air would help. So the family moved.

Meme did recover slowly. But the rheumatic fever left scar tissue on her heart. The doctors told her that she could never bear children. Her heart wasn't strong enough to survive labor and delivery.

But Meme wanted to have children. She had that hope. And she acted on that hope through faith. So Meme had 9 children.

In hope Abraham believed against hope. He had hope in the face of hopelessness, hope when he was past hope.

But Abraham had a promise of God. So he clung to the promise of God for what he hoped. And that hope became faith – faith that was counted to him as righteousness.

Meditation: Consider hopes that you have because of the promises of God. Write down the hopes and the promises on which they are based in your journal.

How does hope in those promises connect to faith? What level of faith do you have for those hopes?

☩   ☩   ☩   ☩   ☩   ☩   ☩

NOTES:_____

_____

_____

_____

_____

_____

_____

_____

_____

_____

_____

_____

_____

_____

> For we know that the whole creation has been groaning together in the pains of childbirth until now. And not only the creation, but we ourselves, who have the firstfruits of the Spirit, groan inwardly as we wait eagerly for adoption as sons, the redemption of our bodies. For in this hope we were saved. Now hope that is seen is not hope. For who hopes for what he sees? But if we hope for what we do not see, we wait for it with patience. Likewise the Spirit helps us in our weakness. For we do not know what to pray for as we ought, but the Spirit himself intercedes for us with groanings too deep for words. And he who searches hearts knows what is the mind of the Spirit, because the Spirit intercedes for the saints according to the will of God. **Rom 8:22-27**

Hope that is seen is not hope.

We have a longing within us. God has placed in us a deep desire to be adopted as His children. It is something that we hope for, but we don't yet see fully. But due to the promises of God, we believe that we are His children.

This hope is a spiritual hope that is analogous to the hope of Abraham. It is a hope for childbirth – for regeneration as God's children. This hope causes groaning too deep for words. And in our weakness, we cannot accomplish it.

But praise be to God! In our longing, He has sent a Helper. The Spirit helps us in our weakness and intercedes for us – with groanings too deep for words.

Meditation: Clear your mind and your heart. Invite the Holy Spirit to come into your heart and to reveal your longings. What type of longings are they? Record these longings in your journal and expound on them.

Next focus on hope for adoption as God's child. Ask the Holy Spirit to intercede for you.

 ╬   ╬   ╬   ╬   ╬   ╬   ╬

> Remember to love God, and to receive His love, as part of your devotions. Loving God in word, in thought, and in action will change your life!

After they had eaten and drunk in Shiloh, Hannah rose. Now Eli the priest was sitting on the seat beside the doorpost of the temple of the LORD. She was deeply distressed and prayed to the LORD and wept bitterly. And she vowed a vow and said, "O LORD of hosts, if you will indeed look on the affliction of your servant and remember me and not forget your servant, but will give to your servant a son, then I will give him to the LORD all the days of his life, and no razor shall touch his head." As she continued praying before the LORD, Eli observed her mouth. Hannah was speaking in her heart; only her lips moved, and her voice was not heard. Therefore Eli took her to be a drunken woman. And Eli said to her, "How long will you go on being drunk? Put your wine away from you." But Hannah answered, "No, my lord, I am a woman troubled in spirit. I have drunk neither wine nor strong drink, but I have been pouring out my soul before the LORD. Do not regard your servant as a worthless woman, for all along I have been speaking out of my great anxiety and vexation."

Then Eli answered, "Go in peace, and the God of Israel grant your petition that you have made to him." And she said, "Let your servant find favor in your eyes." Then the woman went her way and ate, and her face was no longer sad. **1 Sam 1:9-18**

"No, my lord, I am a woman troubled in spirit."

Hannah was barren. The desire of her heart was to bear children. But she could not.

So Hannah poured out her soul to the Lord. She expressed her great anxiety and vexation for what she hoped.

When he understood, the priest, Eli, spoke a word of assurance. And Hannah was no longer sad. Eli's word of assurance birthed something within Hannah.

Meditation: Imagine the anxiety and vexation of Hannah. Try to feel what she felt as she poured out her soul to the Lord for what she desired.

What deep desire do you have? Is there something for which you want to pour out your soul to the Lord?

☩   ☩   ☩   ☩   ☩   ☩   ☩

NOTES:_____

And Hannah prayed and said,

"My heart exults in the LORD; my horn is exalted in the LORD. My mouth derides my enemies, because I rejoice in your salvation.

"There is none holy like the LORD: for there is none besides you; there is no rock like our God. Talk no more so very proudly, let not arrogance come from your mouth; for the LORD is a God of knowledge, and by him actions are weighed.

"The bows of the mighty are broken, but the feeble bind on strength.

"Those who were full have hired themselves out for bread, but those who were hungry have ceased to hunger.

"The barren has borne seven, but she who has many children is forlorn." **1 Sam 2:1-5**

"My heart exults in the Lord; my horn is exalted in the Lord."

This passage is the first part of the "song of Hannah." This song expresses the joy of childbirth – a hope fulfilled. It is a prophetic statement of the glory of a desire for childbirth fulfilled.

Meditation: Read the song of Hannah slowly (If desired, the full song of Hannah is 1 Sam. 2:1-10). What do you feel as you read it?

Ask the Holy Spirit to put the assurance in this song into your heart.

╬   ╬   ╬   ╬   ╬   ╬   ╬

Worship, like the song of Hannah, is a good way start your devotion and to enter into the presence of God. Worship responds to God and to Who He is. There are many ways to begin your devotional time, but worship is a good one to use often.

And there appeared to him an angel of the Lord standing on the right side of the altar of incense. And Zechariah was troubled when he saw him, and fear fell upon him. But the angel said to him, "Do not be afraid, Zechariah, for your prayer has been heard, and your wife Elizabeth will bear you a son, and you shall call his name John. And you will have joy and gladness, and many will rejoice at his birth, for he will be great before the Lord. And he must not drink wine or strong drink, and he will be filled with the Holy Spirit, even from his mother's womb. And he will turn many of the children of Israel to the Lord their God, and he will go before him in the spirit and power of Elijah, to turn the hearts of the fathers to the children, and the disobedient to the wisdom of the just, to make ready for the Lord a people prepared."

And Zechariah said to the angel, "How shall I know this? For I am an old man, and my wife is advanced in years." And the angel answered him, "I am Gabriel. I stand in the presence of God, and I was sent to speak to you and to bring you this good news. And behold, you will be silent and unable to speak until the day that these things take place, because you did not believe my words, which will be fulfilled in their time."

And the people were waiting for Zechariah, and they were wondering at his delay in the temple. And when he came out, he was unable to speak to them, and they realized that he had seen a vision in the temple. And he kept making signs to them and remained mute. And when his time of service was ended, he went to his home. After these days his wife Elizabeth conceived, and for five months she kept herself hidden, saying, "Thus the Lord has done for me in the days when he looked on me, to take away my reproach among people." Luke 1:11-25

He looked on me, to take away my reproach among people.

Help me! Entwine Your names, Yourself, Your Word, Your power and life around mine so that I am strengthened by all You are and have for me, instead of depending on my own strength!

Help me to use the "stamps", REDEEMED, SAVED, DELIVERED, etc. very freely! O God, I thank You for the power of the cross that "stamps" things with Your life, salvation, and freedom!! What a wonderful Savior You are!

Help me as I go through today to be diligent about my "stamping". The truth is that <u>with my mouth and my thoughts I always am stamping things. The problem is that too often I am stamping them with the wrong things: lost, hopeless, defeated, no possible life, unredeemable, etc.</u> Change me and change me and change me!! I need You more!
–Pastor Daniel Martin, 7/7/13

Elizabeth was barren and could not have children. But the Lord knew her plight and sent an angel to appear to her husband, Zechariah, while he was ministering in the temple.

Elizabeth was barren and she was now old. She and her husband longed for children. They had prayed for it – hope against hope. But an angel appeared to Zechariah with a good word – a word of promise and a word of joy.

But Zechariah questioned the word. He did not see how the impossible could be possible. In response to Zechariah's expressed doubt, the angel proclaimed him mute – unable to speak – until the child was born.

But Elizabeth rejoiced that her reproach had been taken away. *They still bear fruit in old age* (Psa 92:14a).

Meditation: Why was Zechariah struck mute when he expressed doubt in the word of promise from Gabriel, the angel? How important was faith in the fulfillment of the promise? Do you think that Zechariah's inability to speak until the child was born was a punishment or was it to encourage words of faith rather than doubt?

Consider your own words. What type of "stamps" do you use? How can you speak words of faith and encouragement?

⼤   ⼤   ⼤   ⼤   ⼤   ⼤   ⼤

NOTES:_____

_____

_____

_____

_____

_____

> So now faith, hope, and love abide, these three;
> but the greatest of these is love. 1 Cor 13:13

Review your journal notes for the week. Consider people of God that hoped for the impossible – the unseen.

Meditation: If you are struck by a theme, a feeling, or a meditation from this past week, explore it further.

Ask the Lord to show you the connections between hope and faith.

☦   ☦   ☦   ☦   ☦   ☦   ☦

NOTES:_____

_____

_____

_____

_____

_____

_____

_____

_____

_____

_____

_____

I.Week Seven, Day 1 (Date:)   **HOPE BUILDERS**

> So when God desired to show more convincingly to the heirs of the promise the unchangeable character of his purpose, he guaranteed it with an oath, so that by two unchangeable things, in which it is impossible for God to lie, we who have fled for refuge might have strong encouragement to hold fast to the hope set before us. We have this as a sure and steadfast anchor of the soul, a hope that enters into the inner place behind the curtain, where Jesus has gone as a forerunner on our behalf, having become a high priest forever after the order of Melchizedek. **Heb 6:17-20**

A sure and steadfast anchor of the soul.

Father, So much hinges on HOPE!! You operate and move through us as we allow our hope/expectations to be the power You use to release life and goodness to us.

- **It is faith's foundation**
- **It is our anchor in life**
- **It is our peace in the middle of storms**
- **It is our glory when all around us is ugly, fearful, impossible, and hopeless**

I thank You that You empower us to hope when in the natural there is No Hope. I thank You for the powerful gift of hope/expectation! I thank You for the energy, freshness, revitalization that all flow with the flow of hope to us, in us, and through us!!

I am so glad for the privilege and power You give us to choose hope in our lives!
–Pastor Daniel Martin, 3/3/13

God guaranteed His promise to His heirs with an oath in which it is impossible for God to lie. Why? So his heirs (which include you) might have strong encouragement to hold fast to the hope set before them.

A ship without an anchor is moved by the waves and currents of the sea. The size of the ship doesn't matter. Even an aircraft carrier has anchors. Otherwise the waves and currents toss it about.

Our hope in God's promises is an anchor for our soul. Our daily circumstances are like waves and currents that try to move us up and down and to and fro. They make a soul without an anchor unstable and double-minded. But our hope acts like an anchor that holds us steady – moored and single-minded. We hold fast to it.

We cannot see the anchor. Like our hope, it is unseen. But if we are connected to it, we remain sure and steadfast. We are not driven by the waves of the sea and tossed about by the wind.

> **Meditation:** What promises of God do you hold onto? Think of these promises. Journal about these promises. Allow them to encourage you as you hold fast to them in hope.

✝ ✝ ✝ ✝ ✝ ✝ ✝

NOTES:_____

_____

_____

_____

_____

_____

_____

_____

_____

_____

_____

_____

_____

_____

> For whatever was written in former days was written for our instruction, that through endurance and through the encouragement of the Scriptures we might have hope. May the God of endurance and encouragement grant you to live in such harmony with one another, in accord with Christ Jesus, that together you may with one voice glorify the God and Father of our Lord Jesus Christ. **Rom 15:4-6**

"That…through the encouragement of the scriptures, we might have hope."

Gargling. Carolyn has been sick the last few days and I woke with a slightly sore throat and a feeling of some congestion below the throat. I have a cup of salt water with me that I every few minutes gargle from. I do it so that the salt can come in contact with the infections and deal with them.

Help me to "gargle" Your word in every situation and issue of my life, so that it can come in contact with and destroy every infection in my mind, will, emotions, and life that the enemy has put there to destroy me, and to prevent me breathing freely.

Help me to "gargle" so fully that there is no pneumonia spiritually blocking Your air going to my body and giving health to every cell in my body.

Show me what it is today to "gargle" spiritually all day long. How good Your word is at removing infections and diseases from me. You really did send Your word and delivered me from ALL my destructions!   –Pastor Daniel Martin, 1/18/13

The scriptures are a gift to us. They were written for our instruction, and their encouragement brings hope.

But a gift must be received. A good gift should be treasured. We need to spend time in scripture in order to build our hope. Let your mind recall it often so that it soaks into your heart. As Pastor Martin encourages, gargle often.

Meditation: Consider how the scriptures birth hope within you. List your favorite scriptures that are "hope builders." Write them down. Then meditate on those scriptures. Call them to mind often.

╬   ╬   ╬   ╬   ╬   ╬   ╬

Take time to read the scripture passages carefully. When we spend time with God's word, it becomes a part of us.

> Give ear, O my people, to my teaching; incline your ears to the words of my mouth! I will open my mouth in a parable; I will utter dark sayings from of old, things that we have heard and known, that our fathers have told us.
>
> We will not hide them from their children, but tell to the coming generation the glorious deeds of the LORD, and his might, and the wonders that he has done.
>
> He established a testimony in Jacob and appointed a law in Israel, which he commanded our fathers to teach to their children, that the next generation might know them, the children yet unborn, and arise and tell them to their children, so that they should set their hope in God and not forget the works of God, but keep his commandments; and that they should not be like their fathers, a stubborn and rebellious generation, a generation whose heart was not steadfast, whose spirit was not faithful to God.
>
> **Psa 78:1-8**

So they [the next generation] should set their hope in God.

I made the trip to Alabama to see my grandparents numerous times. I knew many portions of those highways. But I also had markers that told me that I was on the right road and that reminded me of the path I was on.

In north Georgia, not far away from the Georgia Welcome Center, a tree stood in the median at the top of a hill. It was one of the most beautiful trees I have ever seen. A thick, strong trunk supported a uniform and flourishing orb of branches. I loved that tree. It did not surprise me after a few years to see that someone had tied a yellow ribbon around the trunk. I told many people in my family about that tree.

When you crossed the Chattahoochee River into Alabama, a sign greeted you that said "Welcome to Alabama the Beautiful." That sign made me smile an ironic smile. I had left the glorious, panoramic mountains of North Carolina to travel to the red clay and scrub pine of central Alabama. That was not my idea of beautiful.

And yet the love that awaited me at my destination made it beautiful.

Every journey with the Lord has markers.

A marker is an extraordinary event, a miraculous turn, or a special touch. A marker stands out from the routine of the day to day journey.

We should be mindful our markers. They assure us of our path and journey, and bring to mind that the Lord, with His might, still does wonders.

Our markers give us hope. A sanctified memory – one that brings to mind the great things that God has done – makes hope arise in otherwise desolate circumstances. And we should tell generations to come of our markers so they have hope as well.

Meditation: List some of the markers in your spiritual journey. What special things has God done in your life? How do you feel as you call those markers to mind? Allow them to build hope within you.

✠ ✠ ✠ ✠ ✠ ✠ ✠

NOTES:_____

_____

_____

_____

_____

_____

_____

_____

_____

_____

_____

_____

_____

Put not your trust in princes, in a son of man, in whom there is no salvation.

When his breath departs, he returns to the earth; on that very day his plans perish.

Blessed is he whose help is the God of Jacob, whose hope is in the LORD his God, who made heaven and earth, the sea, and all that is in them, who keeps faith forever;

who executes justice for the oppressed, who gives food to the hungry. The LORD sets the prisoners free; the LORD opens the eyes of the blind. The LORD lifts up those who are bowed down; the LORD loves the righteous.

The LORD watches over the sojourners; he upholds the widow and the fatherless, but the way of the wicked he brings to ruin.

The LORD will reign forever, your God, O Zion, to all generations. Praise the LORD!   **Psa 146:3-10**

God acts with righteousness.

God is a God of the oppressed; a God of the hungry; a God of the imprisoned; a God of the afflicted; a God of the lowly; a God of the righteous; a God of the refugee; a God of the widow; and a God of the orphan. He is a God of hope to all of these because of His righteousness. When treated unjustly, I can hope in Him because He sees my plight and upholds me.

Meditation: Consider the heart of God toward each group listed in this passage. How does that heart differ from the way our culture treats that group?

What hope does the righteousness of God provide within you?

Remember to write your thoughts and ideas in your journal. Writing them down can help define your thoughts and help refine them.

> My son, if your heart is wise, my heart too will be glad. My inmost being will exult when your lips speak what is right.
>
> Let not your heart envy sinners, but continue in the fear of the LORD all the day. Surely there is a future, and your hope will not be cut off. Pro 23:15-18

God is the God of the future.

What awesome and glorious things the riches of Your Presence are!

At Your right hand there is pleasure forevermore!

There is also deep abiding security as my older brother holds my hand, "goes with me to turn the 'lights' on when I am terrified of the dark" and cannot make it alone at all!

You, as my older brother are very willing to go with me through the fearful darkness that makes me tremble, ready to protect me, ready to take me eventually to the Father. Both of You have faced the "booger-man" and have conquered him at the cross. It is nothing for You to defeat him again in all that he tries to bring up and do in my life!

O blessed Savior, wonderful Brother, awesome Defender! Come and help me to know and recognize more and more what I have in You! You are all and more than I need!

Thank You for the horrible price You paid for me, just so You could take me as Your own. This child needs You so much. Come and take over in all the kingdoms of my life, so that your Kingdom is all that matters to me, so that "my petty kingdoms" are seen as nothings, as the trashy, misty, fading, and inconsequential things that they are!

O God, lift me up today and help me to stand on higher ground in You! Show me Your will, way, and glory!

Come and have Your way in me, and let me know the fullness of Your Presence, life, and glory! You and You alone are all that matters!

O great Light of the world! Your presence is with me in all the darkness, but Your Light exposes and eradicates all the darkness! Imagine that night that all of a sudden brilliant light lit up my path and exposed all that was around! You not only protect me in the darkness, You release Your light to Expose all the dark things that terrify me, and cause them to vanish in the brilliance of Who You are! What a wonderful Shepherd I have!

Thank You so much for Your wonderful leading and guiding this morning!
        –Pastor Daniel Martin, 10/12/14

God is the God of the future. He fulfills His plans for man and beast. Whether circumstances seem delightful or dire; whether prospects look bright or bleak; God is still the God of the future. Your future is in His hands.

We often want to control the future. We want our affairs to go a certain way. So we worry about them. Anxiety about the future arises from our attempt to control it. We try to be the God of the future instead of allowing God to be the God of the future.[10]

God is the God of the future. We need to continue in fear of Him all the day. He is good. He will not cut off our hope.

Meditation: Consider the things in your life that trigger stress. Write them down. If needed, repent to God for the stress and anxiety that you have.

Now take them and figuratively put them in your hand. Lift your hand to God and release these things from your hand to Him. Tell God that the hope of your future is in Him. Tell God that you desire for Him to be the God of your future.

✝   ✝   ✝   ✝   ✝   ✝   ✝

NOTES:_____

_____

_____

_____

_____

_____

_____

_____

_____

---

[10] See Appendix A (*Steps To Peace*) for a good discipline to overcome anxiety. Authored by Steve Parker, *Steps To Peace* is based on Psalms 37 and outlines positive steps from that Psalm to fight worry and to find peace in Him.

So we do not lose heart. Though our outer self is wasting away, our inner self is being renewed day by day.

For this light momentary affliction is preparing for us an eternal weight of glory beyond all comparison, as we look not to the things that are seen but to the things that are unseen. For the things that are seen are transient, but the things that are unseen are eternal.

2 Cor 4:16-18

Glory just ahead!

I am so amazed at the Power and Love with which You hold us up, carry us through deep waters of fear, pain, potential loss, and defeat—but with You there is always GLORY JUST AHEAD!

O what a powerful phrase this is—GLORY JUST AHEAD!

And because of Your great sacrifice for us on the cross, there truly, always, no matter what happens or what seems to prevail, is GLORY JUST AHEAD!

Because You are just ahead.

You have gone before us, taken our pains, fears, losses, and hopelessness all on Yourself and made a way for us where there is no way! Eternity holds no tears, pains, scars, losses, defeats, or sorrows.

And You are the center of eternity! What an amazing, awesome, and glorious God You are to us! I love You and thank You for all You are to me!

What an amazing God You are!!   -Pastor Daniel Martin, 7/3/16

This momentary light affliction is preparing for us an eternal weight of glory. God does not just control the future. He has promised an eternal weight of glory. Any affliction that I bear is light in comparison to the eternal weight of glory that will be. In fact, there is no comparison.

My faith in looking to the unseen and to the eternal keeps me from losing heart. The eternal weight of glory gives me hope. Glory just ahead!

Meditation: Explore how you feel about the unseen and the eternal. Record your feelings. Explore whether you have faith or doubt about the glory just ahead. Ask the Holy Spirit to give you insight into that glory. Write about it in your journal.

✝ ✝ ✝ ✝ ✝ ✝ ✝

God's promises; the scriptures; God's mighty works; God's righteousness; His plans for the future; and the eternal weight of glory – these are all sources of hope.

> **Meditation:** Look back over your notes for this week. Identify the areas that build hope within you. As you meditate on those areas, invite the Holy Spirit to build hope in Him within you.

⳨   ⳨   ⳨   ⳨   ⳨   ⳨   ⳨

NOTES:_____

_____

_____

_____

_____

_____

_____

_____

_____

_____

_____

_____

_____

I.Week Eight, Day 1 (Date:)   **LOVE AND HOPE**

> Behold, the eye of the LORD is on those who fear him, on those who hope in his steadfast love, that he may deliver their soul from death and keep them alive in famine.
>
> Our soul waits for the LORD; he is our help and our shield.
>
> For our heart is glad in him, because we trust in his holy name.
>
> Let your steadfast love, O LORD, be upon us, even as we hope in you. **Psa 33:18-22**

Dare to hope.

Great boldness is needed in our time! It is not a time to shrink back, but a time to surge forward!

Tremendous role of HOPE in driving back the darkness, in seeing God's Kingdom come in while we are in the middle of what looks like darkness taking over!

Hope produces BOLDNESS!

Expectation produces great BOLDNESS!   –Pastor Daniel Martin, 8/31/14

Hope driving back the darkness. Deliverance from death. Kept alive in famine. Hope.

Twice the Psalmist expresses his hope. And each time the Psalmist finds that hope in the steadfast love of the Lord.

The steadfast love of God is the primary source of hope.

- Love bears all things.
- Love believes all things.
- *Love hopes all things.*
- Love endures all things.
- Love never ends.

Meditation: Love hopes all things. Slowly repeat this phrase. Allow the love of our Lord to build hope within you.

"But this I call to mind and therefore I have hope."

Lamentations is an incredible book. Many attribute authorship of the book to Jeremiah, the weeping prophet.

Lamentations details the incredible desolation, devastation, and destruction of Jerusalem and of God's people. The book is filled with descriptions of pain, despair, loss, and grief. It is not for the faint of heart. Don't read its forlorn passages if you are suffering from depression.

In our English translation, Chapters 1, 2, 4, and 5 are each 22 verses long. (You can read independently about the acrostic symmetry in Hebrew that some translations try to reflect.)

Although all other chapters are 22 verses long, Chapter 3 of Lamentations is 66 verses long. But centered around verse 22 of Chapter 3 is a key passage in the book. It is a beacon of hope in an otherwise dismal lament:

Lam 3:19 Remember my affliction and my wanderings, the wormwood and the gall!

Lam 3:20 My soul continually remembers it and is bowed down within me.

Lam 3:21 But this I call to mind, and therefore I have hope:

Lam 3:22 The steadfast love of the LORD never ceases; his mercies never come to an end;

Lam 3:23 they are new every morning; great is your faithfulness.

Lam 3:24 "The LORD is my portion," says my soul, "therefore I will hope in him."

Lam 3:25 The LORD is good to those who wait for him, to the soul who seeks him.

Lam 3:26 It is good that one should wait quietly for the salvation of the LORD.

In the middle of hopeless despair, the writer calls one thing to mind and thus has hope. *"The steadfast love of the Lord never ceases; his mercies never come to an end; they are new every morning; great is your faithfulness."*

The steadfast, unfailing, unwavering, and never ending love of the Lord brings hope in the midst of terror, devastation, and hopelessness.

The love of God is the primary source of hope. And hope leads to faith. Hope is a bridge between love and faith.

Meditation: If you are able, read the Book of Lamentations (If you have limited time, read Lamentations 3). As you read it, ask the Holy Spirit to quicken to your heart the love, hope, and faith that the writer expresses while living in the midst of desolation, devastation, and destruction.

Second Lifeline: I trust You, O my God, at all times and in all places.

✠   ✠   ✠   ✠   ✠   ✠   ✠

NOTES:_____

_____

_____

_____

_____

_____

_____

_____

_____

_____

_____

_____

_____

> We love because he first loved us. **1 Jn 4:19**

He loved us first.

I once knew a person who excelled in encouraging the people around her to love and to serve. She didn't give speeches or lessons on it, or even say many words about it. Yes, she did talk about it occasionally. And above the door of her sewing closet was a framed quote of 1 Cor. 13:8a which says "Love never fails."

But her encouragement came as a result of her example to the people around her and maybe more importantly, her outpouring of love for them. And they knew they were loved.

Over the years, I noticed two things that happened as a result of her outflow of love. First, people around her were drawn to her – like a moth is drawn to a light. They may not have fully understood why they were drawn to her, but they wanted to be around her and to share her life.

The second result is that people wanted to love her and to serve her in return. Sometimes I felt that people almost tripped over each other trying to give her things. It was a natural and organic response to the love she showed them.

She loved them first and, as they grew, they loved her in return.

You are loved – deeply, powerfully, intimately, and fully.

And this is the beginning for us. Our life in Him began with love from God.

The initial meditation in this devotion focused on our destination which is fullness of love – perfect love between God and us. The reason we started with this destination was to give vision. But our life in Him began because He loved us first.

His love flows from Who He is and we are its object. He bestows His love freely. We did not earn it. We did not merit it. He loves us because of our status – because of who we are. We are His dearly beloved.

He calls us to abide in His love. We only need receive it.

Meditation: Today is a meditation of rest. Still your mind and quiet your spirit. Then rest in God's love. Allow yourself to fall into the loving arms of God. Rest peacefully in the warmth, peace, and grace of love. Abide in His love now and throughout your day.

✝   ✝   ✝   ✝   ✝   ✝   ✝

> See what kind of love the Father has given to us, that we should be called children of God; and so we are. The reason that the world did not know us is that it did not know him. **1 Jn 3:1**

"Son, I love you!"

As I was traveling by myself late last night to Madison, along the freeway with very little traffic, I had been listening to a CD and then the radio, when I thought that I would just turn it all off and spend some time waiting on You. I paused and looked at the serenity of the sky, the peaceful smooth road I was on, and just said calmly, from the heart as well as my mouth, "Father, I love you."

I instantly, clearer than ever before felt You say to me, "Son, I love you!"

I have never in my life had a deeper sense of Your voice inside me speaking so clearly and freshly, so powerfully. There is power in WHAT You say, but there is also power in HOW You say it. It just overwhelmed me. What power there was in those 4 words. I was in awe of them for awhile. In awe of knowing Your voice. In awe of WHAT You said, and HOW You said it. Human words fail to describe the full impact of them.
    –Pastor Daniel Martin, 5/3/13

God's love has a certain quality – a certain nature - that arises from Who He is.

I often told my children that their father would always love them. It isn't a perfect love, but it will always be there. I would not always agree with them; and I would not always approve of what they did or said. But I committed always to love them.

What kind of love has the Father given? The kind of love that arises from a Father's heart. God is a Father by nature. The love of a father flows from Who He is.

God loves His children. And you are His child.

Meditation: Imagine the perfect Father. What does he do? How does he act? What does he say to his children? Journal your thoughts.

Then imagine that you look into His eyes and see His perfect love for you. What do you see when you look into His eyes? What do they communicate to you?

What type of hope does this love build within you?

☩   ☩   ☩   ☩   ☩   ☩   ☩

NOTES:_____

_____

_____

_____

_____

_____

_____

_____

_____

_____

_____

_____

_____

_____

It is fine to spend more than one day on the same devotion. If you sense God is moving in your heart, allow Him time to finish His work.

> I will arise and go to my father, and I will say to him, "Father, I have sinned against heaven and before you. I am no longer worthy to be called your son. Treat me as one of your hired servants."'
>
> And he arose and came to his father. But while he was still a long way off, his father saw him and felt compassion, and ran and embraced him and kissed him. And the son said to him, 'Father, I have sinned against heaven and before you. I am no longer worthy to be called your son.'
>
> But the father said to his servants, 'Bring quickly the best robe, and put it on him, and put a ring on his hand, and shoes on his feet. And bring the fattened calf and kill it, and let us eat and celebrate. For this my son was dead, and is alive again; he was lost, and is found.' And they began to celebrate. **Luke 15:18-24**

When he saw him and felt compassion, he ran and embraced him and kissed him.

Hourly chime just went off… 8:00-8:03. Told You I loved You, and it seemed I heard You say, "I love You, too, son!" O the glory and thrill of those words!

O, I needed to hear it from You this morning. I knew it. I was content in the truth of it. It can never be different from that because of the cross—but I still needed to hear it from You! How rich and life-giving those words are!   -Pastor Daniel Martin, 7/14/12

This passage is from the parable of the prodigal son. Before the son could speak – before the son could humble himself before his father, the father saw him, ran to him, and hugged him and kissed him.

Unconditional love is not something many of us have experienced. Earthly parents love imperfectly. Love, affection, and approval are often used:

- As a manipulation of behavior;
- As a reaction based on the parent's emotional feeling about the child at that moment; or
- To validate the parent by living vicariously through the child.

But God's fatherly love is unconditional, and it is pure. It is always there – constant. It does not vary. And it is not diminished by our behavior.

Meditation: Is it hard or easy for you to accept the love of a father? Why?

What are the implications of unconditional love? What hope does this love give you?

"What man of you, having a hundred sheep, if he has lost one of them, does not leave the ninety-nine in the open country, and go after the one that is lost, until he finds it? And when he has found it, he lays it on his shoulders, rejoicing.

And when he comes home, he calls together his friends and his neighbors, saying to them, 'Rejoice with me, for I have found my sheep that was lost.'

Just so, I tell you, there will be more joy in heaven over one sinner who repents than over ninety-nine righteous persons who need no repentance." **Luke 15:4-7**

Rejoice with me for I have found my sheep that was lost.

Times with close friends that involve laughter, stories, and camaraderie are a source of great joy. I have had times with friends that I was laughing so hard I was in tears and almost rolling in the floor. In fact, some years I have reviewed the year and decided that a certain shared time was the funniest moment of the year. Those moments involve close friends.

The story of Joe and the monkey is one such occasion. My wife and I have hosted refugee young men at a Bible study on Monday nights for 15 years. These close friends are now adults, but they share stories from their childhoods in Africa or Asia. One Monday around the dinner table, Joe told us his story about the monkey.

When Joe was a very young boy in Congo, someone had tied a monkey behind his house on a leash. Joe decided he would have a little fun with the monkey. He began mocking the monkey and making fun of him. The monkey responded by screeching at Joe and straining at the leash. But Joe stayed just far enough out of the monkey's reach that the monkey could not get him. He kept making faces at the monkey and gesticulating at it with the monkey screaming back at him.

What Joe did not know is how poorly the leash was anchored. Suddenly, the monkey broke free and jumped on top of Joe's head. The monkey began beating Joe and pulling his hair. Joe screamed in pain and began running toward the house. He managed to get the monkey off of him and to run inside – but not before the monkey had given him a good thrashing.

We "rolled in the floor" as Joe described his monkey encounter and his healthy fear of monkeys ever since that encounter.

Luke 15 is my "repentance, reconciliation, and restoration" chapter. But it is also my "joy, joy, and more joy" chapter. In Luke 15, Jesus tells 3 parables – the parable of the Lost Sheep, the parable of the Lost Coin, and the parable of the Prodigal Son. Each parable describes lost, then found – followed by joy.

Relationship is a source of joy. Times with close friends, like hearing Joe's story, are a source of great joy. But you need to be there for it to be that funny. That is because knowing the persons present and sharing the moment together are keys to the hilarity.

The Lord derives great joy from relationship. Reconciliation and restoration through repentance bring Him delight. The father in the parable of the Prodigal Son expresses this delight in his words and with his actions. Relationship is a Source of Joy.

Joy in relationship builds hope. In fact, it is almost impossible not to have hope when you have joyful relationship with the Lord.

> **Meditation:** Think of times that you have experienced hilarity with close friends. What joy did you experience in those times? Consider the connections between relationship, joy, and hope. Write your thoughts in your journal.

＃　＃　＃　＃　＃　＃　＃

NOTES:_____

_____

_____

_____

_____

_____

_____

_____

> His delight is not in the strength of the horse, nor his pleasure in the legs of a man, but the LORD takes pleasure in those who fear him, in those who <u>hope</u> in his <u>steadfast love</u>. **Psa 147:10-11**

- Love is patient.
- Love is kind.
- Love does not envy.
- Love does not boast.
- Love is not arrogant.
- Love is not rude.
- Love does not insist on its own way.
- Love is not irritable.
- Love is not resentful.
- Love does not rejoice at wrongdoing.
- Love rejoices with the truth.
- Love bears all things.
- Love believes all things.
- Love hopes all things.
- Love endures all things.
- *Love never ends.*

Review the entries in your journal for this week.

A realization of God's love leads us to hope. Hope provides a path to faith. Faith fuels a journey where our love grows and our ability to receive God's love grows. Faith, hope, and love lead us to His perfect love.

Meditation: Love never ends. (Other versions: "Love never fails.")

Repeat this passage slowly. Ask God to show you the nature of a love that never fails...a love that never ends.

✠   ✠   ✠   ✠   ✠   ✠   ✠

I.Week Nine, Day 1 (Date:)   **DEMONSTRATIONS OF GOD'S LOVE**

For while we were still weak, at the right time Christ died for the ungodly. For one will scarcely die for a righteous person—though perhaps for a good person one would dare even to die—but God shows his love for us in that while we were still sinners, Christ died for us.

Since, therefore, we have now been justified by his blood, much more shall we be saved by him from the wrath of God. For if while we were enemies we were reconciled to God by the death of his Son, much more, now that we are reconciled, shall we be saved by his life. **Rom 5:6-10**

God demonstrates His love for us.

I saw the cross of Jesus, when burdened with my sin,
I sought the cross of Jesus, to give me peace within;
I brought my soul to Jesus, He cleansed it in His blood;
And in the cross of Jesus I found my peace with God.

I love the cross of Jesus, it tells me what I am—
A vile and guilty creature, saved ONLY through the Lamb;
No righteousness, nor merit, no beauty I can plead;
Yet in the cross of glory, my title there I read.
(WOW, O WOW!!)
I clasp the cross of Jesus in every trying hour,
My sure and certain refuge, my never failing tower;
In every fear and conflict, I more than conqueror am;
Living I'm safe, or dying, thro' Christ, the risen Lamb.

Sweet is the cross of Jesus! There let my weary heart
Still rest in peace unshaken, till with Him, ne'er to part;
And then in strains of glory I'll sing His wondrous power,
Where sin can never enter, and death is known no more.   (Frederick Whitfield 1861)

O the wonder and power of the cross! What awesome life and glory it bestows on me! It Stripped You of all Your splendor and glory—glory that then fell on me! It devastated the wonder of heaven—to give me the wonder of heaven!

It so vividly and powerfully transferred and demonstrated to me how awesome and powerful Your love, acceptance, and desire for me are! -Pastor Daniel Martin, 10/11/13

God shows His love for us. While we were still sinners, Christ died for us.

The cross is the foremost demonstration of God's love for us.

Meditation: Imagine yourself at the foot of the cross. Gaze upon the Son of Man suffering on it. Hear His labored breathing. He occasionally cries out.

What do you feel for Him?

What do you want to say to Him? Write down your meditations.

As you abide at the foot of the cross, contemplate the love that Jesus had for you to die on the cross. Receive His love expressed through His sacrifice.

✠   ✠   ✠   ✠   ✠   ✠   ✠

NOTES:_____

_____

_____

_____

_____

_____

_____

_____

_____

_____

And you were dead in the trespasses and sins in which you once walked, following the course of this world, following the prince of the power of the air, the spirit that is now at work in the sons of disobedience—among whom we all once lived in the passions of our flesh, carrying out the desires of the body and the mind, and were by nature children of wrath, like the rest of mankind.

But God, being rich in mercy, because of the great love with which he loved us, even when we were dead in our trespasses, made us alive together with Christ—by grace you have been saved—and raised us up with him and seated us with him in the heavenly places in Christ Jesus, so that in the coming ages he might show the immeasurable riches of his grace in kindness toward us in Christ Jesus.

For by grace you have been saved through faith. And this is not your own doing; it is the gift of God, not a result of works, so that no one may boast. **Eph 2:1-9**

"Because the great love with which He loved us."

O yes, renew, change, and cleanse my heart from every trifle, every lie!

Thank You so much for how much You have already done, but there is far more left to do than has been done. The farther I go in You and allow You to cleanse me, and free me, the more I realize that has to be done!

Come and help me to see You more and more as Isaiah did, "high and lifted up", and give me such clear revelation of Your holiness, purity, and life that all I can do is cry out and say, "O, Lord, I am a man of unclean lips and I dwell among a people of unclean lips."

Yes, the changes, cleansing, and renewal all flow from the GRACE that I found in You! They are not a result of me at all—they are all because of You and Your great love, mercy, gentleness, and care for me!

O what a Shepherd You have been to me! I need You more!

O the glory of Your love in my life! It has so powerfully impacted me. It was impacting me long before I knew it, long before I even acknowledged to You that I didn't love You, didn't know You.

O how gracious and merciful You were to reveal to me the emptiness and holes in my life. You have been so good to me! I don't know anyone who has experienced You being as good to them, as You have been to me. I am amazed at You, Father!
  – Pastor Daniel Martin, 7/18/14

Meditation: Read carefully through the devotion of Pastor Martin and the scripture passage and pick out the words that are descriptive of the goodness of God. Underline each word if that would be helpful. Embrace His goodness!

Dwell on each word and ask the Holy Spirit to make that word come alive to you in your heart and in your life.

☩   ☩   ☩   ☩   ☩   ☩   ☩

NOTES:_____

_____

_____

_____

_____

_____

_____

_____

_____

_____

_____

_____

_____

The LORD is merciful and gracious, slow to anger and abounding in steadfast love.

He will not always chide, nor will he keep his anger forever.

He does not deal with us according to our sins, nor repay us according to our iniquities.

For as high as the heavens are above the earth, so great is his steadfast love toward those who fear him; as far as the east is from the west, so far does he remove our transgressions from us.

As a father shows compassion to his children, so the LORD shows compassion to those who fear him.

For he knows our frame; he remembers that we are dust.

As for man, his days are like grass; he flourishes like a flower of the field; for the wind passes over it, and it is gone, and its place knows it no more.

But the steadfast love of the LORD is from everlasting to everlasting on those who fear him, and his righteousness to children's children, to those who keep his covenant and remember to do his commandments. **Psa 103:8-18**

Compassion.

You must cultivate confidence in God's affection toward you even when you stumble. If you lack this confidence, then you close your spirit toward Jesus. The revelation that God enjoys you in your weakness transforms you. In my experience, this is the hardest revelation for people to enter into and the place on the spiritual journey where most people stall and stop. The reason?

You will never enjoy God more than your revelation of God enjoying you in your weakness.

But when you do see that He enjoys you in weakness, then you bear fruit. You begin to enjoy God all the time. Your heart responds in affection. You hear the Godhead, the Three in One, say, "We like you." Your heart answers, "I like You, then." Who doesn't enjoy being with people who like him? So when you understand that God likes you all the time, you respond by liking Him. You start smiling just thinking about God. It happens automatically.

[PRAYER STARTER] I rest in the fact that You like me, Lord. You want to spend time with me, and You enjoy me just as I am. What an incredible thought, dear Lord, and it fills me with confidence in Your love for me.

You will never enjoy God more than you experience His enjoyment of you in your weakness.   -Pastor Daniel Martin, 8/14/13 (Portions from a *Charisma* Devotion)

Compassion is the ability to suffer with the weak. Our society exalts strength and beauty, and disdains the frail, the dependent, and the unstable. But God, Who is all powerful, shows His love through compassion for the weak.

Meditation: Think of the people that you know who are frail, infirm, or emotionally unstable. Exercise compassion toward them. Ask God what you can do to show compassion toward them just as God shows compassion toward you. Love does not boast.

☩   ☩   ☩   ☩   ☩   ☩   ☩

NOTES:_____

_____

_____

_____

_____

_____

_____

_____

_____

_____

_____

_____

"You have heard that it was said, 'You shall love your neighbor and hate your enemy.'

But I say to you, Love your enemies and pray for those who persecute you, so that you may be sons of your Father who is in heaven. For he makes his sun rise on the evil and on the good, and sends rain on the just and on the unjust.

For if you love those who love you, what reward do you have? Do not even the tax collectors do the same? And if you greet only your brothers, what more are you doing than others? Do not even the Gentiles do the same?

You therefore must be perfect, as your heavenly Father is perfect."
Matt 5:43-48

Why does God love His enemies?

I had a situation that regularly upset me. For me, a very simple but real offense that seemed to occur daily was driving in traffic. I live in a large city. People drive like maniacs. Challenged drivers cut in front of you. They don't let you merge into oncoming traffic. They drive 20 miles per hour over the speed limit and tailgate you when you don't do the same. People can be so inconsiderate. I even got to the point that I categorized the bumper stickers of the most offensive drivers. I was righteously indignant at some of the worst categories.

Then, I decided to drive with love and grace for my fellow drivers. Determined not to get upset, my focus became blessing the inconsiderate motorist. If someone cut in front of me, I tried to defer. If someone drove recklessly, I tried to bless them and not think bad thoughts of them. My new attitude met with repeated failure, but my driving attitude did change. I allowed love to enter the world of motor vehicle operation.

The nature of love is love. God's love is perfect. His love is constant, consistent, and unchanging. Love is His unchanging attribute. It does not waver.

Our love is imperfect. If another person is mean or spiteful to us, our love may quickly change to anger, pain, or vengefulness. We often want to lash out and to pay back the offense.

But it is not so with God. His love does not change. Whether treated well or treated spitefully, God still loves perfectly. God loves His enemies because His love endures from everlasting to everlasting.

Love bears all things.

Meditation: Consider the situations that make you angry or upset. Write down a list of these situations in your journal. Identify a situation that happens often. Allow love to enter that situation. Take steps to love your enemies.

╬   ╬   ╬   ╬   ╬   ╬   ╬

NOTES:_____

_____

_____

_____

_____

_____

_____

_____

_____

_____

Please do not neglect meeting with your mentor or devotional partner. Godly wisdom from another source is very beneficial in your journey to fullness of love.

I thank him who has given me strength, Christ Jesus our Lord, because he judged me faithful, appointing me to his service, though formerly I was a blasphemer, persecutor, and insolent opponent. But I received mercy because I had acted ignorantly in unbelief, and the grace of our Lord overflowed for me with the faith and love that are in Christ Jesus.

The saying is trustworthy and deserving of full acceptance, that Christ Jesus came into the world to save sinners, of whom I am the foremost.

But I received mercy for this reason, that in me, as the foremost, Jesus Christ might display his perfect patience as an example to those who were to believe in him for eternal life.

To the King of the ages, immortal, invisible, the only God, be honor and glory forever and ever. Amen. **1 Tim 1:12-17**

Mercy to a sinner.

Such commitment, such commitment to what to all others was so small, so insignificant, so corrupt, ugly, and repulsive! Yet You saw worth and value, You GAVE worth and value to this insignificant, repulsive, and corrupt being—so much worth and value that You were willing to suffer, to take great loss, to go through deep rejection, pain, and lose Your holiness and righteousness, even have the Father turn His face away from You—all so You could pay the price to purchase me, to set me free, to have me in Your Presence for eternity!

Amazing GRACE!!!   –Pastor Daniel Martin, 11/27/14

Paul knew that he received mercy and overflowing grace. He saw himself as the foremost of sinners, but he received mercy as a demonstration by Jesus of perfect patience.

Love is patient. That patient love is demonstrated by mercy to sinners like you and me.

Meditation: Think of the ways that God has shown you mercy in your life. How has He been patient with you? Write about God's mercy and patience toward you.

Thank God for His ongoing patience and mercy to you. Thank God that He is not impatient, intolerant, and cruel.

> What then shall we say to these things? If God is for us, who can be against us? He who did not spare his own Son but gave him up for us all, how will he not also with him graciously give us all things?
>
> Who shall bring any charge against God's elect? It is God who justifies. Who is to condemn? Christ Jesus is the one who died—more than that, who was raised—who is at the right hand of God, who indeed is interceding for us. **Rom 8:31-34**

No condemnation.

O come and help me to sing, really sing of Your love and pardon for me! I remember thinking about the absolute joy an inmate would experience if given a complete pardon where he was under an impending death sentence—on his way to the death chamber—with no hope, no expectation, only deep regret for the life he had lived and all he had done.

He might be strongly desiring for the governor to give him more time, to put it off, but knowing his guilt, and what he had done, knowing that there was NO HOPE for anything else.

And then to hear that the governor was going to send his son down to pay the full price—his only son, just to set the prisoner free—that would be unthinkable!

Yet what You did on the cross was far beyond that! I Love it!
–Pastor Daniel Martin, 4/23/15

No condemnation.

God demonstrates His love for us by not condemning us through His grace. But many times we feel condemned even when God has assured us that He has justified us and that He does not condemn us.

Satan is called the accuser of the brethren who *"accuses them day and night before our God"* (Rev 12:10b). He is the one who brings accusation against us.

Meditation: Explore when and why you may feel condemnation against yourself. Write in your journal about these instances.

Allow the love of God to assure you that you are not condemned, but under grace.

NOTES:_____

_____

_____

_____

_____

_____

_____

_____

_____

_____

_____

_____

_____

_____

Strive for consistency in your devotional life, but also give yourself grace. As we realize the great measure of God's love for us, we also realize the great measure of the grace He gives us! Receive grace.

Review this past week and ways in which God demonstrates His love for you.

- Love is patient. *Endures my bad; waits; doesn't need instant results.*
- Love is kind. *Introduces good and positive into my life.*
- Love does not envy. *Doesn't feed off others (comparison); content.*
- Love does not boast. *Satisfied with self; doesn't need to promote.*
- Love is not arrogant. *Doesn't focus on own significance.*
- Love is not rude. *Doesn't treat me as insignificant.*
- Love does not insist on its own way. *Selfless.*
- Love is not irritable. *External peace despite suffering.*
- Love is not resentful. *Internal peace despite offense.*
- Love does not rejoice at wrongdoing. *Not vengeful or retributive.*
- Love rejoices with the truth. *Desires truth and defeats shame.*
- Love bears all things. *Shields and supports me.*
- Love believes all things. *Trusts and confides in me.*
- Love hopes all things. *Looks for and expects what is right and best.*
- Love endures all things. *Never quits.*
- Love never ends. *Never is depleted.*[11]

Meditation: Spend time meditating on God's love embodied in the attributes above.

Compose your own meditation on God's love and His demonstration of His love to you. Based on His demonstration, write what each of these attributes means to you (an example is above).

As you write and then read over your notes, worship, praise, and thank Him for His love.

⊹   ⊹   ⊹   ⊹   ⊹   ⊹   ⊹

---

[11] Meditation notes contributed by Thomas Thurman.

I.Week Ten, Day 1 (Date:)   **RECEIVING LOVE - HINDRANCES**

> In this is love, not that we have loved God but that he loved us and sent his Son to be the propitiation for our sins. **1 Jn 4:10**

How are you at receiving God's love?

I had lunch recently with a friend – a close friend with whom I have an accountability relationship. I asked my friend "How are you at receiving God's love?"

My friend thought for a minute and then answered "Terrible."

It begins with God's love. In fact, John says love exists not because we loved God, but because He loved us.

If we desire a relationship in which we love God, we first must be able to receive His love. His perfect love supplies the foundation for a loving relationship with Him.

But receiving His love may be harder for us than we think.

> **Meditation:** How are you at receiving God's love? Is it easy or hard for you? Write about it in your journal. Ask the Holy Spirit to show you reasons why.

✠   ✠   ✠   ✠   ✠   ✠   ✠

NOTES:_____

_____

_____

_____

_____

_____

_____

_____

And they rose early in the morning and went up to the heights of the hill country, saying, "Here we are. We will go up to the place that the LORD has promised, for we have sinned."

But Moses said, "Why now are you transgressing the command of the LORD, when that will not succeed? Do not go up, for the Lord is not among you, lest you be struck down before your enemies. For there the Amalekites and the Canaanites are facing you, and you shall fall by the sword. Because you have turned back from following the LORD, the LORD will not be with you."

But they presumed to go up to the heights of the hill country, although neither the ark of the covenant of the LORD nor Moses departed out of the camp. Then the Amalekites and the Canaanites who lived in that hill country came down and defeated them and pursued them, even to Hormah. **Num 14:40-45**

Our self sufficiency is a myth.

"So," I asked my friend "why do you think you are terrible at receiving love from God?"

My friend paused again. "Maybe self-sufficiency. I tend to want to do things myself and not to be dependent on anyone."

God told the Israelites that He had given them the Promised Land. He told them to enter in and to take it. When Moses sent spies into the land though, most of the spies brought back a fearful report. When God gave the command to the Israelites to "Go!", the Israelites rebelled in fear and refused.

So God pronounced judgment and told them to turn back to the wilderness. So what did the children of Israel do the next day? They rose early in the morning and tried to march into the Promised Land!

Our self sufficiency is a myth. We are fully dependent on the love of God and we should be opening our hearts to it every hour of every day.

Meditation: Think of areas of your life in which you rely on yourself. What are the areas of your life that you carefully control? List the areas in your journal.

Then open your heart to God and receive His love for you. Commit the areas of self-reliance to God and give Him control of them.

✝   ✝   ✝   ✝   ✝   ✝   ✝

NOTES:_____

_____

_____

_____

_____

_____

_____

_____

_____

_____

_____

_____

_____

_____

_____

_____

_____

> Now as they went on their way, Jesus entered a village. And a woman named Martha welcomed him into her house. And she had a sister called Mary, who sat at the Lord's feet and listened to his teaching.
>
> But Martha was distracted with much serving. And she went up to him and said, "Lord, do you not care that my sister has left me to serve alone? Tell her then to help me."
>
> But the Lord answered her, "Martha, Martha, you are anxious and troubled about many things, but one thing is necessary. Mary has chosen the good portion, which will not be taken away from her."
> Luke 10:38-42

Our performance does not earn the love of God.

An Hour With You: 5:11-6:39 (and counting!) I am nowhere near Finished! I must stay before You all day—always! Thank You for the HOUR, but I need more than an hour! I need You!!

Thank You for giving me the "hour" (daily hour of prayer) back in 2011, but I think now that the "hour" over the last 4 years, was simply to deliver me to the place I got a glimpse of this morning!

This has been a very significant day! How significant it has been will largely be determined by whether I build on it, or allow it to wither where it is!

O come and help me to build on what You have done in me in this last hour +!!

Father, there is so much I want to "get done", the I "need to accomplish" in this day— good things, beneficial, good spiritual things—But more than I need to get anything "Done/Accomplished", I need to <u>Connect with, Share life, Abide in, and Bless You!</u>

O come and help me to "Be in the moment" of each moment of the day, living in You, dwelling in You, blessing You, pleasing You!

Whatever accomplishes those things—that is what is real accomplishment.

It may be nothing more than reading one psalm and soaking in the life of the one, or it may be simply gazing on the beauty of Your holiness, or simply quietly waiting on You!

Whatever You by Your Spirit lead in—that is LIFE, that is true <u>accomplishment</u>!

O come and slow me down and help me to see that a real relationship is far more than going down a check list of "done."

O God, help me to not become so obsessed with doing the work of the Kingdom, that I don't have time for the King of the Kingdom!

You are so worthy of all TIME, surrender, yieldedness, and devotion!

O help me to give You TIME in this hour with You...You and You alone are worthy of my focus in this hour! Come and help me to use what You give to me to draw me closer to You, but help me to keep the focus that it is You that it is all about!!

O, draw me closer to you in this TIME, O God! Show me where I am spending more time focusing on Tools than focusing on the one that the tool is all about—You!

Help me to be a Mary, not a proud, upset, bent out of shape Martha!
-Pastor Daniel Martin, 7/26/15

This story is the source of many sermons. Martha engaged in works. Mary engaged in relationship. The relationship is essential.

And that is true. But consider how Mary and Martha were responding to the love of God. Mary was at Jesus' feet receiving what the Master offered her.

Martha was performing. Martha was trying to serve Jesus. She was showing love through her performance – maybe even seeking approval from Him.

We often experience family dynamics in which love shown to us was conditioned upon performance. Approval and kindness were given if we met the expectations imposed. Disapproval and unkindness were given if we failed to perform.

There is a time when action is appropriate – when action is a part of obedience. But our performance does not earn the love of God. In fact, it may be offensive to the Almighty to believe that our performance is necessary in order for Him to love us.

One thing that is necessary is to receive the love of God in our hearts now - a love that exists because of Who God is, not because of who we are.

Meditation: Spend time discerning ways that you perform to gain love. Do you feel as if you have to earn God's love? As you identify those areas, consider whether they may actually hinder you from receiving God's love.

Allow God to assure you of His love whether you "earn" it or not.

✝   ✝   ✝   ✝   ✝   ✝   ✝

A friend once asked me how we spell love. The answer: T-I-M-E. Spend T-I-M-E with the Lord as Pastor Martin encourages so that you can share in His L-O-V-E.

> At that time Hanani the seer came to Asa king of Judah and said to him, "Because you relied on the king of Syria, and did not rely on the LORD your God, the army of the king of Syria has escaped you. Were not the Ethiopians and the Libyans a huge army with very many chariots and horsemen? Yet because you relied on the LORD, he gave them into your hand. For the eyes of the LORD run to and fro throughout the whole earth, to give strong support to those whose heart is blameless toward him. You have done foolishly in this, for from now on you will have wars."
>
> Then Asa was angry with the seer and put him in the stocks in prison, for he was in a rage with him because of this. And Asa inflicted cruelties upon some of the people at the same time. The acts of Asa, from first to last, are written in the Book of the Kings of Judah and Israel.
>
> In the thirty-ninth year of his reign Asa was diseased in his feet, and his disease became severe. Yet even in his disease he did not seek the LORD, but sought help from physicians. And Asa slept with his fathers, dying in the forty-first year of his reign. **2 Chr 16:7-13**

And he inflicted cruelties upon some of the people.

By all accounts, Asa, king of Judah, ruled as a righteous king for most of his reign. *And Asa did what was good and right in the eyes of the LORD his God* (2 Chr 14:2).

But Asa had some hurtful things occur to him. The king of Israel tried to block access to Judah so that people and goods could not go to Judah.

So Asa retaliated. He hired the King of Syria to attack Israel and to relieve Judah from the blockade. But Hanani the seer rebuked him for turning to Syria for help instead of turning to the Lord. Asa became angry, imprisoned the seer, and then inflicted cruelties on the people.

Then Asa suffered from physical pain - a painful foot disease. Even then, he did not turn to the Lord for help.

The pain we suffer can hinder us from receiving God's love. The pain can be emotional, mental, or physical. It hardens our hearts and blocks the flow of love.

Meditation: Love is not resentful. What wounds or injuries have you sustained? Are they wounds of the heart, wounds of the soul, or physical injuries? Journal about them.

Have these wounds affected your ability to receive love from God? Turn to God and show Him these wounds. Tell Him you do not want these wounds to block His love. Ask Him to pour His love into your heart.

✝ ✝ ✝ ✝ ✝ ✝ ✝

NOTES:_____

_____

_____

_____

_____

_____

_____

_____

_____

_____

_____

_____

_____

> Now concerning food offered to idols: we know that "all of us possess knowledge." This "knowledge" puffs up, but love builds up.
>
> If anyone imagines that he knows something, he does not yet know as he ought to know. But if anyone loves God, he is known by God. **1 Cor 8:1-3**

Love is not arrogant.

O Father, give me a good, healthy, and wholesome fear of You!!

Never let me harden and come to the place of feeling that I don't desperately need You! The truth is that I need You far more than I ever realize.

For sure, I don't need a lower awareness of my deep need for You! I need more and more awareness of it! Draw me into greater awareness of my need!

O Cleanse, Purify, Sanctify, and Deliver me from all wrong, from all wrong attitudes about my deep need of You!!   –Pastor Daniel Martin, 5/26/15

Scripture is clear that the pride of man is repulsive to God. God is close to the humble, but distances Himself from the proud (Psa 138:6).

The idea that we know something can be a significant source of pride. At the point that we think that we know; that we have mastered a life lesson; or that we have an intellectual edge, then our felt need for God's love diminishes. We are hardened.

But we always have a deep need for God's love – every day, every hour, and every moment.

Meditation: Focus on your need for God's love. Tell God that you have a deep need for Him. Ask the Holy Spirit to enter your heart and to reveal that need to you.

Then ask the Holy Spirit to fill your need for God's love. Ask Him to remind you of your need for God's love throughout the day.

✠   ✠   ✠   ✠   ✠   ✠   ✠

> Be encouraged that God is working in your heart and life as you spend time with Him.

He also told this parable to some who trusted in themselves that they were righteous, and treated others with contempt:

"Two men went up into the temple to pray, one a Pharisee and the other a tax collector.

The Pharisee, standing by himself, prayed thus: 'God, I thank you that I am not like other men, extortioners, unjust, adulterers, or even like this tax collector. I fast twice a week; I give tithes of all that I get.'

But the tax collector, standing far off, would not even lift up his eyes to heaven, but beat his breast, saying, 'God, be merciful to me, a sinner!'

I tell you, this man went down to his house justified, rather than the other. For everyone who exalts himself will be humbled, but the one who humbles himself will be exalted."   **Luke 18:9-14**

Love rejoices with the truth.

Christ desires to give forgiven humans a new identity that is the restored son/daughter relationship to his Father...[I]n this way, not only is the guilt of sin addressed (it is forgiven!) but the shame of sin is also taken on (it is healed through the gift of a new identity).[12]

Love rejoices with the truth. And truth about ourselves begins with the way that we perceive ourselves. For many reasons, it is hard to perceive ourselves in truth. There may be issues about pride, guilt, insecurity, pleasure, or shame. We carry a false identity with us that has been craftily and carefully constructed over many years to defend against the sins that we bear and against the shame that we feel.

God's love is intended for a real person – for the true you, a child of God. The tax collector understood grace – that his identity as forgiven was dependent on grace. The Pharisee wrongly thought his identity as a righteous man was dependent on his own works. Our false perceptions hinder the flow of God's love to our inner core.

---

[12] Philip D. Jamieson, *The Face of Forgiveness* p. 41 (IVP 2016).

Meditation: "God, be merciful to me, a sinner!" This confession is the "*kyrie eleison*" – a historic confession of the church. Repeat this confession slowly and carefully. As you do so, ask the Holy Spirit to quicken this confession to your heart so forgiveness and His love can flow to your inner man. Repeat this confession slowly multiple times. Emphasize a different word in the confession each time that you say it.

☩   ☩   ☩   ☩   ☩   ☩   ☩

NOTES:_____

_____

_____

_____

_____

_____

_____

_____

_____

_____

_____

_____

_____

_____

_____

- Love is patient.
- Love is kind.
- Love does not envy.
- Love does not boast.
- Love is not arrogant.
- Love is not rude.
- Love does not insist on its own way.
- Love is not irritable.
- Love is not resentful.
- Love does not rejoice at wrongdoing.
- Love rejoices with the truth.
- Love bears all things.
- Love believes all things.
- Love hopes all things.
- Love endures all things.
- Love never ends.

Meditation: Today use artistic expression to receive love from God. Write a letter or a poem to God about the love that the two of you share. Or draw or create something visual. Or use dance or physical expression. Do whatever best allows you to express your relationship of love with your Heavenly Father!

Be honest and be bold. Tell, illustrate, or demonstrate to God what you think or feel about His love.

Stay in tune with the movement of your heart during devotions. Slow movement over time can be very good as God is building a solid foundation within you for the character necessary to fulfill His call on your life.

SECTION I – FAITH, HOPE, AND LOVE: WEEK ELEVEN

I.Week Eleven, Day 1 (Date:)   **JOURNEY – FAITH, HOPE AND LOVE**

> We give thanks to God always for all of you, constantly mentioning you in our prayers, remembering before our God and Father your work of faith and labor of love and steadfastness of hope in our Lord Jesus Christ. **1Thes 1:2-3**

Work of faith; labor of love; steadfastness of hope.

The whole substance of religion is faith, hope, and love. By the practice of these we become united to the will of God. Everything else is unimportant and should be used as a means to our end, which is to be swallowed up by faith and love.

All things are possible to him who believes. They are less difficult to him who hopes. They are easier to him who loves. And they are easiest to him who perseveres in the practice of all three virtues.[13]

Faith, hope, and love are inseparable. We need all three working together to walk with the Lord.

Paul makes it clear that faith and hope without love are empty (1 Cor 13:1-3).

Without faith, we cannot please God (Heb 11:6).

And hope is an essential component of faith (Heb. 11:1). Hope builds and bolsters faith.

When faith, hope, or love is present, the others are not far away. When they work together, they sometimes seem indistinguishable.

So we are intentional to exercise all three.

Meditation: As you consider faith, hope, and love, ask the Lord to show you if you struggle with one of the three more than the others.

If the Lord shows you a lack of one of the three, seek the Lord as to the reasons why. Write down any struggles that you sense and why.

Then ask the Holy Spirit to show you how you can grow in that one virtue.

✠   ✠   ✠   ✠   ✠   ✠   ✠

---

[13] *The Practice of the Presence of God*, p. 25.

Therefore, since we have been justified by faith, we have peace with God through our Lord Jesus Christ. Through him we have also obtained access by faith into this grace in which we stand, and we rejoice in hope of the glory of God.

Not only that, but we rejoice in our sufferings, knowing that suffering produces endurance, and endurance produces character, and character produces hope, and hope does not put us to shame, because God's love has been poured into our hearts through the Holy Spirit who has been given to us. **Rom 5:1-5**

The interworkings of faith, hope, and love.

The love of God breathes hope into our hearts.

Our hope forms a foundation for faith.

Faith gives us access to grace in which we stand. We exercise our faith to move forward in our journey to perfect love.

Hope gives us joy – a joy that exists even when we suffer. For because of hope and faith, we know the fruit of suffering. Suffering produces endurance; endurance produces character; and the bolstered character gives us more hope.

Suffering can lead to hope! When we have suffered but have exercised faith during the suffering, realizing the character that has been instilled after we have suffered and endured actually increases our hope. The realization of growth affirms and strengthens hope.

Even more, we are never ashamed of our hope, because God's love has been received in our hearts through the Holy Spirit.

Meditation: Focus on the progressions in this scripture passage.

Underline the words Faith, Hope, and Love as they appear in this passage. Then meditate on the roles of faith, hope, and love in the progression.

In what ways do you identify with this progression?

✝   ✝   ✝   ✝   ✝   ✝   ✝

NOTES:_____

_____

_____

_____

_____

_____

_____

_____

_____

_____

_____

_____

_____

_____

_____

_____

_____

_____

_____

_____

> For there is hope for a tree, if it be cut down, that it will sprout again, and that its shoots will not cease.
>
> Though its root grow old in the earth, and its stump die in the soil, yet at the scent of water it will bud and put out branches like a young plant. **Job 14:7-9**

Hope is a bridge between faith and love.

My friend, who was a godly man, was experiencing severe depression. It had been a gradual slide over the course of many months. Now, he was surrounded by darkness and feeling physical and mental pain.

My phone calls with my friend were long, some lasting over an hour. We spoke almost every day and sometimes 2 or 3 times a day. My friend did not feel loved. He could not read scripture because it didn't mean anything to him. He questioned his salvation and whether he could be saved due to mistakes he had made. I spent hours with him, encouraging him. I assured him of salvation and forgiveness. I told him he was loved. I quoted scripture after scripture to him.

When my friend went to a mental health facility, I visited him.

Thankfully, my friend recovered. And after he recovered, he told me this: "You were a bridge of hope to me."

When we journey through life, we rely on faith to keep us moving forward. On most of the journey, we feel God's love and His presence.

But there are challenges on the journey. There are pitfalls of temptation, canyons of despair, torrents of challenge, deserts of desolation, quagmires of addiction, and swamps of grief.

Often during these challenges, we don't see the love of God. We can't feel it. Our faith seems shaky. It is under attack. But, in those times, hope can provide a bridge. During those times, we hope in God and in His goodness. We hope in God's promises and in His word. We hope for a future and for a brighter day.

Hope can lift us up during those seasons and carry us through the storms.

Meditation: Is there a time in your life when you have experienced this dynamic – when the encouragement of hope from another person helped keep your faith alive? Write in your journal about it. How did God work through that person to preserve hope in the midst of darkness?

111

> When neither sun nor stars appeared for many days, and no small tempest lay on us, all hope of our being saved was at last abandoned. Since they had been without food for a long time, Paul stood up among them and said, "Men, you should have listened to me and not have set sail from Crete and incurred this injury and loss. Yet now I urge you to take heart, for there will be no loss of life among you, but only of the ship. For this very night there stood before me an angel of the God to whom I belong and whom I worship, and he said, 'Do not be afraid, Paul; you must stand before Caesar. And behold, God has granted you all those who sail with you.' So take heart, men, for I have faith in God that it will be exactly as I have been told." **Acts 27:20-25**

Encouragement provides a bridge of hope.

O God, I am so exhausted—got home from Red Eagle last night at 10:05, after the last service with <u>We Care—Renewed Hope</u>—one of the most significant weeks of my life!

Unbelievable off the charts, contacts, services, singing groups, hopelessness, devastation, darkness, light, horror stories, victories, battles, salvations, evil, good, terror, desperation, glory, amazing grace, fear, righteousness—all rolled into one week.

I am overwhelmed, tired, energized, ecstatic over things I have seen, crushed by things I have seen and heard, ready to go on, ready to lie down and rest, relieved at what I saw God do, devastated by what the enemy has done and is doing, full of hope for the future, full of awareness of the urgency that we are tipping into total ruin and devastation in our church, families, society, culture, very aware of the gruesome lies and total very wide spread destruction the enemy has dumped on our state, yet also aware that in the darkness the light of God shines bright, that when the enemy comes in like a flood, the Spirit of the Lord will raise up a standard against him!

We went—over 400 of us, into 26 prisons, containing over 33,000 inmates.

Mostly Mennonites, mostly from Pennsylvania, Ohio, Minnesota, and Wisconsin, also from maybe 15 other states, along with many Mennonites from Alabama. (I don't recall there being a non-Mennonite worker from Alabama other than myself.) M had to drop out.

O God, help me to respond, to see, to understand, to hear, to rest, to strive, to look to You in everything and see, understand, and know that YOU ARE GOD, that You are in control, that Your Love still lifts, wins, Never Fails, Never Gives in, Never Gives up...

Help me to see the victories and rejoice.

Help me to be ecstatic over the good I have seen.

Help me to Weep over the brokenness, evil, devastation, and heartache that was everywhere!

O God, help me to be what You want me to be in all things about this week.

Give me deeper prayer life for individuals, as well as groups—deeper than ever before! Come and show me the way You want me to go, the way You want me to respond to everything around me!

What an awesome God You are!

You are so amazing! So Good! So Powerful!   –Pastor Daniel Martin, 1/30/14

Paul was on a boat with 276 persons (Acts 27:37). The boat was adrift in a storm for 14 days. All hope of being saved was lost.

Paul had faith in God and God's promises. Paul could share about his faith, but he could not force his faith on his fellow shipmates. But Paul could encourage them and restore their hope.

We can show love to others. But we can't make them accept or feel God's love.

We can share about redemption with others. But we can't make them come to faith.

Hope is a little bit different. Others don't have to receive the hope we share, but our encouragement can provide a bridge of hope to them.

Encouragement is a great gift. Our encouragement can provide a bridge of hope to another that is in the midst of the storm. When my close friend was in the middle of depression, I shared hope with him to encourage him not to allow his faith to die.

Meditation: Remember a time that you provided hope and encouragement to another person in the midst of felt darkness. What did you do or say to that person that provided a bridge of hope to them?

✝   ✝   ✝   ✝   ✝   ✝   ✝

Speaking of encouragement, don't forget to meet regularly with your mentor or devotional partner. "Ups and downs" are a normal part of the devotional life just as in life. During your meetings you can encourage each other and give perspective during the difficult moments.

113

NOTES:_____

So Satan went out from the presence of the LORD and struck Job with loathsome sores from the sole of his foot to the crown of his head. And he took a piece of broken pottery with which to scrape himself while he sat in the ashes.

Then his wife said to him, "Do you still hold fast your integrity? Curse God and die."

But he said to her, "You speak as one of the foolish women would speak. Shall we receive good from God, and shall we not receive evil?" In all this Job did not sin with his lips. **Job 2:7-10**

Love to hope to faith. The reverse can also occur.

Feeling unloved leads to a loss of hope. Loss of hope leads to a loss of faith.

Job's wife lost everything. She lost hope, which led to a loss of faith in God and in His goodness. *"Curse God and die."*

But Job did not lose faith. He still believed and had hope in God. *Though he slay me, I will hope in him; yet I will argue my ways to his face* (Job 13:15).

When my close friend was severely depressed, I spent many hours on the phone with him. In his time of darkness, my friend did not feel any love. But I told him I loved him and I encouraged him that he was loved. My friend did not lose hope in his trial - in part because of the regular assurances of love.

So being loved supports hope. Hope in turn sustains faith in the face of the catastrophes of our lives. And the preservation of our hope and faith guides us on our journey to His perfect love.

Meditation: Do you blame Job's wife for her reaction – her loss of hope? Why or why not? Record your thoughts in your journal.

Next, consider the interplay between love, hope, and faith in the middle of challenges or trials. Spend time meditating on the connections between them.

⊥⊤   ⊥⊤   ⊥⊤   ⊥⊤   ⊥⊤   ⊥⊤   ⊥⊤

As you go through each day, try to remember you are loved. Walk in His love each day.

We who are strong have an obligation to bear with the failings of the weak, and not to please ourselves. Let each of us please his neighbor for his good, to build him up. For Christ did not please himself, but as it is written, "The reproaches of those who reproached you fell on me."

For whatever was written in former days was written for our instruction, that through endurance and through the encouragement of the Scriptures we might have hope. May the God of endurance and encouragement grant you to live in such harmony with one another, in accord with Christ Jesus, that together you may with one voice glorify the God and Father of our Lord Jesus Christ.

Rom 15:1-6

The God of endurance and encouragement.

I now see that possibly my motto as I face things needs to be, "Love--Pray and Obey", or maybe "PRAY—Love and Obey!"

I was stunned by the power of Your love flowing through K__ and the glory that surrounds her life in the middle of filth, pain, ugliness, smells, and sights of brokenness all day long. Am I to take the position of simplicity—that all You are basically calling me to do in the brokenness around me is:

A. Love-love You, love the broken around me;

B. Pray and Obey?

Live a life of prayer and love, all the while praying/listening to You, listening/hearkening with an ear for whatever You are saying needs to be my response to the situations/problems/people around me, and then DOING whatever You lead in with a happy abandon, knowing that whatever You are saying, as I obey it will end well in eternity!

What an awesome way to live my life! Help me to more diligently live this way all day long—every day!!   –Pastor Daniel Martin, 5/12/13

When we provide the bridge of encouragement – a bridge of hope, we grow in Christ. Christ did not please Himself. He bore the reproaches of another to fulfill all godliness.

God meets us at the place of reproach – at the place that we bear a burden that is not our own. God meets us at the place that we do not please ourselves.

When we provide a bridge of hope to another, we experience Christ and we experience His love and glory.

Meditation: Meditate on the connection between the glory of God, and weakness, reproach, and bearing another's burden. How does bearing the reproach of the cross birth the glory of God?

✝   ✝   ✝   ✝   ✝   ✝   ✝

NOTES:_____

_____

_____

_____

_____

_____

_____

_____

_____

_____

_____

_____

_____

_____

_____

_____

- Love bears all things.
- Love believes all things.
- Love hopes all things.
- *Love endures all things.*
- Love never ends.

Review your notes from the devotions over the past week.

Meditation: Today is a prayer for growth in faith, hope, and love in your life. Ask God to help you grow in these areas. Trust Him to bring that growth in your life.

Write in your journal ways in which you see growth in these areas.

☩   ☩   ☩   ☩   ☩   ☩   ☩

NOTES:_____

_____

_____

_____

_____

_____

_____

_____

_____

_____

_____

> Everyone who believes that Jesus is the Christ has been born of God, and everyone who loves the Father loves whoever has been born of him. By this we know that we love the children of God, when we love God and obey his commandments. For this is the love of God, that we keep his commandments. And his commandments are not burdensome.
>
> For everyone who has been born of God overcomes the world. And this is the victory that has overcome the world—our faith. 1 Jn 5:1-4

Love and faith empower us to overcome.

How much Clearer I can see so many things now than I saw 24 hours ago!

It is like a wiper went across my field of vision and opened it up to so many realities that I thought were already realities in my life, giving me greater intensity about things I had struggled for intensity for.

O how Great You are, my God and my King!! There really is None Like You!!

You are the Holy One of Israel, the Great I AM, the Almighty One, the Eternal One, the Everlasting One!

You just now brought back to my mind what I told Bethel years ago—BIG BATTLE = BIG VICTORY! How much truer that rings in my heart this morning!

Where I am facing BIG BATTLE, the flesh often sees BIG DEFEAT, but the truth is that we are more than CONQUERORS in everything. So when the enemy shows up, I am to run to You, believe You, wait on You, draw from You, and believe You just that much more intensely.

O God, help me to grow in Faith and deeper Resting in You as well.

Help me to grow from the "academics" of things, to the realities of those things! O there is so much change I am needing in You!

Come and take over completely in me with all that You are!

You are so absolutely, completely, totally in charge, on the throne, reigning, ruling, sovereign, almighty, conquering, victorious, mastering, overwhelming, prevailing, unfailing, availing, supreme, and Lord of All!   – Pastor Daniel Martin, 7/3/16

We will overcome the world. In fact, this scripture says that we have overcome the world...through faith.

When we love Him, we obey His commands. The commands may seem burdensome, but they are not. As we begin to obey, his commandments seem lighter. At that point, we are beginning to overcome.

Meditation: What does it mean to overcome the world in your life? Ask the Lord to show you ways in which you are overcoming the world even now.

╬   ╬   ╬   ╬   ╬   ╬   ╬

NOTES:_____

_____

_____

_____

_____

_____

_____

_____

_____

_____

_____

_____

_____

_____

_____

_____

> May the God of hope fill you with all joy and peace in believing, so that by the power of the Holy Spirit you may abound in hope.
> **Rom 15:13**

That you may abound in hope.

Now may the God of Hope fill you with all Joy and Peace in believing, that you may ABOUND in Hope By the Power of the Holy Spirit!

And right now, my spirit does overflow with hope, sings with deep assurance that You have everything in full control, that You are leading me every step of the way, that You are covering Carolyn in every way!

O God, come and take over in my life, changing me in every way I need changing, giving me to grace and glory to rise above all the storms that are pounding right now!

O the glory of Your Hope!!   –Pastor Daniel Martin, 7/3/16

Hope leads us to joy.

Pastor Martin used his hope to find joy and peace in the middle of "pounding storms." Love is my destination. Faith is the fuel to get me there. Hope is a bridge between faith and love. Faith, hope and love enable me to overcome and they lead to joy, peace, and delight.

Meditation: Overcoming is a concept that we usually apply to a completed victory. But overcoming occurs in the middle of the pounding storms.

Note Pastor Martin's focus on hope and glory. Meditate on the connection between glory and the child of God exercising hope in the middle of pounding storms.

✝ ✝ ✝ ✝ ✝ ✝ ✝

Resting in God is important. God calls us to work and to pursue Him. But He also provides rest when we are weary. Set aside time to rest and to lean fully into Him.

> And we know that for those who love God all things work together for good, for those who are called according to his purpose.
>
> For those whom he foreknew he also predestined to be conformed to the image of his Son, in order that he might be the firstborn among many brothers. And those whom he predestined he also called, and those whom he called he also justified, and those whom he justified he also glorified. **Rom 8:28-30**

There is joy in the process.

Creativity is a source of great joy. The Creation was a joyful event. *When the morning stars sang together and all the sons of God shouted for joy* (Job 38:7).

A major source of this joy was making man and woman in His own image (Gen 1:26-27). It is actually a little bit of a puzzle. Each one of us is fearfully and wonderfully made, and each one of us is fearfully and wonderfully unique. God has a role for each one of us and a destiny for each one of us that is different.

Yet God has called each one of us to a destiny that conforms to the image of His Son. There is such diversity in the Body of Christ, but each member conforms to One image. There is joy in that process because it is fulfilling God's marvelous creativity.

Creativity is a way to express my inner being. My ideas, my perspectives, and my emotions are put into a tangible form. Joy arises from creativity because I am able to express and to define my identity that God has created and placed with me.

Similarly, an outlet to exercise my spiritual gifts brings me joy. Spiritual gifts are a large part of the identity that God has given me. The expression of my gifts expresses my identity in Him and conforms me to His image in greater and greater measure.

Meditation: In the context of Romans 8, what does "the image of His Son" mean to you? What are the attributes of His image to which we are conformed?

What does it mean to be conformed to the image of His Son? Write your thoughts in your journal. (We will further explore the concept of being conformed to His image later in this devotional.)

NOTES:_____

_____

_____

_____

_____

_____

_____

_____

_____

_____

_____

_____

_____

_____

_____

_____

_____

_____

Blessed be the God and Father of our Lord Jesus Christ! According to his great mercy, he has caused us to be born again to a living hope through the resurrection of Jesus Christ from the dead, to an inheritance that is imperishable, undefiled, and unfading, kept in heaven for you, who by God's power are being guarded through faith for a salvation ready to be revealed in the last time.

In this you rejoice, though now for a little while, if necessary, you have been grieved by various trials, so that the tested genuineness of your faith—more precious than gold that perishes though it is tested by fire—may be found to result in praise and glory and honor at the revelation of Jesus Christ.

Though you have not seen him, you love him. Though you do not now see him, you believe in him and rejoice with joy that is inexpressible and filled with glory, obtaining the outcome of your faith, the salvation of your souls. **1 Pet 1:3-9**

Gushing springs of joy.

O You do Cheer every winding path we are treading. You give us joy in our journey, hope for the future, life for what looks like it leads to death, grace for despair, faith for worry, and freedom from the bondage of horrible things!

O what Grace is ours for every trial, grace to provide all we need in every detail and destructive thing in our lives. You are so amazing.

O thank You for the <u>Gushing Springs Of Joy</u> that are in front of us, ahead of us, gushing from the Rock, Christ Jesus who gave His all for us!   –Pastor Daniel Martin, 7/3/16

Joy that is inexpressible. Joy that is filled with glory. Peter tells us to rejoice despite trials. What we realize is the genuineness of our faith in the middle of our trials. That genuine faith results in praise, glory, and honor.

> **Meditation:** In the context of this scripture passage, to whom does the praise, glory, and honor result? Is it to God; or is it to the faithful believer; or is it both? Ask the Holy Spirit to illuminate this praise, glory, and honor to you.

✝   ✝   ✝   ✝   ✝   ✝   ✝

Who shall separate us from the love of Christ? Shall tribulation, or distress, or persecution, or famine, or nakedness, or danger, or sword? As it is written, "For your sake we are being killed all the day long; we are regarded as sheep to be slaughtered."

No, in all these things we are more than conquerors through him who loved us.

For I am sure that neither death nor life, nor angels nor rulers, nor things present nor things to come, nor powers, nor height nor depth, nor anything else in all creation, will be able to separate us from the love of God in Christ Jesus our Lord. **Rom 8:35-39**

We are more than conquerors through Him who loved us.

This is the end of Romans 8 where Paul speaks of love – and the overcoming and victorious nature of love. Love triumphs, even in the midst of dire events.

When I read Paul's list of challenges, I wonder if he was thinking of what he faced in fulfilling the very specific and powerful call that God placed on Paul's life as an apostle of Jesus Christ. The list here of tribulation, distress, persecution, famine, nakedness, danger, or sword is reminiscent of the list of what Paul endured in II Cor. 6 ("afflictions, hardships, calamities, beatings, imprisonments, riots, labors, sleepless nights, hunger") and in II Cor. 12. I wonder if Paul had in mind what he endured and overcame to fulfill God's call on his life.

My friend, Glyn Hasty, says this: *"When you have fulfilled what God has called you to do, then you experience the manifestation of the fullness of His love."*

God's call on my life leads me to my destiny in Him – and conforms me to the image of His son in a way that I experience the fullness of His love.

Meditation: Meditate on the call (or calls) that God has placed on your life. What have you endured and overcome to fulfill that call? Write down your experiences.

Next focus on the victorious and triumphant nature of God's love. How have you experienced God's love as you have moved toward your destiny in Him?

Tell God that you want to experience more of His love – even when you are called to endure hard things in fulfilling His call.

NOTES:_____

_____

_____

_____

_____

_____

_____

_____

_____

_____

_____

_____

_____

_____

_____

_____

_____

_____

> The LORD your God is in your midst, a mighty one who will save; he will rejoice over you with gladness; he will quiet you by his love; he will exult over you with loud singing. **Zeph 3:17**

He will exult over you with loud singing.

O the glory of this truth—

<u>You delight in every detail of my life—even the messups, etc. You do delight in my growth, my immaturity, my feeble attempts to walk, to move, to follow You.</u>

Help me to actually grow day by day in all the above and learn to delight You more as I mature and am empowered to love You, delight You, please You, understand You, and live in relationship with You more.

(I know how rich my relationship is with my children now, as I see them walking with You, leading their families, and relating to me as adults. O God, what a treasure I have in them—I want to be more and more what You treasure as well. Mature me, change me, cause me to grow in being a delight to You!!)

O, Father, show me what You want me to see. Come and change me, correct me, instruct me, admonish me, lift me, and exhort me.

I want to be more and more a vessel of honor for You. Give me deep abhorrence for all that dishonors You, and deep desire and commitment to what honors You.

You are so worthy of honor, praise, glory, weightiness, and sincere devotion!

Help me to increasingly approach Your devotion to me day by day. O, YOU ARE SO WORTHY, LAMB OF GOD!!   –Pastor Daniel Martin, 1/20/14

I experience joy in the Lord when I walk with Him. But the delight is not mine alone. God rejoices over me.

The singing is not mine alone. God sings over me loudly.

The love of God is shared with me. The joy of the Lord is shared with me. The victory of the Lord is shared with me as well.

> **Meditation:** What sources of joy do you experience in your life? As you dwell on these sources of joy, praise and thank God for them. Write them down.
>
> Next, seek God for greater, wider, and deeper springs of joy. Ask Him for His joy to flow in your life!

127

Review your journal notes over the past week.

Today is a meditation of rest and quiet. *He will quiet you by his love (Zeph 3:17b).*

"He assumes the person of a mortal man, because, unless He stammers in this manner, He cannot sufficiently show how much He loves us. Thy God will therefore be quiet in His love, i.e., this will be the greatest delight of thy God, this His chief pleasure, when He shall cherish thee. As a man caresses his dearest wife, so will God then quietly repose in thy love." – John Calvin[14]

Meditation: Try to clear your mind and your emotions. Try to empty yourself of thoughts and distractions. Then ask God to put His joy and delight deep within you – in your soul.

---

*(You are a living soul. At times, I have heard the word "soul" equated with emotion, passion, the mind, or even "in the blood." But a living soul is what you are. **And the LORD God formed man of the dust of the ground, and breathed into his nostrils the breath of life; and man became a living soul (Gen 2:7)(KJV).** My uneducated interpretation is that God took dust (matter) and breathed spirit into it to make a living soul (man) – a separate, self-existent, and animated being.*

Internally, I view my soul as the core or essence of my being. I am not a theologian, but in my meditation time, I sense my soul in my stomach area. For whatever reason, for myself that is where I sense the core of my being.)

NOTES:_____

_____

_____

_____

_____

_____

---

[14] Quoted by Keil & Delitzsch, *Commentary on the Old Testament* (Hendrickson 1989).

SECTION I – FAITH, HOPE, AND LOVE: WEEK THIRTEEN

(This week is a practicum to grow in the relationship of love between you and God. There will be some meditation verses, but most of the time will be spent receiving God's love and loving God.)

I.Week Thirteen, Day 1 (Date:)   **PRACTICUM – LOVING GOD**

> One of his disciples, whom Jesus loved, was reclining at table at Jesus' side. **John 13:23**

The disciple whom Jesus loved.

The "disciple whom Jesus loved" – this phrase appears multiple times in the Gospel of John. Many leading scholars believe John is referring to himself. John knew Jesus loved him and he felt that Jesus loved him. John had experienced the love of Jesus. He felt His love so strongly that it shaped his identity. "I am the disciple whom Jesus loved."

Meditation: You are the disciple whom Jesus loves. Jesus loves you deeply, fully, wholly, and completely. Take time to focus on Jesus' love and to receive that love.

Next, think of the busiest part of your upcoming day. Commit to take some time out – even if only a few minutes – during the busiest part of your day. During that time, focus again on the love of Jesus and receive His love.

✝   ✝   ✝   ✝   ✝   ✝   ✝

NOTES:_____

_____

_____

_____

_____

_____

> "No one can serve two masters, for either he will hate the one and love the other, or he will be devoted to the one and despise the other. You cannot serve God and money." Matt 6:24

Devote yourself to the right master.

Help me to Set myself to Seek You, to DEVOTE myself to this Daily, Hourly, to grow in this more and more every day, to engage my Heart to Approach You!

O Father, help me to DEVOTE myself to You daily, hourly, to set myself aside to be Yours, to dwell in Your Presence, to Seek You with All my heart, will, soul, strength, and mind! I need You and Your Life in me, I need to live the Shared Life with You! Come and increase my Hunger and Desire for this!

O Father, help me to guard and grow in this powerful treasure I have in You, in Your Presence, in Your Word!! O, thank You, for this!

Father, I will answer the question!

I will be one who will devote himself to YOU!

I will come close to You as You bring me near!

I will engage my heart to approach unto you! Jer. 30:21 (KJV).

O anoint me, empower me, lead me, inspire me to Engage My Heart.

Show me more and more of what that means and entails and help me to do it daily!

O help me to connect my heart, to get my heart involved and entangled with You and You alone!

I want my life to be on this higher plane that I have found this morning! O come and take me closer and closer to Yourself, O my God!!
–Pastor Daniel Martin, 1/8/14

Meditation: Focus on using your will to love God. Choose to love Him. Be devoted to Him. Without regard for your feelings of the moment, without regard for your mood, and without regard for your circumstances, take time to love God by choice. His love for you is constant. Make time to love God now and continually through the day.

☩   ☩   ☩   ☩   ☩   ☩   ☩

When Jesus saw his mother and the disciple whom he loved standing nearby, he said to his mother, "Woman, behold, your son!" Then he said to the disciple, "Behold, your mother!" And from that hour the disciple took her to his own home. **John 19:26-27**

Receiving love at the worst moments.

This exchange occurred at Jesus' crucifixion. Jesus' mother and the disciple that Jesus loved watched Jesus suffer on the cross. But the disciple still knew Jesus loved him.

Meditation: Consider the things that make you feel bad about yourself – maybe a bad memory, maybe a mistake or an accident, maybe an outburst or an embarrassment, or maybe a burden that you carry. Write these things down in your journal.

Now focus on Jesus' love for you. During the day, at the moments that you feel the worst about yourself, stop and receive Jesus' love for you, the disciple whom Jesus loves. Make time to receive Jesus' love.

✝   ✝   ✝   ✝   ✝   ✝   ✝

NOTES:_____

_____

_____

_____

_____

_____

_____

_____

> Because he holds fast to me in love, I will deliver him; I will protect him, because he knows my name. **Psa 91:14**

Holding fast to Him in love.

O, what a Gold Mine I have found this morning! I had the words to "Close to Thee" come to my mind as I was writing the first lines of the devotion this morning. >> That led me to look the words of the song up. >> I had just highlighted them to copy and paste them when I saw that below the words of the song, there was something about the author, Fanny Crosby. >> I read the words:

"Fanny Crosby

"Who is he who will devote himself to be close to Me?" Jeremiah 30:21 (NIV).

"Toward the close of a day in the year 1874 I was sitting in my room thinking of the nearness of God through Christ as the constant companion of my pilgrim journey, when my heart burst out with the words – Close to Thee."

And my heart soared with the inspiration of them in NIV that is seen above. O what a daily treasure I can have from meditating and dwelling on this truth! –Pastor Daniel Martin, 4/12/13

Meditation: Use your mind to love God. Use your memory to recall the great and awesome things He has done in your life. Use your imagination to envision the Father in His splendor and glory; to envision Jesus as the good and caring Shepherd; and to envision the Holy Spirit coming to surround you with comfort and grace.

Now worship God with your mind in praise, thankfulness, and blessing. Worship Him with love for Him.

☩   ☩   ☩   ☩   ☩   ☩   ☩

Stay faithful in keeping a journal while you engage in your devotions. Record the times that you sense God's love touch your heart. Markers are important in our journey, and a journal is a good written reminder of these markers.

NOTES:_____

_____

_____

_____

_____

_____

_____

_____

_____

_____

_____

_____

_____

_____

_____

_____

_____

_____

> That disciple whom Jesus loved therefore said to Peter, "It is the Lord!" When Simon Peter heard that it was the Lord, he put on his outer garment, for he was stripped for work, and threw himself into the sea.
> **John 21:7**

"It is the Lord!"

As I lay in bed, I turn my heart of affection toward Him. I don't intercede, worship or plan the next day. I just turn my affections toward Him until I become aware of His presence upon me.

Going to sleep in that condition works wonders in the night. Our day actually begins at night: *"The evening and the morning were the first day"* Gen. 1:5 (KJV). It's time to learn how to set up the day with rest, worship and an affectionate embrace.[15]   –Pastor Daniel Martin, 5/17/12

Realization of a beloved elicits an immediate response.

Meditation: Spend time receiving God's love. Meditate on "It is the Lord!"

Tonight, right before you go to sleep, ask the Lord to bless your rest. Then spend time receiving His love. Continue receiving His love as you drift off to sleep. Ask the Lord to allow your spirit to rest in His love during your sleep.

"In the spiritual life, not to advance is to retreat. Those who have the wind of the Holy Spirit go forward even in sleep." – Brother Lawrence[16]

⊹   ⊹   ⊹   ⊹   ⊹   ⊹   ⊹

> Speaking of a retreat, a quarterly retreat with your mentor could be beneficial. A day or a weekend to review the last 90 days of devotions can be meaningful.

---

[15]Quoted from a *Charisma Leader* article by Bill Johnson (2012).

[16] *The Practice of the Presence of God*, p.41.

> [Solomon] said, "O LORD, God of Israel, there is no God like you, in heaven above or on earth beneath, keeping covenant and showing steadfast love to your servants who walk before you with all their heart." **1 Kings 8:23**

"With all of their heart."

O Blessed Redeemer, I now lift my mind, will, and emotions to You! Come and bring me word of Your unfailing love in my life. Let me hear You tell me: "You are my own!", "I love You!"

Cause me to KNOW that You love, accept, delight, and take pleasure in me, no matter what I am or am about!

O, this child loves You, and he is so glad he knows and experiences Your love!

O, I must KNOW Your way for me to go! Show me how You want me to respond to every detail of my life!

Let Your Kingdom come and Your will be done in me and my life today!

I lift up my MIND (Change it and change it to go Your way more and more!), WILL (O give me Your will, willingness to go Your way in every detail of my life), and EMOTIONS (Cause me to not allow my feelings to go wherever they want, but help me to bring every thought, feeling, and attitude under Your control, ruled over by Your Word!).
–Pastor Daniel Martin, 4/22/15

> **Meditation:** Love God with all of your heart. To the extent He allows and you are able, feel love for Him. Open your emotions to lavish on Him your kindness, compassion, respect, awe, and devotion. Give to Him your heart of love.

✠ ✠ ✠ ✠ ✠ ✠ ✠

NOTES:_____

_____

_____

_____

135

Review your journal entries over the past week. What have you experienced as you focused on giving, receiving, and sharing God's love during this time?

- Love is patient.
- Love is kind.
- Love does not envy.
- Love does not boast.
- Love is not arrogant.
- Love is not rude.
- Love does not insist on its own way.
- Love is not irritable.
- Love is not resentful.
- Love does not rejoice at wrongdoing.
- Love rejoices with the truth.
- Love bears all things.
- Love believes all things.
- Love hopes all things.
- Love endures all things.
- Love never ends.

> **Meditation:** We end this section (Faith, Hope, and Love) where we began – meditating on the attributes of love. Ask the Lord to help you continue to grow in these attributes in your life. Ask Him to reveal to you ways in which you can grow in Him and in His love.

╬   ╬   ╬   ╬   ╬   ╬   ╬

NOTES:_____

_____

_____

SECTION II - SURRENDER

Week One: Surrender – Discipleship

Week Two: Surrender – The Temptation

Week Three: Desire and Destiny

Week Four: Deny Yourself

Week Five: Torment

Week Six: Brokenness

Week Seven: Indifference

Week Eight: Comfort - Things

Week Nine: Comfort – People

Week Ten: Truth – Inner Being

Week Eleven: Surrender and Call

Week Twelve: Disordered Desires

Week Thirteen: Practicum - Drip, Trickle, Flow

A WORD BEFORE SECTION II - SURRENDER

You have reached the beginning of Section II – Surrender. Congratulations on the completion of Section I! Now might be a good time to review the suggestions contained in *Preliminary Matters for This Devotional Journey* in the prefatory section of this book.

Please also take some time to review what God is doing in your heart and in your life as you have journeyed through Section I – Faith, Hope, and Love. God works in different ways in different people – according to His Wisdom and His timetable.

God is sovereign. When Jesus ministered on earth, He had the power and authority to work wondrous and instantaneous miracles. But just as powerfully, He worked slowly and meticulously in the lives of His followers – through teaching, transformative living, modeling, and training. At times the changes in the lives of His followers were almost imperceptible, but He was working nonetheless.

The same is true for His work in the lives of His followers today. He can bestow a touch of grace that is miraculous and instantaneous. He can illuminate a scripture or give a powerful personal revelation. But He also can implement changes that are slow but life-giving.

All His ways are a blessing, and we grow both through the miraculous touch and through the slow changes. Often He works step by step – first one area, and when that area has changed, then another area. Each step takes us closer to maturity, closer to His love, and closer to fullness in Him. Our transformation is the work of a lifetime that He patiently, lovingly, and meticulously accomplishes.

His timing is perfect. Some things that we want Him to do, He delays or even refuses. There are things that may be painful or difficult for us. He uses these things for our good although we can't see it. They are a part of His plan for our growth in holiness and in character.

Godly character is built step by step – brick by brick. I want things to happen instantly in my life. But slow and meticulous growth builds a foundation of strength. We are a product of what we have learned and experienced. He works within us to instill what is needed for us to fulfill our destiny in Him and to take our place in His Body that He has ordained.

Surrender and trust are keys to our growth and to our destiny. Allow Him to work within you at His pace and with His good intention for you.

And I am sure of this, that he who began a good work in you will bring it to completion at the day of Jesus Christ. **Php 1:6**

SECTION II – SURRENDER: WEEK ONE

> For this reason I bow my knees before the Father, from whom every family in heaven and on earth is named, that according to the riches of his glory he may grant you to be strengthened with power through his Spirit in your inner being, so that Christ may dwell in your hearts through faith
>
> —that you, being rooted and grounded in love, may have strength to comprehend with all the saints what is the breadth and length and height and depth, and to know the love of Christ that surpasses knowledge, that you may be filled with all the fullness of God.
>   **Eph 3:14-19**

I bow my knees before the Father.

Come and increase my "knee time"!
I remember Tuesday morning, CK telling us about those in medieval days who would kneel before the king, place their clasped hands inside the king's hands, and looking up declare their loyalty, their homage, their total surrender to the king.
O God, help me to do the same!
Help me to daily place my Life, my hands, my all into Your hands.
(As I did that this morning, I sensed that You might be then placing Your hands on my life, and on my world as I continue in doing this! What glory there is in this!)
O help me to faithfully, HOURLY, place my hands in Yours!
Come and show me what it means to place my hands, my life in Your hands and declare to You,
"I am Your man.
I will walk with You.
I will do whatever You say.
I place all I am and have in Your hands.
I put my life in Your hands.
I will live for You.
I will even die for You if necessary!
I am Yours."   –Pastor Daniel Martin, 8/13/15

Perfect love is our destination. In his prayer that we fully comprehend the scale of God's love through faith, Paul begins with the key – the one response from the people of God that is appropriate and desirable: Surrender. *"I bow my knees before the Father."*

Surrender is the key to the exercise of faith, hope, and love. Surrender is the key to realization of the fullness of God. Surrender allows God to dwell in me, and to work through me. Surrender allows the power of God instead of the depravity of man.

Surrender means mind, will, and emotions. Surrender means heart, spirit, and body. Surrender means every part, every organ, and every cell of my being.

Surrender is fundamentally what God asks of me.

Meditation: Today we bow before the Father. To the extent you are able, physically bow on your knees before the Lord. As you bow, surrender every part of your being to Him.

Part by part, spend time surrendering each part of your being you can conceive – first your heart, then your mind, then your will, then your emotions, then your body, then your hands, your feet, your eyes, etc.

Write down what you feel as you surrender. Do you feel a resistance? Do you feel a release?

☦   ☦   ☦   ☦   ☦   ☦   ☦

NOTES:_____

_____

_____

_____

_____

_____

_____

_____

_____

> Then Jesus told his disciples, "If anyone would come after me, let him deny himself and take up his cross and follow me." Matt 16:24

The conditions of discipleship.

O Father, I now confess wandering heart and selfishness, placing my comfort, my plans, my ways, my...my...my above Yours!

Come and give me total surrender to You and Your ways, Your plans. Give me total yieldedness to You, so that no matter what You called for in my life, my response would be <u>total denial of self and total acceptance of whatever You were calling for</u>. This child needs the Shepherd so much!

Come and take over—Take possession of me!! Melt me, making me very pliable and soft toward You!

Wherever I am resisting You, break me down to submit to You. Give me a deeper desire to walk obediently with You, to give You the highest place in all my decisions.

Mold me into Your image from glory to glory!   –Pastor Daniel Martin, 12/28/14

A disciple is a person who follows another person – a pupil who not only learns from his teacher, but imitates him.

Jesus clearly delineates His conditions for discipleship:

Deny yourself (Ouch!).

Take up your cross (Double Ouch!).

Follow Him in His steps (Oh my!).

Each of these conditions requires surrender on my part – full, complete, and whole.

Meditation: One by one, review these conditions of discipleship in detail. Consider what each of the three conditions means to you.

How are you living out these conditions at the present time?

How do you want to live out these conditions? Share your desire with Jesus and ask Him to help you live them out.

✠   ✠   ✠   ✠   ✠   ✠   ✠

NOTES:_____

_____

_____

_____

_____

_____

_____

_____

_____

_____

_____

_____

_____

_____

_____

_____

_____

_____

_____

> Then Jesus told his disciples, "If anyone would come after me, let him deny himself and take up his cross and follow me.
>
> For whoever would save his life will lose it, but whoever loses his life for my sake will find it.
>
> For what will it profit a man if he gains the whole world and forfeits his soul? Or what shall a man give in return for his soul?" **Matt 16:24-26**

What does it mean to take up my cross?

Jesus clearly delineates His conditions for discipleship. The second condition is to take up your cross.

Then Jesus makes the matter more clear. It is a matter of life or death. It is a matter of life or death - for my flesh, my desires, my will, and the life that I possess.

To take up my cross means that I live as a dead person – my flesh, my desires, and my will have been sentenced to die. I have no rights because I have surrendered them to Him.

But it is not just a matter of life or death for my flesh, it is a matter of life or death for my soul. Surrender of my life means that my soul finds life in Him – His deep, loving, rich, and satisfying life. It is the only true life from the Source of life.

Meditation: Imagine Jesus taking up His cross on the way to Calvary. Think of the surrender that has just occurred – surrender to beatings, mocking, ridicule, injustice, and scourging. What did it mean for Jesus to give up His rights in surrender to the Father?

Now imagine yourself carrying your cross. What do you see? What do you feel as you carry your cross? What are the implications for you to carry your cross every day?

Are you willing to surrender the same rights that Jesus did as you take up your cross? Record your thoughts and feelings in your journal.

> Listening during your devotional time is important especially as we discern surrender and what it means.

From that time Jesus began to show his disciples that he must go to Jerusalem and suffer many things from the elders and chief priests and scribes, and be killed, and on the third day be raised. And Peter took him aside and began to rebuke him, saying, "Far be it from you, Lord! This shall never happen to you."

But he turned and said to Peter, "Get behind me, Satan! You are a hindrance to me. For you are not setting your mind on the things of God, but on the things of man."

Then Jesus told his disciples, "If anyone would come after me, let him deny himself and take up his cross and follow me. For whoever would save his life will lose it, but whoever loses his life for my sake will find it. For what will it profit a man if he gains the whole world and forfeits his soul? Or what shall a man give in return for his soul?

For the Son of Man is going to come with his angels in the glory of his Father, and then he will repay each person according to what he has done. Truly, I say to you, there are some standing here who will not taste death until they see the Son of Man coming in his kingdom." **Matt 16:21-28**

Thy kingdom come; Thy Will be done.

Woke up and I realized that I needed deeper <u>pursuit</u> of righteousness, holiness, cleanliness, purity, and Your KINGDOM, Your rule, control, and dominion in my life! If I am not in pursuit of these things, there is great danger of slipping from whatever level I am on, and then finding myself on lower levels, losing ground.

O God, I want You! I want to be overtaken and consumed with the <u>pursuit</u> of, the Seeking, Searching, and Making it my Chief Aim—Your Kingdom and Your righteousness!

There is a reason You tell me to "Seek First" Your Kingdom and Your righteousness! I need Your KINGDOM coming into my life, becoming the goal, aim, and chief pursuit of my life. When this is happening all other good and Godly things will fall into place as well.

O God, give me deeper hungers for Your life, Your holiness, righteousness, faithfulness, love, and desire for Your Kingdom, Your rule, control, dominion, and supremacy coming about in my life! I need You so much.   -Pastor Daniel Martin, 12/16/13

Understand the context of Jesus' conditions of discipleship. The issue was one of kingship.

Jesus' disciples thought Jesus was the Messiah, but in their book that meant he was destined to seize power and to become the king at that time (Luke 19:11). Jesus would defeat the Romans and rule an earthly kingdom. And Jesus' disciples were very interested in the trappings of royalty – power, pleasure, and glory (Mark 10:35-37).

So when Jesus began to talk about going to Jerusalem to suffer, die and be raised, Peter took Jesus aside and said "No way, Jesus! This isn't how the script is supposed to read!"

Jesus immediately rebuked Peter. Jesus would not entertain the temptation of worldly power, pleasure, and glory, and He did not desire His disciples to do so either. Jesus was careful to distinguish His discipleship from the discipleship of the world.

So the question is one of life and death. But it is also one of kingship. Whose kingship will reign in our lives - the kingship of worldly power, or the Kingship of the King of Kings?

Meditation: "Thy Kingdom come; Thy will be done." Slowly repeat the Lord's Prayer. Dwell on each line as you repeat it.

Next repeat the first four lines of the Lord's Prayer slowly. Yield your heart to the Lord as you seek His Kingship in your life. Ask Him to enter into your heart and life as your King.

☩   ☩   ☩   ☩   ☩   ☩   ☩

NOTES:_____

_____

_____

_____

_____

_____

_____

And as they led him away, they seized one Simon of Cyrene, who was coming in from the country, and laid on him the cross, to carry it behind Jesus. And there followed him a great multitude of the people and of women who were mourning and lamenting for him.

But turning to them Jesus said, "Daughters of Jerusalem, do not weep for me, but weep for yourselves and for your children. For behold, the days are coming when they will say, 'Blessed are the barren and the wombs that never bore and the breasts that never nursed!'

Then they will begin to say to the mountains, 'Fall on us,' and to the hills, 'Cover us.' For if they do these things when the wood is green, what will happen when it is dry?" Luke 23:26-31

And there followed Him a great multitude of people.

In the cross is salvation, in the cross is life, in the cross is protection against our enemies, in the cross is infusion of heavenly sweetness, in the cross is strength, in the cross joy of spirit, in the cross the height of virtue, in the cross the perfection of holiness. There is no salvation of the soul, or hope of everlasting life, but in the cross. Take up your cross therefore and follow Jesus, and you shall go into everlasting life...For if you be dead with Him, you shall in like manner live with Him. And if you share His punishment, you shall also share His glory.[17]

Jesus instructed His disciple to take up his cross and to follow Him.

Meditation: Imagine Jesus on the way to Calvary. Now you are walking behind Him with others as He is going to His sure and certain death. What do you see? What do you feel?

Then Jesus turns to those mourning Him and speaks a word not focused on Himself, but focused on them. "Daughters of Jerusalem, do not weep for me..." What do you think when you hear Jesus speak those words? What do you feel?

What does it mean to you to carry your own cross?

---

[17] *The Imitation of Christ*, p.86.

NOTES:_____

_____

_____

_____

_____

_____

_____

_____

_____

_____

_____

_____

_____

Please remember to keep a journal
about your devotional times. Notes
are good, but a journal details
moods, movements, and markers.

Now great crowds accompanied him, and he turned and said to them,

"If anyone comes to me and does not hate his own father and mother and wife and children and brothers and sisters, yes, and even his own life, he cannot be my disciple. Whoever does not bear his own cross and come after me cannot be my disciple.

For which of you, desiring to build a tower, does not first sit down and count the cost, whether he has enough to complete it? Otherwise, when he has laid a foundation and is not able to finish, all who see it begin to mock him, saying, 'This man began to build and was not able to finish.'

Or what king, going out to encounter another king in war, will not sit down first and deliberate whether he is able with ten thousand to meet him who comes against him with twenty thousand? And if not, while the other is yet a great way off, he sends a delegation and asks for terms of peace.

So therefore, any one of you who does not renounce all that he has cannot be my disciple." Luke 14:25-33

Poor recruitment methods.

This passage is Jesus' discipleship recruitment speech to the masses. His standards are rigorous and His words are hard. One might say Jesus was lucky to find 12 guys willing to sign up, even if they were not exactly the "cream of the crop."

But Jesus knew exactly the type of person He wanted and the type of person that pleased Him. Jesus' qualifications did not relate to education, talent, skill, or social standing. The qualifications related to devotion, self denial, abandonment, and surrender.

Jesus knew that if a person with those qualifications signed up, Jesus could supply all else that was needed to bring the Kingdom of God.

Meditation: Focus on the qualifications that Jesus required in this passage. In what ways do you meet these qualifications? Is there anything that you need to change? Write down your answers in your journal.

This day is a review day. Review your journal notes from the past week.

Pastor Late is a beloved man of God who fathered many spiritual children. He regularly exhorted us, "Like Peter did, we are fond of saying that we will die for the Lord. But the question is not whether we will die for Him. The question is whether we will live for Him! If we are not living for Him now, and carefully obeying everything He tells us to do, then we are not willing to die for Him. We demonstrate our willingness to die for Him every day that we die to ourselves and conduct our lives for His glory. Otherwise, it is just idle talk."[18]

Meditation: Consider the tension between life and death – the contradiction that dying to our self yields life. How do you deal with this dichotomy in your life? In what ways do you die to your own self and live to Him?

Ask God to help you surrender your life to Him.

✝ ✝ ✝ ✝ ✝ ✝ ✝

NOTES:_____

_____

_____

_____

_____

_____

_____

_____

---

[18] David Thurman, *The Call: Book Two – Foundational (Progressive Fivefold Function),* p. 61 (2009).

II.Week Two, Day 1 (Date:)   **SURRENDER – THE TEMPTATION**

> Then Jesus was led up by the Spirit into the wilderness to be tempted by the devil. **Matt 4:1**

Spirit led.

For not every desire proceeds from the Holy Spirit, even though it seems right and good. It is difficult to judge truly whether a good spirit or the contrary drive you to desire this or that; or whether by your own spirit you be moved thereto. Many have been deceived in the end, who at the first seemed to be led on by a good spirit.

Therefore, whatever occurs to the mind as desirable must always be desired and prayed for in the fear of God and with humility of heart. You must commit the whole matter to Me with special resignation of yourself, and say: "O Lord, Thou knowest what is the better way, let this or that be done as Thou shalt please. Give what Thou wilt, and how much Thou wilt, and when Thou wilt. Deal with me as Thou knowest, and as best pleaseth Thee, and is most for Thy honor. Set me where Thou wilt, and deal with me in all things just as Thou wilt. I am in Thy hand; turn me round, and turn me back again, even as a wheel. Behold, I am Thy servant, prepared for all things; for I desire not to live unto myself, but unto Thee; and oh, that I could do it worthily and perfectly."[19]

The temptation of Jesus did not occur by accident. The Spirit led Jesus into the wilderness to be tempted by the devil. Jesus submitted Himself to the leading of the Spirit when He faced the temptation. His temptation was an act of surrender on His part. Jesus committed the matter to His Father.

The devil intended the temptation for evil. He wanted to test Jesus and to thwart the purposes for which Jesus came to earth. But God allowed the temptation in order to affirm Jesus' character and role, and to show us an example of holiness resisting evil.

Sometimes, we face something evil that God intends to convert to good. It may be for our own good or it may be for the glory of God. Other times, God asks us to surrender to Him in order to face evil, so that we may overcome it.

Meditation: Do you think that the man, Jesus, understood the reasons for the temptation as it was happening?

Meditate on the surrender that Jesus demonstrated in being led by the Spirit to be tempted by the devil.

---

[19] *The Imitation of Christ*, p.125.

> And after fasting forty days and forty nights, he was hungry.
>
> And the tempter came and said to him, "If you are the Son of God, command these stones to become loaves of bread."
>
> But he answered, "It is written, "'Man shall not live by bread alone, but by every word that comes from the mouth of God.'" **Matt 4:2-4**

He was hungry.

If we really want to know if something is a temptation, let us examine our obedience. It is the best light in time of temptation, and we will know exactly where we are and what we are doing. It is the best light in that terrible darkness. Even for Jesus, the devil wanted to find out who he was. He was not sure. The devil will stoop to anything to find out where our weak point is. He will do anything to get us to accept that one wrong thought, to say that one unkind word, to do that one impure act, that one act of disobedience, that one instance of giving something away without permission, that one neglect of prayer – just that one thing. If there is an award to be given for patience it should be given to the devil. He has a lot of patience.[20]

This temptation appealed to the hunger that Jesus felt. Numerous commentators analogize the three temptations of Jesus to the three categories of worldly desire listed in I Jn. 2:16 – the desires of the flesh, the desires of the eyes, and the pride of life.[21]

> Do not love the world or the things in the world. If anyone loves the world, the love of the Father is not in him. For all that is in the world— the desires of the flesh and the desires of the eyes and pride of life— is not from the Father but is from the world. And the world is passing away along with its desires, but whoever does the will of God abides forever. **1 Jn 2:15-17**

This first temptation related to a desire of the flesh. Jesus was hungry – maybe even starving. His hunger was natural and Jesus had the liberty to eat food. But many times temptation hinges not on what is lawful or permissible, but on what is profitable to the soul.

---

[20] Mother Teresa, *Total Surrender,* p. 77 (Servant 1985).

[21] E.g., Jamieson, Fausset, and Brown, *A Commentary On the Old and New Testaments*, I Jn. 2:16.

In order to fight this temptation, Jesus acted in self denial. He denied his flesh and its hunger. His purity did not allow the devil any traction.

Meditation: Focus on your flesh – your body, its cravings, its desires, and its hunger. What temptations of the flesh do you experience? Write them down.

As the Lord shows you each temptation of the flesh, surrender it to the Lord. Tell the Lord that you acknowledge the desire exists. Ask the Lord to help you overcome that desire and to use it in a way that pleases Him.

✠   ✠   ✠   ✠   ✠   ✠   ✠

NOTES:_____

_____

_____

_____

_____

_____

_____

_____

_____

_____

_____

_____

> But the serpent said to the woman, "You will not surely die. For God knows that when you eat of it your eyes will be opened, and you will be like God, knowing good and evil."
>
> So when the woman saw that the tree was good for food, and that it was a delight to the eyes, and that the tree was to be desired to make one wise, she took of its fruit and ate, and she also gave some to her husband who was with her, and he ate. **Gen 3:4-6**

Sources of temptation.

The devil directly tempted Jesus just as he directly tempted Eve. And he utilized other sources of temptation in his temptation of Eve. Besides his direct work, the devil used two other sources of temptation – the flesh and the world. The tree was good for food (flesh), was a delight to the eyes, and desired to make one wise (world). Some teachers list three main sources of temptation as the world, the devil, and the flesh.[22]

In the first temptation of Jesus, the devil used the flesh as one source of temptation. The devil communicated the temptation, but he appealed to a desire of the flesh –hunger - for maximum effect. But Jesus did not succumb to the temptation of the flesh or the temptation of the devil.

Meditation: Consider the role that Eve's senses played in her temptation. What role do your senses play as a source of temptation in your life?

Next, consider the role that curiosity played in Eve's temptation. What role does curiosity play as a source of temptation in your life?

Consider the sources of your temptations. Identify your most difficult struggles. What are the sources of those temptations – the flesh, the world, the devil? Consider how those sources enter into your life. Write about your temptations and their sources. Are there steps that you can take to eliminate the sources of your temptations?

What areas of your life do you need to surrender in order to eliminate those sources?

╬   ╬   ╬   ╬   ╬   ╬   ╬

---

[22]E.g., St. John of the Cross, *The Spiritual Canticle*, Stanza 3 Commentary (ICS Publications 1991).

_____

_____

_____

_____

_____

_____

_____

_____

_____

_____

_____

_____

Rest in the Lord! Even in times of temptation and struggle, the Lord desires for us to have an inner core that rests in Him.

> Then the devil took him to the holy city and set him on the pinnacle of the temple and said to him, "If you are the Son of God, throw yourself down, for it is written, "'He will command his angels concerning you,' and "'On their hands they will bear you up, lest you strike your foot against a stone.'"
>
> Jesus said to him, "Again it is written, 'You shall not put the Lord your God to the test.'" **Matt 4:5-7**

The pride of life.

Set yourself always in the lowest place (Luke 14:10) and the highest shall be given to you; for the highest cannot stand without the lowest. The chiefest saints before God are the least before themselves, and the more glorious they are, so much within themselves are they humbler. Those who are full of truth and heavenly glory are not greedy of vainglory. Those who are firmly settled and grounded in God can no wise be puffed up. And they who ascribe all unto God, whatever good they have received, seek not glory of one another, but wish for that glory which is from God alone.[23]

The next temptation is one of a public demonstration. The devil solicits a public display of Who Jesus is. It is a temptation of pride, reputation, and self glory. It is a temptation of adulation.

Ironically, this temptation arises from the very heart of the devil. The devil desires the adulation and glory that belong only to God.

"How you are fallen from heaven, O Day Star, son of Dawn! How you are cut down to the ground, you who laid the nations low!

You said in your heart, 'I will ascend to heaven; above the stars of God I will set my throne on high; I will sit on the mount of assembly in the far reaches of the north; I will ascend above the heights of the clouds; I will make myself like the Most High.'" **Isa 14:12-14**

So the devil tried to lure Jesus into the same fall that the devil had cast himself – through pride and self glory.

Meditation: Ask the Lord to show you areas of pride in your life. Consider your work, your family, your relationships, your achievements, and your possessions. Write a list of your sources of pride.

As He shows you each area, ask Him to help you surrender it to Him.

---

[23] *The Imitation of Christ,* pp.82-83.

Again, the devil took him to a very high mountain and showed him all the kingdoms of the world and their glory. And he said to him, "All these I will give you, if you will fall down and worship me." Then Jesus said to him, "Be gone, Satan! For it is written, "'You shall worship the Lord your God and him only shall you serve.'" **Matt 4:8-10**

The means of sinful nature.

For the third temptation, the devil used the world. He appealed to the lust of the eyes by showing Jesus all the kingdoms of the world. Then he offered Jesus control of human endeavor – complete earthly power.

Human power is the means by which sinful nature is exercised. Marva Dawn quotes Bill Wylie Kellermann saying that the three temptations were all temptations to worldly power. The first temptation was a temptation to economic power – changing stones to bread. The second temptation was located at the temple – a temptation to religious power. The third temptation offered military and political power.[24]

Human power is the means used by the devil to influence and corrupt men and women. The strength of man is the fundamental premise of legalism. The attraction of power is deceptive because of its appeal to man. <u>Human strength serves the devil as a counterfeit for divine grace.</u>

The temptation to power is insidious. Through His humility and surrender, Jesus discerned the deception immediately and responded that all power belonged to God. God is the only true Power and the only true Source of power.

Meditation: Put yourself in the shoes of Jesus. The devil shows you all the kingdoms of the world and their glory. He offers it to you. What do you feel as you observe the vastness of worldly power and glory?

What are your feelings as this vast power and glory is offered to you? In what ways does it appeal to you? Ask God to show you the sources of those feelings. Ask Him to help you surrender those sources to Him.

╬   ╬   ╬   ╬   ╬   ╬   ╬

---

[24] Marva Dawn, *Powers, Weakness, and the Tabernacling of God* p.76 (Eerdmans 2001).

NOTES:_____

_____

_____

_____

_____

_____

_____

_____

_____

_____

_____

_____

_____

_____

_____

_____

_____

_____

> A word fitly spoken is like apples of gold in a setting of silver. **Pro 25:11**

Apples of gold in a setting of silver.

Help me to come closer to the point where when the enemy pokes at me, all that can come out of me is You and Your Word, because that is all that is in me! O deliver me more and more, change me more and more today!! –Pastor Daniel Martin, 8/27/14

"It is written." To each temptation, Jesus responded *"It is written."*

After Jesus used the rebuke of scripture in the first temptation, the devil tried to use scripture in presenting the second and third temptations. But the use of scripture by the devil emanated from a carnal and fallen spirit. The word was not fitly spoken.

Jesus' use of scripture arose from inspiration and illumination. He was full of the Holy Spirit, and He was fully surrendered to the Holy Spirit. *And Jesus, full of the Holy Spirit, returned from the Jordan and was led by the Spirit in the wilderness...* (Luke 4:1). The words of Jesus were fitly spoken.

Meditation: Consider the use of scripture by the devil and the use of scripture by Jesus. What are the differences in how scripture was used?

Meditate on how you can use scripture properly. Ask God to help you plant scripture into your heart, mind, and soul so that it becomes a part of you so that through it, you can resist temptation.

☨   ☨   ☨   ☨   ☨   ☨   ☨

Jesus was the Word made flesh – the Word Incarnate. Take time with the scriptures in this devotional. Read them carefully and slowly. Go over them deliberately. Ask God to put the Word in your heart and to make it a part of you. The Word is a sword with which we fight and we overcome. Implant it!

> Then the devil left him, and behold, angels came and were ministering to him. **Matt 4:11**

Today is a day of simplicity and rest.

Father, how simple You have made things.

I am to just follow You, step where You say step, go where You say go, do what You say do, and REST in You, Your Word, Your love, and Your truth!

Help me to keep things simple and follow You all the days of my life, living in the center of Your presence and love.   -Pastor Daniel Martin, 9/12/14

Jesus relied on the provision of the Lord only. He refused to receive provision from any other source.

Meditation: Be silent before the Lord. Eliminate all outside distractions. Quiet your heart and mind.

Now ask the Lord to send His angels to come and to minister to you. Wait quietly to give the Lord the opportunity to minister to you. Rest in Him and in His love.

☩   ☩   ☩   ☩   ☩   ☩   ☩

NOTES:_____

_____

_____

_____

_____

_____

_____

_____

II.Week Three, Day 1 (Date:)   **DESIRE AND DESTINY**

> And we know that for those who love God all things work together for good, for those who are called according to his purpose. **Rom 8:28**

Called according to His purpose.

O God, help me to not count my life (in my flesh) dear to myself. Help me instead to count Your life in me, Your CALLINGS on my life dear to myself.

The life of my flesh is empty, drains my emotional, physical, and spiritual energy, causing those energies to be poured out on "nothings."

Help me today, as I now set my hourly chime to see to it that my energies are poured out on Life-giving things, Your CALLINGS, my Course, and the Ministry I have received from You!

O thank You for the ministry of testifying of the Good News (gospel) of Your Grace!!
        -Pastor Daniel Martin, 3/9/14

This verse is well known. "God works all things together for my good" is how this verse is often quoted. And there is merit in that interpretation although the "good" in the verse may not be so personalized.

But there are a couple of conditions in this verse. One condition is "for those who love God." We have focused on loving God in this devotional, and we will continue to do so.

A second condition is "for those who are called according to His purpose." God calls people to Himself for His purpose – not for their purposes, but for His purpose.

God has called you for a reason. God has a role, purpose, and destiny for you. He is your primary destiny, but He has a role and a purpose for you in your journey to Him.

A key to fulfilling the destiny of God is seeking, discerning, and obeying the call which God has on your life.

Meditation: Spend time with God reviewing His work in your life. What has He shown you about His call on your life? [You can review your notes from I. Week Twelve, Day 3.

Write down what He has shown you about your role, purpose, and destiny in Him.

---

‡   ‡   ‡   ‡   ‡   ‡   ‡

And seeing one of them being wronged, he defended the oppressed man and avenged him by striking down the Egyptian. He supposed that his brothers would understand that God was giving them salvation by his hand, but they did not understand.

And on the following day he appeared to them as they were quarreling and tried to reconcile them, saying, 'Men, you are brothers. Why do you wrong each other?' But the man who was wronging his neighbor thrust him aside, saying, 'Who made you a ruler and a judge over us? Do you want to kill me as you killed the Egyptian yesterday?'

At this retort Moses fled and became an exile in the land of Midian, where he became the father of two sons. **Acts 7:24-29**

He supposed that his brothers would understand that

God was giving them salvation by his hand.

This account of Moses comes from the martyr, Stephen. Moses was the deliverer of Israel. Deliverance was his call and destiny. Moses had an understanding of that call before he left Egypt – before God empowered him to fulfill that call at the burning bush. Within him while he was still in Egypt, Moses had a desire to deliver Israel.

At this stage of Moses' life, Moses was not ready. He was raised in Pharaoh's house and understood deliverance in terms of human power, human political skill, and human strength. His desire was disordered. So Moses acted on his desire according to human devices. He killed the Egyptian.

Only after Moses toiled as a shepherd for 40 years as an exile in Midian was he ready to fulfill his destiny with proper desire in a godly way. At that point, he was ready to walk in surrender in leading Israel out of Egypt.

God puts desires within us that align with His call and purpose in our lives. Those desires are both true and godly. David Benner says "The human journey – particularly our spiritual journey – is shaped by our deepest desires."[25] Many times though, we act on those desires in an ungodly way. We need to discern our call and purpose in God, and to identify the desires He has placed within us, so that we can fulfill those desires in the godly way that He intends.

---

[25] David Benner, *Desiring God's Will* p.76 (IVP 2015).

Meditation: Spend time with God discerning the desires in your heart. The desires can be holy desires or wicked desires. Try to discern which desires are on the surface and which desires are deep and heartfelt. Write them down.

Ask God to show you which desires are true desires placed in your heart by Him.

☩   ☩   ☩   ☩   ☩   ☩   ☩

NOTES:_____

_____

_____

_____

_____

_____

_____

_____

_____

_____

_____

_____

_____

_____

> Have this mind among yourselves, which is yours in Christ Jesus, who, though he was in the form of God, did not count equality with God a thing to be grasped, but emptied himself, by taking the form of a servant, being born in the likeness of men. And being found in human form, he humbled himself by becoming obedient to the point of death, even death on a cross.
>
> Therefore God has highly exalted him and bestowed on him the name that is above every name, so that at the name of Jesus every knee should bow, in heaven and on earth and under the earth, and every tongue confess that Jesus Christ is Lord, to the glory of God the Father. **Phil 2:5-11**

Jesus emptied Himself.

Show me lies and trifles, vanities and emptiness, evil and sin that I follow after, set my heart on, allow my mind to dwell on, etc.

Deliver me from my addictions to things that do not glorify You, that have no good effects in my life, that lead me away from You and what You have planned for my life. I don't want the flows from my life to contain ANYTHING of the enemy. I want the flow from my life to be those streams that are of You, that originate and flow from my life lived abiding in You, drawing from You, resting/abiding in You, connecting with You, and sharing life with You!

When these things are going on in me, there is no room or desire for anything of the enemy in me! Come and draw me more and more into the life You have for me!
–Pastor Daniel Martin, 12/17/14

Jesus emptied Himself. He poured out himself.

Jesus walked in complete surrender when, although He was God the Son, He humbled Himself to become a Servant. He also humbled Himself in obedience to the point of death – death on a cross. Jesus surrendered to the will of the Father in fulfilling the destiny that God had for Him.

Surrender is the key to realizing and fulfilling the destiny which we have in God.

Meditation: Keep asking God to show you desires within your heart, soul, and spirit. As God shows you each desire, surrender that desire to Him. Tell God that you want to walk in complete surrender to Him. Ask Him to help you walk in that surrender for each desire that you have. That is a part of taking up your cross.

NOTES:_____ ⁄ _____

_____

_____

_____

_____

_____

_____

_____

_____

_____

_____

_____

Take your time to explore each meditation well. It is fine to take more than one day on a single devotion if that is needed to explore the topic of the devotion and to instill its full application.

> Have this mind among yourselves, which is yours in Christ Jesus, who, though he was in the form of God, did not count equality with God a thing to be grasped, but emptied himself, by taking the form of a servant, being born in the likeness of men. And being found in human form, he humbled himself by becoming obedient to the point of death, even death on a cross.
>
> Therefore God has highly exalted him and bestowed on him the name that is above every name, so that at the name of Jesus every knee should bow, in heaven and on earth and under the earth, and every tongue confess that Jesus Christ is Lord, to the glory of God the Father. **Phil 2:5-11**

Jesus has a destiny.

Jesus has a destiny. That destiny is one of glory, power, and exaltation. Every knee will bow to Him and every tongue will confess that He is Lord, to the glory of God the Father.

Jesus had desires in His heart that aligned with His destiny. Here is the insidious nature of the temptations that the devil presented to Jesus: Each temptation connected to a godly desire in the heart of Jesus. If the desire in Jesus' heart were disordered, misunderstood, or misaligned, then the temptation would have been effective and Jesus could have acted on that desire on the spot.

The third temptation was a temptation to rule the earth. Jesus is the King of Kings Who is destined to rule the earth.

The second temptation was a temptation to glory and exaltation. Jesus is the King of Glory Who is and Who will be highly exalted.

The first temptation concerned the supply of bread. Jesus is the Bread of Life given for mankind. He is the One who multiplies bread to feed His followers.

Each temptation connected to a godly desire in Jesus' heart. But the means to that desire offered by the devil was earthly and ungodly. Jesus rejected the paths that the devil offered to fulfill His desires. His desires were godly, and Jesus determined to fulfill them through the godly path that His Father willed.

> Meditation: Focus on the desires in your heart that the Lord has identified over the last few days. For each desire, ask God to show you if that desire has a true and godly source. Ask Him to reveal godly ways in which you act on that desire, and ungodly ways in which you act on that desire. Seek Him about His intended fulfillment of each desire.

> Delight yourself in the LORD, and he will give you the desires of your heart. **Psa 37:4**

He will give you the desires of your heart. [26]

O the glory of Your desires becoming my desires!

Thank You for gifting me with these desires. They are so wholesome, life-giving, fulfilling, gratifying, and satisfying—the desires themselves!

And the reality of the things You have given me to desire are far beyond the desires themselves! O what a wonderful life You have for me. I like Your ways far better than mine! Yours are so packed with life and glory!

I love You, O my God and King! How awesome and great You are!! My soul Sings this morning of Your greatness, of Your majesty, love, will, ways, word, and life! You are so GOOD! -Pastor Daniel Martin, 8/28/13

When I read the verse above, I have theological confusion: "Lord, you can't give me the desires of my heart, because they are so evil."

But this statement is a statement of faith. First, this statement requires faith that God has and will put desires in my heart that are true, righteous, and godly. My true longings may not be fully understood, but they are not evil.

Second, this statement requires faith that, as I surrender my desires to Him, He will reveal my true desires to me. He will lead me on a path where those desires are fulfilled.

Third, part of my surrender to Him involves blind obedience. He sees what I cannot. Many desires that I feel are actually destructive to me. Many ways in which I act on those desires are detrimental to my soul and hinder my destiny in Him. I must trust Him, His words, and His ways whether or not I see how they fulfill the desires of my heart. Surrender.

Meditation: When He was tempted, did Jesus, the Son of Man, fully understand how the Father would fulfill His desires? I don't know that answer but scripture says that Jesus was tempted in all respects as we are (Heb 4:15).

Consider what it means to surrender to God even when you do not see, understand, or feel how that surrender impacts you or your desires.

---

[26] For further application of Psalm 37, see Appendix A: *Steps To Peace.*

> And when Jesus was baptized, immediately he went up from the water, and behold, the heavens were opened to him, and he saw the Spirit of God descending like a dove and coming to rest on him; and behold, a voice from heaven said, "This is my beloved Son, with whom I am well pleased."
>
> Then Jesus was led up by the Spirit into the wilderness to be tempted by the devil. **Matt 3:16-4:1**

After all, He desires good things for us.

O the glory of Your Presence!

This child/sheep needs You, Your Presence, and Your LAD (Love, Acceptance, and Desire)!

<u>Your DESIRE for me</u>:

- Staggers my imagination (but the cross overcomes any doubt of its reality)
- Fulfills me
- Makes me whole
- Satisfies deep longings and needs in me
- Puts a smile on my face
- Overcomes doubts about You
- Gives me HOPE when I feel like I am hopeless
- Floods me with Joy
- Gives me strength to go on in anything
- Gives me deeper desires to honor, love, glorify, bless, and please You
- Lets me know that the grace that I need is greater than my faults - that it abounds farther than my sin
- Helps me to understand the cross
- Makes me know that whatever I need, really need, You will supply according to Your wisdom, knowledge, and understanding of the entire issue.
  -Pastor Daniel Martin, 12/27/14

His desire for us empowers us to fulfill our destiny.

The last words in scripture that Jesus heard before the temptation were words of delight. *"This is my beloved Son, with whom I am well pleased."* These words arise out of a loving relationship.

The Father spoke these words to His Son when His Son began His earthly ministry. The Father knew that the Son needed to hear these words at this launching point. This is the key to realization of our destiny – that the Father loves us, the Father desires us, and the Father is well pleased with us.

Meditation: Love is our destination. How much will love, acceptance, and desire from the Lord impact that journey?

What will it look like when you reach that destination? Meditate on the experience of fullness of love. Describe it in your journal.

---

‡   ‡   ‡   ‡   ‡   ‡   ‡

NOTES:_____

_____

_____

_____

_____

_____

_____

_____

_____

_____

_____

Today is a day of faith. As you review the devotions from this week, also review the godly desires that God has placed in your heart. Review the call and destiny that you sense from the Lord.

> **Meditation:** Now as you review those areas, exercise faith toward God in the fulfillment of those desires; fulfillment of that call; and fulfillment of that destiny. Tell God you trust Him for fulfillment in His time and for His pleasure.

☧   ☧   ☧   ☧   ☧   ☧   ☧

NOTES:_____

_____

_____

_____

_____

_____

_____

_____

Be faithful in meeting regularly with your mentor or devotional partner. A wise friend can help you understand and define the desires of your heart and how they relate to destiny and call from God.

II.Week Four, Day 1 (Date:)   **DENY YOURSELF**

> And those who belong to Christ Jesus have crucified the flesh with its passions and desires. **Gal 5:24**

Passions and desires.

O Jesus, keep me near the cross, even for this issue!

Come and search me in such a way that I know what is in my heart!

Reveal it to me in such a powerful way that I turn to You, take up my cross, and die daily to what my flesh is demanding! This is <u>healthy!</u>

It is Good for my flesh to be denied, so that You can be honored, glorified, exalted, praised, pleased, and delighted!

O the Glory that I feel and know when I glorify, magnify, please, delight, and bless You! Help me to spend more quality time in my days doing this! You are so worthy of it!!
   –Pastor Daniel Martin, 5/26/13

Passions and desires. Appetites. An initial struggle for many followers of Christ is in the area of fleshly appetites.

What I desire becomes what I crave. What I crave becomes what I need. Obtaining what I need seems pretty reasonable. So I act on what I desire.

But Paul says I have crucified the flesh with its passions and desires. This crucifixion is a part of "deny yourself" and a part of bearing your own cross.

Meditation: Consider your foremost appetites. What are the fleshly appetites with which you struggle? As the Holy Spirit shows them to you, write them down and then surrender them to God. Ask the Holy Spirit to help you deny yourself.

Then slowly say "I want to follow Christ." Repeat the phrase as you make it your prayer.

   ✠   ✠   ✠   ✠   ✠   ✠   ✠

> If your mind wanders during devotions, it is okay. Bring it back. If your mind wanders to a temptation or to an appetite, surrender that to God and ask for His forgiving grace.

NOTES:

> For the desires of the flesh are against the Spirit, and the desires of the Spirit are against the flesh, for these are opposed to each other, to keep you from doing the things you want to do.
>
> But if you are led by the Spirit, you are not under the law.
>
> Now the works of the flesh are evident: sexual immorality, impurity, sensuality, idolatry, sorcery, enmity, strife, jealousy, fits of anger, rivalries, dissensions, divisions, envy, drunkenness, orgies, and things like these. I warn you, as I warned you before, that those who do such things will not inherit the kingdom of God. **Gal 5:17-21**

The desires of the flesh are against the Spirit.

O, how wonderfully life-giving Your LAD (Love, Acceptance, and Desire) is! Thank You for the power of it in my life! I need You so much, O my blessed Redeemer and Friend! What an awesome God You are to me!

Thank You for the flood of life You give me each morning as I open up to You and allow You to remove the blockages from my life!!

As I wrote the word "blockages" above, I instantly had the picture of the sewage flowing so full and free after I finally broke through the blockage in my home sewer line Wednesday! As I first saw it coming and then a full flow of it passing through for quite some time, it was glory—we had ability to use our water, take baths, use the toilets, wash—do everything our supply of water allows us to do!

Until the blockage was removed, the supply of water was there, but it was useless to us, all because of a small blockage, less than 6 inches in diameter!

But O the glory now as it is cleaned out and there can be a flow of all that is needed in the house!

O God, come and show me the blockages in my life that prevent the free flow of Your Love, Acceptance, and Desire into my life, through my life, and out of my life into my world around me!

Show me not only the blockages—I need to know:

- **Where the blockages are...**
- **What is causing the blockage to form...**
- **What the blockages are made of...**
- **How to prevent the blockage from forming...**
- **What I need to not allow in my life that could cause a blockage (excess "toilet tissue")...**

- What "roots" there are in me that create the beginning stages of a blockage...
- How to clear out any of these problems...
- How to access Your SWK (Salvation, Wisdom, and Knowledge) about the above!

O Father, I need You so much!!

Come and deliver me from myself, from all evil in me!

I need Your love more and more alive and at work in me, along with deep understanding of Your acceptance and desire!

Come and help me to access them so powerfully that they keep all the lines clear and flowing with Your life!!   -Pastor Daniel Martin, 12/27/14

The works of flesh oppose the works of the Spirit. Our fleshly appetites deprive us of the Holy Spirit. Oh, that we could remove these blockages!

Meditation: Spend time with the Lord asking Him about blockages in your life. For a reference point, you can use the "works of the flesh" listed by the Apostle Paul in the scripture above.

As the Lord shows you areas of possible blockage, write them down and then ask Him to remove them so there can be a flow of life from the Holy Spirit. Ask Him if there is anything that you need to do to remove the blockage.

☩ ☩ ☩ ☩ ☩ ☩ ☩

NOTES:_____

_____

_____

_____

_____

_____

_____

_____

For the wrath of God is revealed from heaven against all ungodliness and unrighteousness of men, who by their unrighteousness suppress the truth.

For this reason God gave them up to dishonorable passions. For their women exchanged natural relations for those that are contrary to nature; and the men likewise gave up natural relations with women and were consumed with passion for one another, men committing shameless acts with men and receiving in themselves the due penalty for their error.

And since they did not see fit to acknowledge God, God gave them up to a debased mind to do what ought not to be done. They were filled with all manner of unrighteousness, evil, covetousness, malice. They are full of envy, murder, strife, deceit, maliciousness. They are gossips, slanderers, haters of God, insolent, haughty, boastful, inventors of evil, disobedient to parents, foolish, faithless, heartless, ruthless.

Though they know God's righteous decree that those who practice such things deserve to die, they not only do them but give approval to those who practice them. **Rom 1:18; 26-32**

God gave them up to a debased mind.

O Jesus, I want to know You more. I want to be transformed into a new person, over and over again! I want to have the way I think changed, to have my thought patterns and processes changed from the ones that hold me to my flesh, to the ones that hold me to You and Your ways.

I want to be one whose thoughts are being increasingly corralled and brought into captivity to what You are thinking, to what You have for me to be meditating on.
    –Pastor Daniel Martin, 1/20/14

Part of the mercy of God is that He gives loving parental care to His own children through discipline. But He often does not discipline those persons who do not follow Him. Instead, He gives them over to their animalistic passions. He allows them to act on those passions and to experience the awful consequences of those actions, desirous that the experience will lead them to turn and to repent.

Our moral law is based on the idea that God established it, and that God has placed His Spirit in man which enables man to follow His law. Contrary to that view, a prevalent philosophical application of evolutionary theory is that man is simply another animal. He does not have a spirit or a soul. As another animal, man is "free" to fulfill his animalistic passions.

The world and the flesh glorify animalistic passions. They exalt the debased mind.

Meditation: Spend time asking God about your own passions. Ask Him to show you which passions are based on godly desires, and which passions are based on the flesh. Write about them in your journal.

Then ask God to renew your mind. Seek Him about your own thoughts and ask Him to change any thoughts that do not glorify Him.

✝ ✝ ✝ ✝ ✝ ✝ ✝

NOTES:_____

_____

_____

_____

_____

_____

_____

_____

_____

_____

> For the wrath of God is revealed from heaven against all ungodliness and unrighteousness of men, who by their unrighteousness suppress the truth. For what can be known about God is plain to them, because God has shown it to them. For his invisible attributes, namely, his eternal power and divine nature, have been clearly perceived, ever since the creation of the world, in the things that have been made. So they are without excuse.
>
> For although they knew God, they did not honor him as God or give thanks to him, but they became futile in their thinking, and their foolish hearts were darkened. Claiming to be wise, they became fools, and exchanged the glory of the immortal God for images resembling mortal man and birds and animals and creeping things.
>
> Therefore God gave them up in the lusts of their hearts to impurity, to the dishonoring of their bodies among themselves, because they exchanged the truth about God for a lie and worshiped and served the creature rather than the Creator, who is blessed forever! Amen.
>
> For this reason God gave them up to dishonorable passions.
> **Rom 1:18-26a**

They worshiped and served the creature rather than the Creator.

Many in our society today look to animal behavior to instruct our human behavior. The world justifies acting on dishonorable passions because that is how "human animals" behave. Foolish hearts have become darkened.

But the Apostle Paul indicates that the fundamental issue is not philosophy or human behavior. The fundamental issue is about worship. The truth of God has been exchanged for a lie. The world worships and serves the creature rather than worshipping and serving the Creator.

Worship of the creature through lusts of the heart is idolatry. Idolatry is not just putting something else above God. An idol is anything that keeps God from His rightful place in your heart. An idol is any longing, any thought, or any possession that keeps you from a total surrender to God.

Lust of the flesh is worship of a creature rather than the Creator. It is an idol.

Meditation: Ask God to show you any idols in your heart. List any idols in your journal. If God reveals an idol to you, ask Him to tear it down and to remove it.

"But the hour is coming, and is now here, when the true worshipers will worship the Father in spirit and truth, for the Father is seeking such people to worship him.

"God is spirit, and those who worship him must worship in spirit and truth." **John 4:23-24**

Worship in spirit and in truth.

To worship God in spirit and in truth means to offer to Him the worship that we owe. God is a Spirit; therefore we must worship Him in spirit and in truth. The means to present to Him true and humble spiritual worship in the very depth of our being. Only God can see this worship. If this is offered unceasingly, it will eventually become natural for us. It will be as if He were one with our soul, and our soul one with Him. Practice will make this clear.[27]

Jesus is speaking to the Samaritan woman at the well. He is teaching her about true worship – worship in spirit and in truth.

The fundamental issue regarding fleshly desires is worship. God has chosen the form of worship for Himself. True worship does not occur through worldly passion or through human strength.

God has chosen true worship to occur in the spirit and not in the flesh. For that reason, a follower who desires to enter into true worship must deny himself and crucify the flesh with its passions and desires. When the old, fleshly man is dead, the Spirit can thrive.

Meditation: Take time to worship God in spirit. Remove all distractions and all outside interference. Quiet your mind.

Invite the Holy Spirit into your heart to glorify God. Worship in spirit and in truth.

Remember to live in God's love – giving and receiving His love. Love covers a multitude of sins (1 Pet 4:8).

---

[27] *The Imitation of Christ*, p. 66.

NOTES:_____

> Jesus answered, "Truly, truly, I say to you, unless one is born of water and the Spirit, he cannot enter the kingdom of God.
>
> "That which is born of the flesh is flesh, and that which is born of the Spirit is spirit." **John 3:5-6**

That which is born of the spirit is spirit.

Part of Tuning my heart is making me to see spiritual realities clearer than I see physical realities! I need You so much, O my God! Come and take over in me, lift me up into Your glory and grace, into the things You know I need to see, and <u>cause me to walk "In Alignment" with Your ways and truth, instead of walking in alignment with my flesh,</u> the desires of the physical, the prevailing philosophies of this world, etc. Come and OPEN my eyes to see You! O, I need Your help in this, O my God.

We respond to things according to what we see. Our SIGHT dictates our RESPONSE!

Correct my sight, my vision, and help me to see according to the eye of faith, the eyes of Your Word, the eye of Your Spirit!   –Pastor Daniel Martin, 8/22/13

In the chapter before Jesus encounters the Samaritan woman at the well, he teaches the religious leader, Nicodemus, about the kingdom of God.

Flesh does not inherit the kingdom of God. The desires, appetites, and deeds of the flesh do not lead one into the kingdom of God. It is necessary to be born of the Spirit, not the flesh.

> **To practice [the Presence of God] correctly, the heart must be empty of all other things. God will possess the heart alone. He cannot possess it solely without emptying it of everything else. He cannot act in the heart, and do what He wants in it, unless it is empty.**   -Brother Lawrence[28]

Like Brother Lawrence, many noted contemplative Christians teach that a believer must empty himself of fleshly and worldly desires, thoughts, imaginations, and actions before the Holy Spirit can work in the manner He desires. The believer must fully turn his back on the world before the Spirit can have His way and bring fullness of Presence.

Meditation: Meditate on the idea of emptiness and what it means to you. Why does Paul say we have crucified the flesh and its desires (See Day 1 of this week)?

How can we empty ourselves of all things except the Spirit of God?

---

[28] *The Practice of the Presence of God*, p. 42.

Today is a day of worship in Spirit. As you review your journals over the last week, let them lead you to worship of the Lord.

Meditation: Eliminate distractions and hindrances. Try to nullify any fleshly desires or thoughts. Spend time loving God and receiving His love.

Next, ask the Holy Spirit to lead you to worship. Through His Spirit, worship Him in glory and majesty. Worship Him in Spirit and in truth.

☩   ☩   ☩   ☩   ☩   ☩   ☩

NOTES:_____

_____

_____

_____

_____

_____

_____

_____

_____

_____

_____

_____

_____

II.Week Five, Day 1 (Date:)   **TORMENT**

> Beloved, I urge you as sojourners and exiles to abstain from the passions of the flesh, which wage war against your soul. **1 Pet 2:11**

The passions of the flesh wage war against your soul.

O Father, come and show me the trifles and lies in my life that I have lifted up and follow after! Deliver me from chasing after the "shell" when the pearls are in reach, in my hand, if I would only recognize and honor them.

Show me where I SPEND TIME, GIVE TIME to empty nothings, and bask in their cheap thrills (Auburn football, etc).

Help me to evaluate things on the basis of Real worth and value, Real nourishment and life, instead of surface, fleshly evaluations! I need You more!!

O help me to "listen and obey the Voice of Truth"!

Show me where I am "hearing" the Voice of Truth, but Following the voice of lies and trifles! O I want to SPEND my time and days following You, O blessed Savior and Friend! You and You alone have the words, the ways of life!

Come and Tune my heart to sing Your Grace. How easy it is for my heart to get out of tune with You, to follow tunes of the flesh instead of Your tunes! O come and help me to sing Your grace, the things which glorify, honor, bless, and please You. These are the only ones which end in delight!

<u>The enemy has many things that bring very temporary, tasteful delights, delights that are no more substantive than thin mists, which quickly disappear, but leave a thick coating of scum on our lives that cry out for more scum.</u>

-Pastor Daniel Martin, 10/23/13

St. John of the Cross says that appetites (which include worldly and fleshly appetites) "cause harm in two principal ways within those in whom they dwell: They deprive them of God's Spirit; and they weary, torment, darken, defile, and weaken them."[29]

The will of God is that your soul may prosper (3 Jn 1:2). God desires that your "inner man" be strengthened (Eph. 3:16).

But the passions of the flesh wage war against your soul in many ways.

---

[29] *The Ascent of Mount Carmel*, I.6.1.

Meditation: Consider what it means for your soul to prosper. What does that look like? Write in your journal what you see.

Now consider ways that fleshly passions wage war against your soul. In what ways do they weary, torment, darken, defile or weaken your soul? How have they had a destructive effect on your life? Record your answers in your journal.

╬   ╬   ╬   ╬   ╬   ╬   ╬

NOTES:_____

_____

_____

_____

_____

_____

_____

_____

_____

_____

_____

_____

_____

_____

> And when she pressed him hard with her words day after day, and urged him, his soul was vexed to death. **Jdg 16:16**

His soul was vexed to death.

Proverbs 31:3 - "Do not give your strength to women, your ways to those who destroy kings." Father, today and in the coming year, free me from all vestiges of lust, wandering thoughts, any evil in this area.

Give me an intensity in this that is unwavering. This is one battle that requires constant diligence, no matter how free I am.

Don't even let me be drawn to faces—help me to see Hearts! O God, I need the vision that You have about the people around me. <u>Help me to not value people because of outward appearance at all.</u> Outward appearances are so deceiving, covering all kinds of things. I must be led by You, Spirit of God!!   -Pastor Daniel Martin, 12/31/11

Samson is a prime example of how our fleshly desires weaken our souls. Through His Spirit, God gave Samson a gift of strength. The purpose of the gift was to deliver Israel from its enemies, the Philistines.

But physical prowess like that (and probably the physique that goes with it) is hard to tame. Samson had fleshly appetites. He loved women, and the woman that attracted him the most was Delilah. Delilah was a charming and no doubt beautiful woman. But she did not truly love Samson and was willing to betray him to the Philistines. Yet Samson was so attached to Delilah, he could not stay away. Samson had an inordinate attachment.

So Delilah kept asking Samson about the secret to his strength. She wore him down until his soul was vexed to death. So Samson told her his holy secret. The result of Samson's desire for Delilah was weakness, defeat, loss of eyesight, and imprisonment.

Meditation: Samson's fleshly desire resulted in a loss of strength. But his spiritual resistance was also worn down. Samson's ability to fight a spiritual war and to fulfill his spiritual destiny was severely weakened due to the impact of his fleshly desire.

Meditate on how fleshly desires weaken the spiritual being. Ask the Lord to show you areas of your spiritual life that are weakened by appetites. Write about them. As the Lord shows them to you, surrender those areas to Him and ask Him for grace to overcome those appetites.

NOTES:_____

_____

_____

_____

_____

_____

_____

_____

_____

_____

_____

_____

_____

_____

"Ups and downs" are a normal part of devotional life just as they are of life itself. Don't be thrown by them. Just try to be consistent in your devotions and allow time for gradual positive change in your soul.

See to it that no one fails to obtain the grace of God; that no "root of bitterness" springs up and causes trouble, and by it many become defiled; that no one is sexually immoral or unholy like Esau, who sold his birthright for a single meal. For you know that afterward, when he desired to inherit the blessing, he was rejected, for he found no chance to repent, though he sought it with tears. **Heb 12:15-17**

A mess of pottage.

Esau is the poster child of the person whose soul is defiled by fleshly appetite. Esau came in from hunting and he was "starving." Jacob was cooking some delicious stew. Driven by his appetite, Esau agreed to sell his birthright to Jacob in exchange for bread and lentil stew. *Thus Esau despised his birthright* (Gen 25:34).

Esau could not deny his fleshly appetite and thus lost his birthright. Think of the immensity of Esau's birthright – his lineage from Abraham and Isaac. The family patriarchs were Abraham, Isaac, and Jacob, but by birthright, they were Abraham, Isaac, and Esau. Esau exchanged his lasting heritage for a "mess of pottage."

We face many choices of our will each day. We may think that a decision is a small one. But "*one who is faithful in a very little is also faithful in much*" (Luke 16:10a).

So many times we focus on our immediate desire rather than the eternal consequence. We exchange purity of soul for a "mess of pottage." Because of the "little" thing, we become defiled and experience bitterness, like Esau.

Compare Esau to Jesus Who did not allow His hunger to overcome Him during the temptation to turn the stones into bread. When Jesus was hungry on another occasion and the disciples brought Him food, Jesus said "*I have food to eat that you do not know about.*" And then, "My *food is to do the will of Him who sent Me and to accomplish His work*" (John 4:32, 34).

In John 4, we read that Jesus was both thirsty and hungry. But we also do not read that He took a drink at the well or that He ate the food that His disciples brought. Jesus was focused on matters of more eternal consequence. He had drink to offer and food to eat of a different nature.

Don't allow immediate gratification of fleshly desires to hinder fulfillment of your eternal destiny in the Lord!

Most men willingly listen to the world than to God. They follow the desire of their own flesh rather than God's good pleasure. The world promises things temporal and mean, and is served with great eagerness. I (Jesus) promise things most high and eternal, and the hearts of mortals grow dull. Who is there that in all things serves and obeys Me with so great care as the world and its lords are served withal?...For a small income, a long journey is made; for everlasting life, many scarce lift a foot from the ground.[30]

✝ ✝ ✝ ✝ ✝ ✝ ✝

NOTES:_____

_____

_____

_____

_____

_____

_____

_____

_____

_____

_____

_____

---

[30] *The Imitation of Christ*, pp.98-99.

> And Ahab went into his house vexed and sullen because of what Naboth the Jezreelite had said to him, for he had said, "I will not give you the inheritance of my fathers." And he lay down on his bed and turned away his face and would eat no food. **1 Kings 21:4**

Vexed and sullen.

My friend, Dan, made fortunes and he lost fortunes. At one point, he was a very wealthy person.

"David," he said "at one time I had so many things. I had houses, cars, and boats. I had my own mansion, and a house in the mountains, and a house at the lake. I had so many toys that I couldn't keep up with them. It wore me out. Then, one morning I realized that for every single thing that I had, I lost 10 minutes of sleep each night. And I had so much stuff that it added up."

Dan lost everything. He reached the point of brokenness and surrendered his life to the Lord. He told me that he was the poorest he had ever been in his life, and also the happiest.

Ahab was the king of Israel. As the king, he had an abundance of every possession – palaces, wealth, and luxury. Despite this abundance, Ahab wanted more. He coveted the vineyard of his neighbor, Naboth. But Naboth was a righteous man who refused to sell the inheritance of his fathers in exchange for a better vineyard or money. Naboth treasured his birthright.

So Ahab grew vexed and sullen. His desire so consumed him that he refused to eat. He allowed his own desires to torment him. St. John of the Cross says "This is the characteristic of those with appetites; they are always dissatisfied and bitter, like someone who is hungry."[31]

Meditation: Consider how our worldly appetites torment us. Why do these appetites rule our lives? What harm do they inflict on our souls?

Read the quote above from St. John of the Cross. Why does he say that our appetites leave us dissatisfied and bitter? What dissatisfaction and bitterness have you experienced in your life? Journal about them.

Then consider brokenness and surrender. How can we surrender these appetites to the Lord in our brokenness?

---

[31] *The Ascent of Mount Carmel*, I.6.

And as soon as Ahab heard that Naboth was dead, Ahab arose to go down to the vineyard of Naboth the Jezreelite, to take possession of it.

Then the word of the LORD came to Elijah the Tishbite, saying, "Arise, go down to meet Ahab king of Israel, who is in Samaria; behold, he is in the vineyard of Naboth, where he has gone to take possession. And you shall say to him, 'Thus says the LORD, "Have you killed and also taken possession?"' And you shall say to him, 'Thus says the LORD: "In the place where dogs licked up the blood of Naboth shall dogs lick your own blood."'"

Ahab said to Elijah, "Have you found me, O my enemy?" He answered, "I have found you, because you have sold yourself to do what is evil in the sight of the LORD. Behold, I will bring disaster upon you. I will utterly burn you up, and will cut off from Ahab every male, bond or free, in Israel. And I will make your house like the house of Jeroboam the son of Nebat, and like the house of Baasha the son of Ahijah, for the anger to which you have provoked me, and because you have made Israel to sin.

And of Jezebel the LORD also said, 'The dogs shall eat Jezebel within the walls of Jezreel.' Anyone belonging to Ahab who dies in the city the dogs shall eat, and anyone of his who dies in the open country the birds of the heavens shall eat." (There was none who sold himself to do what was evil in the sight of the LORD like Ahab, whom Jezebel his wife incited. He acted very abominably in going after idols, as the Amorites had done, whom the LORD cast out before the people of Israel.)

And when Ahab heard those words, he tore his clothes and put sackcloth on his flesh and fasted and lay in sackcloth and went about dejectedly.

And the word of the LORD came to Elijah the Tishbite, saying, "Have you seen how Ahab has humbled himself before me? Because he has humbled himself before me, I will not bring the disaster in his days; but in his son's days I will bring the disaster upon his house." **1 Kings 21:16-29**

Consumed.

Jezebel was the daughter of the king of Sidon. In violation of God's commands to Israel, Ahab married Jezebel for political purposes. Jezebel brought with her the worship of Baal and Astarte, and she imposed that worship on Israel.

As a king's daughter, Jezebel understood worldly power and how to use it. When Ahab expressed torment from his desire for Naboth's property, Jezebel assured him she would take care of it. Jezebel arranged the framing and execution of Naboth, an innocent man, so that Ahab could have his heart's worldly desire.

But the desires of Ahab resulted in judgment through the word of Elijah. Ahab's desires tormented him, and then consumed him.

Meditation: Think of the great wickedness of Ahab's desires and actions – covetousness, seizure of property, and murder. They resulted in Ahab's judgment. Then think of the greater mercy and compassion of God. Despite the horrible sins and unfaithfulness of Ahab, God showed mercy when the wicked Ahab humbled himself. God is a God of great mercy!

☩   ☩   ☩   ☩   ☩   ☩   ☩

NOTES:_____

_____

_____

_____

_____

_____

_____

_____

_____

For I delight in the law of God, in my inner being, but I see in my members another law waging war against the law of my mind and making me captive to the law of sin that dwells in my members.

Wretched man that I am! Who will deliver me from this body of death?

Thanks be to God through Jesus Christ our Lord! So then, I myself serve the law of God with my mind, but with my flesh I serve the law of sin. **Rom 7:22-25**

Who will deliver me from this body of death?

Vaults in the BANK of my time, will, emotions, and thoughts!

Come and set me free from all those things that hinder me seeking Your kingdom and righteousness. Show me what they are and help me to deal ferociously with them, to not pamper them, OK them in any way, or allow them entrance into the BANK of my time, will, emotions, and thoughts!

<u>**When I allow them access to any of those "banks", they rob the vaults!**</u>

Empower me to deal harshly with them!!   –Pastor Daniel Martin, 11/20/14

The hallmarks of fleshly appetites to which we have yielded are: (1) They are never satisfied because they never go away; and (2) We need greater amounts of them (or stronger doses) in order to achieve the same excitement.

Paul experienced the same struggles with his flesh that we do. In fact he cries out in his wretchedness *"Who will deliver me from this body of death?"*

Meditation: Who will deliver you from this body of death? Present yourself before the Lord and ask Him for keys to deliverance from your fleshly appetites.

✝   ✝   ✝   ✝   ✝   ✝   ✝

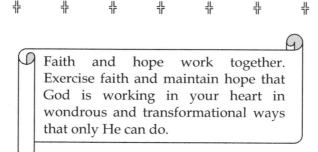

Faith and hope work together. Exercise faith and maintain hope that God is working in your heart in wondrous and transformational ways that only He can do.

Today is a day of humbling. Review your notes over the past week.

> **Meditation:** As you review your journal notes about appetites and desires, come to the Lord in humility. Like Ahab, you are allowed to use outward signs such as kneeling, tearing your clothes, wearing sackcloth on your body, or fasting, if you desire. Humble yourself before God bringing your appetites and desires to light before Him.
>
> As you are moved, repent. Surrender your feelings to God in prostrate bowing, tears, or other outward manifestations.
>
> Ask God to deliver you from this body of death. Seek the mercy and compassion of God.

☦   ☦   ☦   ☦   ☦   ☦   ☦

NOTES:_____

_____

_____

_____

_____

_____

_____

_____

_____

_____

_____

_____

_____

> "Not many days later, the younger son gathered all he had and took a journey into a far country, and there he squandered his property in reckless living. And when he had spent everything, a severe famine arose in that country, and he began to be in need.
>
> "So he went and hired himself out to one of the citizens of that country, who sent him into his fields to feed pigs. And he was longing to be fed with the pods that the pigs ate, and no one gave him anything.
>
> "But when he came to himself, he said, 'How many of my father's hired servants have more than enough bread, but I perish here with hunger! I will arise and go to my father, and I will say to him, "Father, I have sinned against heaven and before you. I am no longer worthy to be called your son. Treat me as one of your hired servants."'
>
> "And he arose and came to his father. But while he was still a long way off, his father saw him and felt compassion, and ran and embraced him and kissed him." Luke 15:13-20

But when he came to himself...

O the glory of lifting up my mind, will, emotions to You and saying in effect, "Here they are, Lord!"

<u>They are broken, out of sorts, wounded, messed up, and not in good operating order. I have misused them, let them get out of bounds, fed them with my flesh, given them to things that did them great damage, and now all I can do is give them to You and say, 'HELP'!</u>

O the glory that You willingly take them, begin to work on them, take the wrong that has been imbedded in them out of them, and begin to pour Your mind, Your will, and Your emotions into them!

O Father, everywhere I have yielded my mind, will, and emotions to the fear of man, to seeking the approval of man,--reverse this and make me so I have great fear, reverence, and respect for You, but none for the pressure to adhere to what pleases people! <u>I don't want to be a people pleaser—I want to be a Father pleaser!</u>

Change me and change me and change me, O my God!!

I need You so much in this, O Father! To You I lift up my soul, my mind, will, and emotions!   –Pastor Daniel Martin, 2/6/14

This story is part of the parable of the Prodigal Son. The son wasted all his father had given him – his inheritance – in reckless and worldly living. He experienced the consequences of his worldly desires.

But then he came to himself. The prodigal son realized his true condition. He became broken – broken to the point that he was willing to be a servant rather than a son. Brokenness is a key to restoration of the soul.

Meditation: Spend time imagining the plight of the prodigal son. He has pursued his desires and appetites. Now he is feeding pigs and he longs to eat what the pigs are eating. Consider the mercy of God to bring him to this point that he longs to eat the pig's food. Imagine the brokenness that the son must feel.

Now imagine the feelings of his father. The father might be angry or vengeful toward a son who defied him and spurned him. Maybe the son's pitiful plight served him right!

Now imagine the reunion of the father and the son. Meditate on the compassion and love of a father who joyfully receives back his son in his broken condition. Write down the feelings the Lord gives you as you walk through this story.

☩   ☩   ☩   ☩   ☩   ☩   ☩

NOTES:_____

_____

_____

_____

_____

_____

_____

_____

_____

_____

> So to keep me from becoming conceited because of the surpassing greatness of the revelations, a thorn was given me in the flesh, a messenger of Satan to harass me, to keep me from becoming conceited.
>
> Three times I pleaded with the Lord about this, that it should leave me. But he said to me, "My grace is sufficient for you, for my power is made perfect in weakness." Therefore I will boast all the more gladly of my weaknesses, so that the power of Christ may rest upon me. For the sake of Christ, then, I am content with weaknesses, insults, hardships, persecutions, and calamities. For when I am weak, then I am strong. **2 Cor 12:7-10**

Full dependence.

My friend was in full time ministry. He was discerning, talented, and charismatic. His ministry was growing and thriving. People loved him.

But my friend began to feel the burdens and the grind of long term sacrificial ministry. My friend experienced increasing mental health issues. Finally, my friend had a collapse. His ministry came to a screeching halt. My friend was incapacitated for six months and had to take a season off in order to recover his sanity.

Now, my friend has been back in ministry for a few more years. The ministry is thriving. But he is much more careful. My friend tells me this: "I used to be invincible. But now I walk with a limp."

I respond: "Good! Now you can do the work of the Lord in His strength and not in your own strength."

So why does God allow us to experience struggles with our flesh, with our desires, or with our appetites that we cannot seem to overcome? We may pray, cry out, and beg that God remove them from us. But the hindrance remains and we continue to stumble.

My belief is that God allows each follower to have at least one area of significant struggle. Maybe I should just say that is my experience. But the Apostle Paul pleaded with the Lord three times only to be told the key: *"My grace is sufficient for you."*

God allows that struggle because He wants us to come to a place of full dependence on Him. We so often believe that we can do it on our own. Human power is the counterfeit for divine grace. If we overcame it on our own strength, we would not be fully dependent on God and on His grace.

Meditation: Consider your own life and the way that you live it. Review your day to day activities. In those activities, how dependent are you upon yourself? How dependent are you on God? Write down the areas of dependence and independence.

What steps can you take to have an attitude of full dependence on God and on His grace throughout your day?

† † † † † † †

NOTES:_____

_____

_____

_____

_____

_____

_____

_____

_____

_____

_____

_____

_____

> The LORD is near to the brokenhearted and saves the crushed in spirit. **Psa 34:18**

Why is the heart of the Lord so close to the poor?

Scripture is clear that the heart of God is close to the poor – to the oppressed, to the widow, to the orphan, and to the alien. In fact, in the tithe commanded in Deuteronomy, every third year the tithe was handled differently. The tithe was not given to the priest. Every third year the tithe was given directly to the Levite, the alien, the orphan, and the widow in the giver's own town (Deut. 14:28-29; 26:12). Giving to the poor was giving to the Lord.

Why is the heart of the Lord so close to the poor? The answer lies in part in the compassion and mercy of the Lord. But it isn't just that God is merciful.

The answer also lies in the heart of the poor. The poor are already brokenhearted in many ways. They are vulnerable and oppressed. But because of their brokenness, their hearts are closer to the Lord than the hearts of persons who are independent and self sufficient.

The Lord is close to the broken.

Meditation: For the next few days, we will focus on the Beatitudes from Matthew 5. They closely relate to brokenness and surrender.

And he opened his mouth and taught them, saying:

"Blessed are the poor in spirit, for theirs is the kingdom of heaven.

"Blessed are those who mourn, for they shall be comforted." **Matt 5:2-4**

Meditate on these verses. Why are the poor in spirit and those who mourn blessed? Are they closer to the heart of God than the rich in spirit and those who are unburdened?

✝   ✝   ✝   ✝   ✝   ✝   ✝

> Remember to eliminate all distractions or interruptions when you engage in your devotions. The lack of interruption will help you sense the movement and work of the Holy Spirit in your spirit.

NOTES:_____

_____

_____

_____

_____

_____

_____

_____

_____

_____

_____

_____

_____

_____

_____

_____

_____

_____

_____

> For you will not delight in sacrifice, or I would give it; you will not be pleased with a burnt offering.
>
> The sacrifices of God are a broken spirit; a broken and contrite heart, O God, you will not despise. **Psa 51:16-17**

Brokenness has value when the will is surrendered.

My friend, Keith, has quite a story. Keith was a licensed pastor. But he had a secret. Keith says:

"I was struggling with homosexual desires. I wasn't acting on them, but my heart was eaten up with them. I met a wonderful woman and we married. I thought that would be the end of my desires, but they got worse. I eventually ended up telling her about it and she was devastated. She left me, our marriage ended, and this put an end to my ministry as well. I waited a few months for God to 'fix' things, but that didn't happen. Meanwhile, the sexual issues just kept getting worse, so I started secretly going to gay bars to meet other men. Eventually, I ended up in drug rehab where my counselor designed my recovery program around coming to terms with the fact that I was gay.

"I followed his advice. I wrote a letter of self-acceptance to myself. I 'came out' to my counseling group and wrote a letter to my parents. The freedom I experienced through this was amazing. For the first time in my life, I wasn't worrying what others thought about me. It felt so good, in fact, that I thought it had to be from God. So I embraced the world of gay Christianity, and I became an activist for gay rights within the church and society. I completed a Bachelor's in sociology at UNC-Asheville and went off to seminary. I became the first openly gay student to be accepted into the M.Div. program at Union Theological Seminary.

"But I hadn't really found freedom from drugs. Every so often, I would go off on a bender, but not so bad as to do irreparable damage. I would quickly get my life back together before anyone found out. But in my second year in seminary, I completely lost it. My drug dealer stole my car, so I rented one and didn't return it. I stole my landlord's checkbook (with about $10,000 in the account) and went off into a time of craziness. I ended up becoming involved in Satanism, and finally got arrested in the stolen rental car two months later trying to buy crack cocaine at 3:00 AM in downtown Asheville."

Keith's life unraveled in the next few years. Keith jumped bail and fled from the law to San Francisco. Keith lived on the streets and shot speed into his veins. He was homeless and ate out of trash cans. Keith reached the point that he no longer had anything to live for. In fact, one day he told God that he did not want to live anymore. Keith was broken.

Shortly thereafter, Keith was arrested. Because of pending charges in North Carolina, he was transported back there. During the van ride, Keith recommitted his life to the Lord.

Keith's life has been restored. Keith has been working in full time Christian ministry for the last 15 years. He is happily married to a wonderful Christian woman and he heads an outreach ministry to a minority people group. Keith says:

"I always saw myself as intelligent and talented. Even when I was homeless and eating out of trash cans, I saw myself as having something to offer. It wasn't until I was fully broken and did not want to live that God could work in my life. At that point, I was willing to surrender everything to Him including my will. In fact I told him that I thought I was born a homosexual – created that way. But if He had different plans, I was willing to follow them. Only at that point was I willing to do what He wanted, not what I wanted."

Brokenness alone is not sufficient. Brokenness can lead to bitterness; or brokenness can lead to a surrender of the will to the Lord which leads to life. <u>Brokenness has value when it results in a will surrendered to the Lord and not to its fleshly desires.</u>

There is a fundamental question that every human must answer: Is it His will, or is it my will? Is it what He wants, or is it what I want? Am I willing to surrender my will and its appetites to Him?

That choice is made in life changing terms, but it is also made in little decisions throughout the day – scores of seemingly small decisions that face us each day.

Meditation: *"Blessed are the meek, for they shall inherit the earth.*

"Blessed are those who hunger and thirst for righteousness, for they shall be satisfied." Matt 5:5-6

In the Beatitudes, Jesus did not only focus on brokenness. He also focused on a hunger and thirst for righteousness – a will set not on its fleshly desires, but a will that longs for righteousness.

Spend time with the Lord asking Him about your own state – if you are...poor in spirit...mourning...meek...hungering and thirsting for righteousness. Journal about it.

✝   ✝   ✝   ✝   ✝   ✝   ✝

Remember to seek the Presence of the Lord when you enter into devotions and throughout your day. Invite Him into your heart with open arms and with open mind.

One of the Pharisees asked him to eat with him, and he went into the Pharisee's house and reclined at the table. And behold, a woman of the city, who was a sinner, when she learned that he was reclining at table in the Pharisee's house, brought an alabaster flask of ointment, and standing behind him at his feet, weeping, she began to wet his feet with her tears and wiped them with the hair of her head and kissed his feet and anointed them with the ointment.

Now when the Pharisee who had invited him saw this, he said to himself, "If this man were a prophet, he would have known who and what sort of woman this is who is touching him, for she is a sinner."

And Jesus answering said to him, "Simon, I have something to say to you." And he answered, "Say it, Teacher."

"A certain moneylender had two debtors. One owed five hundred denarii, and the other fifty. When they could not pay, he cancelled the debt of both. Now which of them will love him more?"

Simon answered, "The one, I suppose, for whom he cancelled the larger debt." And he said to him, "You have judged rightly."

Then turning toward the woman he said to Simon, "Do you see this woman? I entered your house; you gave me no water for my feet, but she has wet my feet with her tears and wiped them with her hair. You gave me no kiss, but from the time I came in she has not ceased to kiss my feet. You did not anoint my head with oil, but she has anointed my feet with ointment. Therefore I tell you, her sins, which are many, are forgiven—for she loved much. But he who is forgiven little, loves little."

And he said to her, "Your sins are forgiven." Then those who were at table with him began to say among themselves, "Who is this, who even forgives sins?"

And he said to the woman, "Your faith has saved you; go in peace." **Luke 7:36-50**

Now which of them will love him more?

In this story, the sinful woman (some traditions say Mary Magdalene) was broken. In her brokenness, she surrendered herself to Jesus - weeping, washing, and kissing His feet. Her act of repentance and surrender led to forgiveness of her sins, and to righteousness and purity in the sight of God.

Meditation: As you meditate on the Beatitudes below, focus on mercy and purity in the story of the sinful woman. Sometimes in my devotional time, I need repentance and contrition. I kneel and reach out my arms. Figuratively, I embrace the feet of Jesus and then I kiss them. Seek God for mercy and for purity of heart.

"Blessed are the merciful, for they shall receive mercy.

"Blessed are the pure in heart, for they shall see God." **Matt 5:7-8**

✝ ✝ ✝ ✝ ✝ ✝ ✝

NOTES:_____

_____

_____

_____

_____

_____

_____

_____

_____

_____

_____

> "And because lawlessness will be increased, the love of many will grow cold." **Matt 24:12**

Whatever is exciting pleases the will.

Whatever is exciting pleases the will; that is the way that will works. Remember that God is beyond our understanding. To be united with God it is necessary to deny the will all tastes and pleasures, both physical and spiritual. When detached in this manner, it is free to love God above all things. If the will can know God at all, it can do so only through love. There is a great difference between the preferences and feelings of the will and its work. The will's preferences and feelings are bound up in the human soul, while its work, which is love, finds its only purpose in God.[32]

Jesus' disciples asked Him about the signs of His coming and the end of the age. In His answer, Jesus describes the juxtaposition of lawlessness and love. When lawlessness increases, love grows cold.

Brother Lawrence says that the will is what craves fleshly and worldly tastes and pleasures. We may feel physical, emotional, or spiritual longings, but our will is what seeks and desires them.

The will craves excitement. That explains why people long to "fall in love." One would think that permanent, long term love that has depth, character, and meaning would be more desirable. But our movies, shows, culture and media focus on "falling in love." It feels more exciting. The problem is that the initial excitement diminishes over time and the lover feels something is wrong. So a search occurs to renew the excitement or to find the excitement elsewhere, which destroys many relationships and marriages. But the truth is that deep love that stands the test of many years and the trials of a lifetime is pretty exciting too!

The true work of the will is the love of God. We must be willing to surrender our desire for excitement to God. Only when the will has surrendered all of its tastes and pleasures can the will engage in its true work – the love of God. Surrender is the key to the love of God.

Meditation: Seek God about your own will. Write down the things that excite your will. Then ask God to show you how those things impact your walk with Him. Seek to surrender your will to Him and ask Him to lead you in a path to His love.

---

[32] *The Practice of the Presence of God*, p. 68.

NOTES:_____

_____

_____

_____

_____

_____

_____

_____

_____

_____

_____

_____

_____

> The idea that our will craves excitement is an important one. If you think of the areas of desire and flesh with which you struggle, many of them probably connect to a desire for excitement. Commit to surrender in this area.

And he opened his mouth and taught them, saying:

"Blessed are the poor in spirit, for theirs is the kingdom of heaven.

"Blessed are those who mourn, for they shall be comforted.

"Blessed are the meek, for they shall inherit the earth.

"Blessed are those who hunger and thirst for righteousness, for they shall be satisfied.

"Blessed are the merciful, for they shall receive mercy.

"Blessed are the pure in heart, for they shall see God.

"Blessed are the peacemakers, for they shall be called sons of God.

"Blessed are those who are persecuted for righteousness' sake, for theirs is the kingdom of heaven.

"Blessed are you when others revile you and persecute you and utter all kinds of evil against you falsely on my account. Rejoice and be glad, for your reward is great in heaven, for so they persecuted the prophets who were before you." **Matt 5:2-12**

Review your journal for this week.

I have followed Jesus for many years. But I must confess that the Beatitudes really did not mean much to me. Sure, I read them and I tried to meditate on them. But I could not identify with them. My thought when I read them is that they mainly applied to persons before they came to faith, or to persons who had faith but were in terrible circumstances.

It only shows how wrong a person can be.

Meditation: Spend time with the Beatitudes. Then place yourself into the Beatitudes. "Blessed am I when…" Ask the Lord to show you how the Beatitudes apply to you. How are you living them out?

> "I shall no longer speak many things with you, for the ruler of this world comes, and he has nothing in Me.
>
> "But that the world may know that I love the Father, and as the Father has given Me commandment, even so I do. Arise, let us go away from here." **John 14:30-31 (MKJV)**

He has nothing in Me.

O, come and help me to drive back the darkness, to be so positioned and filled with all You are, that there is nothing in me that Welcomes, satisfies, pleases, or increases the enemy or his work.

I want Your life, character, holiness, purity, love, and Ways to be known by me, through me, and into the world around me! Help me to know and acknowledge, to cling to Your Ways, Truth, Life, and commandments. Help my life to mirror You and what You are about.

Deliver me from any ideas, thoughts, motives, actions, or words that are like the enemy. Flood my life with all You are so that only You are exalted and released from me into the world around me! O, I want to be more Like You, Jesus!!

Help me increasingly come to the place where it can be said, "The ruler of this world comes, but he has NOTHING in me."   –Pastor Daniel Martin, 8/27/14

Jesus is preparing His disciples for His Passion and for His departure. He makes an amazing statement regarding the enemy: He has nothing in Me. Jesus has no appetite, no desire, no passion, no attachment, and no sin upon which the enemy could lay claim. Jesus was truly free – free of the things which the enemy could use. Jesus has purity and integrity of heart, mind, and soul. We are back to the concept of emptying. Jesus emptied Himself and has nothing of the world in Him.

Then Jesus immediately speaks of His love for the Father. His will is set on the love of the Father. The Father's love commands Jesus' actions.

Meditation: Oh that I could be as Jesus – wholly unattached to things of the world and the flesh! Oh that I could be empty of anything of the flesh, of the world, or of darkness. Oh that my will would be set on love of the Father, and directed only by love for Him!

Write a prayer in your journal about your desire for purity and integrity of your heart, mind and soul, and your desire for the love of the Father.

> I appeal to you therefore, brothers, by the mercies of God, to present your bodies as a living sacrifice, holy and acceptable to God, which is your spiritual worship.
>
> Do not be conformed to this world, but be transformed by the renewal of your mind, that by testing you may discern what is the will of God, what is good and acceptable and perfect. **Rom 12:1-2**

The role of created things.

O come and help me to make a COMPLETE sacrifice, to present my body to You Daily, Hourly for You and Your will to be done in my life!

I need Your help in obeying Romans 12:1, Lord. Come and take me deeper and deeper into it. Come and show me how to walk in Your footsteps.

I am sure that I don't see the cross as fully as I should and this failure hinders my sacrifice. Come and show me the cross of Jesus! –Pastor Daniel Martin, 10/14/15

St. Ignatius lived in the 16th century. He wrote <u>The Spiritual Exercises of St. Ignatius</u> which has been crucial in the spiritual growth of many believers. As the First Principle and Foundation in his <u>Exercises</u>, St. Ignatius describes the concept of indifference:

Man is created to praise, reverence, and serve God our Lord, and by this means to save his soul. The other things on the face of the earth are created for man to help him in attaining the end for which he was created. Hence, man is to make use of them in as far as they help him in the attainment of his end, and he must rid himself of them in as far as the prove a hindrance to him.

Therefore, we must make ourselves indifferent to all created things, as far as we are allowed free choice and are not under any prohibition. Consequently, as far as we are concerned, we should not prefer health to sickness, riches to poverty, honor to dishonor, a long life to a short life. The same holds for all other things.

Our one desire and choice should be what is more conducive to the end for which we are created.[33]

Indifference is based on the will of God for my life – the holy, acceptable, and perfect will of God. My heart, mind, and will should conform to His will through being transformed, and that instructs my desires and choices. Since created things are a means and not an end, my desire for them should be guided only by the perfect will of God.

---

[33] St. Ignatius, *The Spiritual Exercises of St. Ignatius*, §23 p. 12 (Translated by Louis J. Puhl, S.J. 1951).

Indifference means that I am not attached to created things. I am attached only to the Father and to His will.

> **Meditation:** Review yesterday's devotion. Consider Jesus and His desire to please His Father. How did Jesus live out indifference in His ministry, life, and death?

‡   ‡   ‡   ‡   ‡   ‡   ‡

NOTES:_____

_____

_____

_____

_____

_____

_____

_____

_____

_____

_____

_____

_____

_____

And Abiathar came up, and behold, Zadok came also with all the Levites, bearing the ark of the covenant of God. And they set down the ark of God until the people had all passed out of the city.

Then the king said to Zadok, "Carry the ark of God back into the city. If I find favor in the eyes of the LORD, he will bring me back and let me see both it and his dwelling place. But if he says, 'I have no pleasure in you,' behold, here I am, let him do to me what seems good to him." **2 Sam 15:24-26**

Let Him do to me what seems good to Him.

Most kings historically have guarded their position, power, and honor jealously. Any hint of a threat is met with brute force such as beheadings or firing squads.

But David was a man after God's own heart. He is facing a rebellion by his own son, Absalom. Absalom's forces are so great that David has been forced to flee. So is David concerned about his position and reputation? Does he want to fight to keep his kingdom?

David is so surrendered to His Lord that he is willing to be restored to his throne…or not. It depends only on what the Lord wants. *"Let Him do to me what seems good to Him."*

David was indifferent to his own honor and position. He was willing to suffer honor or dishonor. David wanted only what God ordained in God's good time and favor. David released full control of his life to God. He trusted God.

Meditation: Consider your own reputation in the circles in which you walk. How do you exercise power and influence to enhance your reputation? List these areas in your journal.

Are you willing to let go of your reputation? Imagine that you are subjected to reproach and dishonor. What does that feel like? Are you able to release it to the Lord and to submit to Him as you experience reproach and dishonor?

He was despised and rejected by men; a man of sorrows, and acquainted with grief; and as one from whom men hide their faces he was despised, and we esteemed him not. Isa 53:3

NOTES:_____

_____

_____

_____

_____

_____

_____

_____

_____

_____

_____

_____

_____

During your devotional time, spend time listening - listening to the Lord and listening to the movements of your heart. Be a student willing and eager to be instructed by the Good Teacher.

> So Satan went out from the presence of the LORD and struck Job with loathsome sores from the sole of his foot to the crown of his head. And he took a piece of broken pottery with which to scrape himself while he sat in the ashes. Then his wife said to him, "Do you still hold fast your integrity? Curse God and die."
>
> But he said to her, "You speak as one of the foolish women would speak. Shall we receive good from God, and shall we not receive evil?" In all this Job did not sin with his lips. **Job 2:7-10**

Shall we receive good from God, and shall we not receive evil?

Father Damien grew up in Belgium, but when his brother was too ill to go to Hawaii as a priest, Father Damien obtained permission to go serve in his brother's place.

Father Damien served as a priest in Hawaii for nine years. He learned of a need for priests to serve a leper colony on the island of Molokai. Father Damien felt a call to serve the lepers there. Despite the health risks, Father Damien moved to Molokai in order to minister to the persons to whom he was called. He did many things to improve the living conditions and the health care of those afflicted with the disease.

After twelve years serving his flock, Father Damien was diagnosed with leprosy. The disease progressed until Father Damien died at the age of 49. Before his death, he wrote his brother that "I am gently going to my grave. It is the will of God, and I thank Him very much for letting me die of the same disease and in the same way as my lepers. I am very satisfied and very happy."

Father Damien was canonized by the Catholic Church and is now referred to as Saint Damien.[34]

Job was stricken and afflicted. Yet he was willing to receive good or evil – health or sickness.

Some theologians teach that God guarantees good health to His followers in this world. If a follower of Jesus becomes ill, the fault lies at the feet of that follower because of a lack of faith. If healing does not occur, the follower may feel condemned.

God is a healing God. He desires for His children to be whole. But the state of the souls of His children is of vastly greater importance than their physical person. In His divine Will, He allows sickness or even death for their benefit. Both Job and Father Damien testified to His goodness and to His mercy, even in sickness or in death.

---

[34] Source: *Father Damien*, **www.nps.org** (2019)

Meditation: Spend time with the Lord reviewing your beliefs about health and sickness. Consider your spiritual state when you are ill – how much you pray; how much you focus on God; and whether you are inclined to commit sin or not.

Then explore whether you are willing to suffer physically if God wills and if the suffering will bring you closer to the end for which you were created. Are you willing to surrender your health to God?

Surely he has borne our griefs and carried our sorrows; yet we esteemed him stricken, smitten by God, and afflicted. Isa 53:4

NOTES:_____

_____

_____

_____

_____

_____

_____

_____

_____

_____

_____

_____

> Jesus looked up and saw the rich putting their gifts into the offering box, and he saw a poor widow put in two small copper coins.
>
> And he said, "Truly, I tell you, this poor widow has put in more than all of them. For they all contributed out of their abundance, but she out of her poverty put in all she had to live on." **Luke 21:1-4**

She out of her poverty put in all she had to live on.

By two wings a man is lifted up from things earthly; namely by simplicity and purity. Simplicity ought to be in our intention; purity in our affection. Simplicity tends toward God; purity apprehends and tastes Him.

No good action will hinder you, if you be inwardly free from inordinate affection. If you intend and seek nothing else but the will of God and the good of your neighbor, you shall thoroughly enjoy inward liberty.[35]

The widow did not have an inordinate attachment to money. She not only put all her money into the offering, she put all of her means of support – all of her livelihood. The widow surrendered all she had.

Indifference means that we do not prefer to be rich or to be poor. We are not bound by money and possessions. We only want what God wants in our lives, and we are free to choose Him because we are not bound by things.

Meditation: Consider the role of money in your life. How much aggravation, irritation, or stress does money cause you? Why?

Reread the quote above. How does indifference toward wealth contribute to inward liberty?

For he grew up before him like a young plant, and like a root out of dry ground; he had no form or majesty that we should look at him, and no beauty that we should desire him. Isa 53:2

---

‡   ‡   ‡   ‡   ‡   ‡   ‡

---

[35] *The Imitation of Christ*, p. 69.

NOTES:_____

_____

_____

_____

_____

_____

_____

_____

_____

_____

_____

_____

Try to remember the devotional theme as you go through your day. Many devotees have set times during the day – Noon or 3 PM - to pause for a few minutes and recollect themselves toward God. Give God time to work His words into your heart and spirit.

> Thus all the days of Enoch were 365 years. Enoch walked with God, and he was not, for God took him. **Gen 5:23-24**

Life cut short.

Father, You have been so good and precious to me, and I love You for Your great love and mercy in my life. I am reminded of Isaiah 53:10, *"It was the Lord's good plan to CRUSH him and fill him with grief."*

O Father, when I consider that with all the love You had for Your Son, deeper love than I can fathom, You were willing to CRUSH Him as He became sin, with My Sin on Him. Why were You so willing to do this?

ALL BECAUSE OF YOUR DEEP DESIRE TO MAKE A WAY TO REDEEM WHAT YOU LOVED MOST ON EARTH—YOUR CREATED PEOPLE—ME!!

O what amazing love You have had—and Have—for me! O the tremendous Power Of Your Love! Love that was strong for me/us, that if it took You having to CRUSH Your Son to save me/us, You were willing to do it!

Amazing Love, How could it be, that You my God, would die for me!!! But You did!!
    –Pastor Daniel Martin, 1/12/15

Enoch lived 365 years, which sounds like a pretty long life. But Enoch's father, Jared, lived 962 years. Enoch's son, Methusaleh, lived 969 years. So by comparison, Enoch didn't do very well in the longevity department. He was shorted by 600 years.

But that is not the point. The point is that Enoch walked so closely with God that God took him. The important thing to Enoch was not his mortal life. Enoch was willing to live a long life or a short life. The important thing to Enoch was that he walked closely to God and that he fulfilled God's plan and design for his life.

Meditation: Consider your plans for your life. How long do you think you will live?

Next consider how precious your life is to you. Are you willing for your life to be cut short if it is God's will and if it will help fulfill the end for which you were created? Are you willing to surrender the length of your life to God? Write down your thoughts and feelings in your journal.

By oppression and judgment he was taken away; and as for his generation, who considered that he was cut off out of the land of the living, stricken for the transgression of my people? Isa 53:8

Review your journal notes for the past week.

But because I am as yet weak in love, and imperfect in virtue, I have need to be strengthened and comforted by Thee. Visit me therefore often, and instruct me with all holy discipline. Set me free from evil passions, and heal my heart of all inordinate affections; that being inwardly healed and thoroughly cleansed, I may be made ready to love, strong to suffer, steady to persevere.

Love is a great thing, yea, altogether a great good; it makes light everything that is heavy, and it bears evenly all that is uneven. For it carries a burden which is no burden (Matt 11:30) and makes every bitter thing sweet and tasteful. The noble love of Jesus drives a man to do great things, and stirs him to always long for what is more perfect. Love wills to be on high, and not to be kept back by anything low and mean. Love wills to be free, and estranged from all worldly affections, so its inward sight may not be hindered; that it may not be entangled by any temporal prosperity, or by any adversity subdued.

Nothing is sweeter than love, nothing stronger, nothing higher, nothing wider, nothing more pleasant, nothing fuller or better in Heaven and earth; because love is born of God (1 John 4:7) and cannot rest but in God, above all created things. A lover flies, runs, and rejoices; he is free and is not bound. He gives all for all, and has all in all; because he rests in One highest above all things, from whom all that is good flows. He respects not the gifts, but turns himself above all goods unto the Giver.[36]

> **Meditation:** Today meditate on the connection between love, and indifference to created things and beings. Above is a passage for meditation. Note especially the freedom that arises from indifference.

☩   ☩   ☩   ☩   ☩   ☩   ☩

NOTES:_____

_____

_____

_____

---

[36] *The Imitation of Christ*, pp. 103-104.

> These also reel with wine and stagger with strong drink; the priest and the prophet reel with strong drink, they are swallowed by wine, they stagger with strong drink, they reel in vision, they stumble in giving judgment.
>
> For all tables are full of filthy vomit, with no space left. **Isa 28:7-8**

They stagger...they reel...they stumble.

My father lived in Asheville, North Carolina where the mountains are beautiful and the winters are cold. My father had a tabby cat named Niffy. Niffy was a fluffy orange fur ball who was a good "mouser" – an endearing trait for a cat in rural North Carolina. My father loved Niffy.

My father came home from the store one cold winter day and parked his truck in the carport. He went inside for a while but then had to go back out. He got into his truck and turned the key to start the engine. When he did, he heard an awful screeching racket from his engine, and it didn't stop. Surprised, he turned the key off and got out to investigate.

What he found was Niffy lying on the ground below the engine – barely alive. What had happened? Niffy had discovered that truck engines emit comforting heat after use. When Daddy arrived home, Niffy crawled under the engine and jumped up on it to nestle in for some good warmth. The warmth must have felt pretty good to Niffy on that cold wintry day. But when Daddy started the engine, Niffy got caught in the turning engine belt and its wheel pulleys. She shrieked as she tried to extricate herself. Niffy was cut, bruised, and had lost 80% of her fur. Niffy burned one of her nine lives on that occasion, but she miraculously managed to recover and to survive. That poor cat looked piebald for months thereafter with patches of fur splotched over large areas of bare skin.

We often seek comfort in areas that are potentially dangerous or life threatening to our souls. If Daddy had been able to communicate with Niffy, he would have admonished Niffy not to seek comfort in the truck engine. God does communicate with us. He lovingly warns us not to seek comfort in harmful places. They are like truck engines to a cat – comforting, yet dangerous.

The priest and the prophet have a call. The priest has a call to minister to the Lord and to the people. He is a mediator between God and man. The prophet has a call to speak the divinely inspired word to the people.

But Isaiah says they did not fulfill their call. Their love of wine and strong drink prevented them from true vision and from giving judgment.

There are many reasons why people indulge in harmful things and even allow themselves to be overcome by them. One primary reason is feeling. A person may feel badly about himself, badly about others, or badly about the world. That person wants to change that feeling. So he turns to something to change that feeling. That person seeks comfort in a created thing.

When a person seeks comfort in a thing, it becomes an attachment. Sometimes the attachment is slight. Other times, the attachment is so strong that it becomes an addiction or a dependency.

Meditation: During the next two weeks, we will explore sources of comfort. Eliminate all distractions and try to quiet your mind. Then explore your feelings about yourself. Are there negative feelings for which you want comfort?

Explore your feelings about others. Then explore your feelings about the world.

Ask the Holy Spirit to show you things that you indulge in, or are addicted to, that give you comfort. [You can review your notes on I.Week Two, Day 5]. What are the things that you use to change the feelings that you have? Write them down in your journal. How destructive are they to your soul?

Then, seek the Lord about how you can surrender those things to God. Seek comfort from Him instead – the God of all comfort Who desires to comfort His children.

✠   ✠   ✠   ✠   ✠   ✠   ✠

NOTES:_____

_____

_____

_____

_____

_____

_____

_____

And as he was setting out on his journey, a man ran up and knelt before him and asked him, "Good Teacher, what must I do to inherit eternal life?"

And Jesus said to him, "Why do you call me good? No one is good except God alone. You know the commandments: 'Do not murder, Do not commit adultery, Do not steal, Do not bear false witness, Do not defraud, Honor your father and mother.'"

And he said to him, "Teacher, all these I have kept from my youth."

And Jesus, looking at him, loved him, and said to him, "You lack one thing: go, sell all that you have and give to the poor, and you will have treasure in heaven; and come, follow me."

Disheartened by the saying, he went away sorrowful, for he had great possessions. And Jesus looked around and said to his disciples, "How difficult it will be for those who have wealth to enter the kingdom of God!"

And the disciples were amazed at his words. But Jesus said to them again, "Children, how difficult it is to enter the kingdom of God! It is easier for a camel to go through the eye of a needle than for a rich person to enter the kingdom of God." **Mark 10:17-25**

Disheartened by the saying, he went away sorrowful, for he had great possessions.

The story of the rich young ruler is a story about inordinate attachment and its impact on destiny. The rich young ruler was attached to his possessions. But he was a good man. He was a devout man who practiced his religion virtuously.

Jesus' response, however, forced a choice: Cut the attachment to possessions and become a disciple of Jesus, or not. The rich young ruler chose "not." His attachment to possessions was so strong he was unwilling to surrender them to follow Jesus.

But Jesus was offering him something more. The story says that Jesus loved him. Jesus was offering a relationship of love to him. Even that love was not strong enough to overcome the rich man's attachment to possessions.

The story of the rich, young ruler is not just a story about a destiny unfulfilled. It is a story about a love unfulfilled.

Meditation: What things are most dear to your heart? Ask the Holy Spirit to reveal them to you. How attached to them are you?

Then ask Jesus to look on you with love. Ask Him to love you in the same way that He loved the rich young ruler. How will you respond to that love?

✠ ✠ ✠ ✠ ✠ ✠ ✠

NOTES:_____

_____

_____

_____

_____

_____

_____

_____

_____

_____

_____

_____

_____

_____

And he said to them, "Take care, and be on your guard against all covetousness, for one's life does not consist in the abundance of his possessions."

And he told them a parable, saying, "The land of a rich man produced plentifully, and he thought to himself, 'What shall I do, for I have nowhere to store my crops?'

And he said, 'I will do this: I will tear down my barns and build larger ones, and there I will store all my grain and my goods. And I will say to my soul, "Soul, you have ample goods laid up for many years; relax, eat, drink, be merry."'

But God said to him, 'Fool! This night your soul is required of you, and the things you have prepared, whose will they be?'

So is the one who lays up treasure for himself and is not rich toward God." **Luke 12:15-21**

Soul, you have ample goods laid up for many years.

Do we try to make our lives so secure that no matter what comes we are safe, secure, taken care of? Our whole idea of a retirement nest egg can lead us to that place.

We trust government, our bank account, our stocks and bonds, our whatever to get us through. How many of us feel that if can just get to the place of a "guaranteed income" whether from a good paying job in a "sound" company or a monthly check for the rest of our life from the government—that we have arrived at a safe and secure place? TRUTH: Neither the government nor any company has an eternal existence, and their life spans could all end tomorrow.

But You are eternal and never failing!

Show me where my trust is in a weekly check from the church, or the fact that there is a surplus in the church account, or in the fact that some in the church have funds, etc., and bring me back to where my trust, hope, expectation is TOTALLY in YOU, no matter what "hoses" You are using right now to deliver Your provision to me!
–Pastor Daniel Martin, 5/30/15

This parable is commonly called the parable of the rich fool. In this parable, the rich man's life consisted of his possessions. He was attached to them. He was obviously a good businessman who knew how to produce more and more. The rich man understood kingdom principles of reproduction that potentially had beneficial applications. But he loved wealth, so he used his knowledge and talent to increase possessions. It was an inordinate attachment.

First, note the feeling of security the rich man had. *"You have ample goods laid up for many years; relax, eat, drink, be merry."* The rich man had a fat 401(k) retirement plan. He kept increasing his goods to feed his need for security.

Second, note that the rich man had plenty. But he always wanted more – more crops and bigger barns. When people use created things to try to satisfy worldly appetites, satisfaction is always just around the corner, but it never arrives. There may be moments of a temporary feeling of satisfaction, but true fulfillment is never achieved. Things are never enough.

Finally, the sober truth is that the rich man lost his soul in his riches. He fed his worldly need for security, but not his soul. Ironically, the rich man speaks to his <u>soul</u> about his ample goods as if his wealth benefited his soul! *"Soul, you have ample goods laid up for many years."* He was sadly mistaken. *"This night your soul is required of you."*

One's life does not consist in the abundance of his possessions. Security for the soul – true security - is found only in the Lord.

Meditation: *"So is that one who lays up treasure for himself and is not rich toward God."* Consider any things that you pursue, or have, that may be treasures for yourself and not for God. Ask the Holy Spirit to reveal them to you. Explore how you can surrender them to the Lord.

What does it mean to be rich toward God? What steps can you take to be rich toward God? Write your thoughts in your journal.

Please be faithful in keeping a journal about your devotions. Impressions, convictions, and insights are vital, but, like riches, they can be fleeting. Honor what the Lord shows you by recording it in your daily journal so you can refer to it later.

Blessed be the God and Father of our Lord Jesus Christ, the Father of mercies and God of all comfort, who comforts us in all our affliction, so that we may be able to comfort those who are in any affliction, with the comfort with which we ourselves are comforted by God. For as we share abundantly in Christ's sufferings, so through Christ we share abundantly in comfort too.

If we are afflicted, it is for your comfort and salvation; and if we are comforted, it is for your comfort, which you experience when you patiently endure the same sufferings that we suffer. Our hope for you is unshaken, for we know that as you share in our sufferings, you will also share in our comfort.

For we do not want you to be unaware, brothers, of the affliction we experienced in Asia. For we were so utterly burdened beyond our strength that we despaired of life itself. Indeed, we felt that we had received the sentence of death. But that was to make us rely not on ourselves but on God who raises the dead. He delivered us from such a deadly peril, and he will deliver us. On him we have set our hope that he will deliver us again.

You also must help us by prayer, so that many will give thanks on our behalf for the blessing granted us through the prayers of many.

For our boast is this, the testimony of our conscience, that we behaved in the world with simplicity and godly sincerity, not by earthly wisdom but by the grace of God, and supremely so toward you. **2 Cor 1:3-12**

We behaved in the world with simplicity and sincerity.

Sincere.

That is the word that came to me as I sat down and started typing.

You want me to be sin-cera! Solidly whole, with full integrity about all I say and do, not stretching truth, not bending anything, but letting what IS be what is spoken, thought, said, and acted upon.

Give me deeper and deeper integrity, O God. Help me to be diligent about all I say and do, to not try to impress others, myself, or You with what is going on, etc.

Lord, show me where I lack sincerity, where my life is not solidly, totally going Your way.   -Pastor Daniel Martin, 10/13/13

Paul looks to God for comfort, not to things of the world. In fact, the response of the world to Paul's kingdom message was to inflict sufferings and affliction on Paul. But Paul understood that the despair and sentence of death have a good purpose. The purpose is so Paul and Timothy would rely not on themselves, but on God Who raises the dead.

God is the God of all comfort. His desire is that all of His children find comfort in Him, not in things created. When his children have feelings of despair, feelings of pain, or feelings of insecurity, He wants His children to turn to Him for comfort.

God is the only Source of true comfort for us.

Meditation: Paul's "testimony of conscience" is behaving in the world with simplicity and godly sincerity, not by earthly wisdom, but by the grace of God. What did Paul mean by this statement?

Why would Paul make this statement after writing about the God of all comfort? What is the connection between simplicity and sincerity as to the world and experiencing the comfort of God? Meditate on the difference between comfort from material things and comfort from the God of all comfort.

✝   ✝   ✝   ✝   ✝   ✝   ✝

NOTES:_____

_____

_____

_____

_____

_____

_____

_____

_____

Now the sons of Eli were worthless men. They did not know the LORD. The custom of the priests with the people was that when any man offered sacrifice, the priest's servant would come, while the meat was boiling, with a three-pronged fork in his hand, and he would thrust it into the pan or kettle or cauldron or pot. All that the fork brought up the priest would take for himself. This is what they did at Shiloh to all the Israelites who came there.

Moreover, before the fat was burned, the priest's servant would come and say to the man who was sacrificing, "Give meat for the priest to roast, for he will not accept boiled meat from you but only raw." And if the man said to him, "Let them burn the fat first, and then take as much as you wish," he would say, "No, you must give it now, and if not, I will take it by force."

Thus the sin of the young men was very great in the sight of the LORD, for the men treated the offering of the LORD with contempt.

1 Sam 2:12-17

Now the sons of Eli were worthless men.

The sons of Eli, Hophni and Phinehas, were ordained to serve as priests. The Lord called them to serve. Their duties were to minister to the Lord and to present offerings to him.

But food was important in the house of Eli. Eli himself was grossly overweight (1 Sam. 4:18). Eli's sons had such an obsession for food that they stole the offering intended for the Lord to feed their own flesh. Such was their desire for food, and their contempt for the Lord.

Food can be a primary source of comfort. Our society has a name for emotional eating: "comfort food." Chocolates, ice cream, and chips are prominent comfort foods.

Food also can gratify lust of the flesh. Cooking shows permeate the culture and whole networks cater to the "foodie." Food has become an idol of pleasure instead of a source of sustenance.

Meditation: Spend time exploring your perspective of food – food as sustenance; food as a part of fellowship; food as pleasure; and food as comfort. How do you view food? How do you use it? Journal about it. Then spend time in surrender to God in this area. What fleshly appetites do you need to surrender to God and to change?

NOTES:_____

_____

_____

_____

_____

_____

_____

_____

_____

_____

_____

_____

_____

Turn toward God. Devotions are an excellent
way to turn our hearts, minds, and spirits
toward God. We are moving toward Him or
we are drifting away from Him. Devotions
help us move toward Him with intent.

> "Come, everyone who thirsts, come to the waters; and he who has no money, come, buy and eat! Come, buy wine and milk without money and without price.
>
> Why do you spend your money for that which is not bread, and your labor for that which does not satisfy? Listen diligently to me, and eat what is good, and delight yourselves in rich food.
>
> Incline your ear, and come to me; hear, that your soul may live; and I will make with you an everlasting covenant, my steadfast, sure love for David." **Isa 55:1-3**

Delight yourselves in rich food!

O the power and grace of the life You have given me to live! I look back at the twists and turns, developments and radical changes You have brought me through, and I am stunned at the way You have been able to guide my life! You have brought me into things I would never have chosen for myself, things that I would have been horrified at, at one time.

I would have never chosen them for myself, would have never thought I could stand them, but now <u>they are some of the richest delights and pleasures of my life</u>!
    –Pastor Daniel Martin, 3/18/14

God is a God of pleasure. He wants His children to experience goodness and delight. That goodness and delight is in the Lord, not in the flesh or in the world.

God is a God of restoration. He restores water to the thirsty and food to the hungry – a type of water and food that cannot be bought with money.

God is a God of satisfaction. He wants us to experience satisfaction in our soul. He wants us to experience life through growth and through His work. He always has steadfast and sure love.

God tells us to come. Come to the feast!

Meditation: Today is a day of seeking the Lord. Eliminate all distractions. Try to quiet your mind.

Then come to the Lord. Go to Him and ask Him to reveal to you the heart of God. Seek the Lord for His heart. Ask Him about His desires and specifically, His desires for you. Write down what the Lord reveals to you about His heart and His desires.

> Though the fig tree should not blossom, nor fruit be on the vines, the produce of the olive fail and the fields yield no food, the flock be cut off from the fold and there be no herd in the stalls, yet I will rejoice in the LORD; I will take joy in the God of my salvation.
>
> GOD, the Lord, is my strength; he makes my feet like the deer's; he makes me tread on my high places. To the choirmaster: with stringed instruments. **Hab 3:17-19**

Today is a review day. Review the past week and see what the Lord has revealed to you about comfort.

> **Meditation:** Meditate on the final verses of the Book of Habakkuk above. As you meditate, consider the attitude of the great men and women of God toward God and toward possessions.

✝   ✝   ✝   ✝   ✝   ✝   ✝

NOTES:_____

_____

_____

_____

_____

_____

_____

_____

II.Week Nine, Day 1 (Date:)   **COMFORT - PEOPLE**

Now King Solomon loved many foreign women, along with the daughter of Pharaoh: Moabite, Ammonite, Edomite, Sidonian, and Hittite women, from the nations concerning which the LORD had said to the people of Israel, "You shall not enter into marriage with them, neither shall they with you, for surely they will turn away your heart after their gods." Solomon clung to these in love. He had 700 wives, who were princesses, and 300 concubines. And his wives turned away his heart.

For when Solomon was old his wives turned away his heart after other gods, and his heart was not wholly true to the LORD his God, as was the heart of David his father. For Solomon went after Ashtoreth the goddess of the Sidonians, and after Milcom the abomination of the Ammonites. So Solomon did what was evil in the sight of the LORD and did not wholly follow the LORD, as David his father had done. Then Solomon built a high place for Chemosh the abomination of Moab, and for Molech the abomination of the Ammonites, on the mountain east of Jerusalem. And so he did for all his foreign wives, who made offerings and sacrificed to their gods. **1 Kings 11:1-8**

Now Solomon clung to these in love.

The evil of the empty wish lies in the fact that the wisher is not Adjusted to the Will of God. He allows his desires to play over things that are entirely out of God's will and dreams of possessing what he well knows he should not have. Five minutes of this futile dreaming and he has lost the fine edge of his spiritual life.

Should the act ripen into a habit, his Christian life may be seriously injured...

Unless he corrects his fault sharply, he will degenerate into a spineless dreamer of empty dreams.

Every desire should be brought to the test of God's Will. If the desire is out of the will of God, it should be instantly dismissed as unworthy of us. To continue to Long for something that is plainly out of the will of God for us is to prove how unreal our consecration actually is.

If, however, the desired object is legitimate and innocent, then there are three possible ways by which it may be obtained.

- **WORK for it.**
- **PRAY for it.**
- **WORK and PRAY for it.**[37]

Things are a source of comfort. People are a source of comfort as well. Solomon loved many foreign women. He was attached to them. He clung to them in love. And they turned his heart away from the Lord. Solomon had inordinate attachments to women.

Romance and sex are primary sources of comfort. The pursuit of romance or sex can be thrilling. Falling "in love" is exciting and that excitement pleases the will. Whole lives are spent seeking gratification and satisfaction through romance and sex.

Romance and sex can be good things if longing for them is surrendered to the Lord in such a way that His created purpose for them is honored.

Meditation: Consider the call of the Lord on the life of Solomon. Solomon built the temple dedicated for the worship of the Lord and for His Presence. Solomon sat on the throne of David which was established as the throne of God's kingdom.

Now meditate on the impact of Solomon's attachment to women on Solomon's heart. Focus on the competition between Solomon's desire for women and Solomon's desire for the Lord. How did this competition impact Solomon in the fulfillment of his call?

☫   ☫   ☫   ☫   ☫   ☫   ☫

NOTES:_____

_____

_____

_____

_____

_____

---

[37] A. W. Tozer, *Prayer: Communing with God in Everything*, p.93 (Moody 2016) (Compiled by W.L. Seaver).

> Now Absalom, David's son, had a beautiful sister, whose name was Tamar. And after a time Amnon, David's son, loved her. And Amnon was so tormented that he made himself ill because of his sister Tamar, for she was a virgin, and it seemed impossible to Amnon to do anything to her. **2 Sam 13:1-2**
>
> She answered him, "No, my brother, do not violate me, for such a thing is not done in Israel; do not do this outrageous thing. As for me, where could I carry my shame? And as for you, you would be as one of the outrageous fools in Israel. Now therefore, please speak to the king, for he will not withhold me from you."
>
> But he would not listen to her, and being stronger than she, he violated her and lay with her.
>
> Then Amnon hated her with very great hatred, so that the hatred with which he hated her was greater than the love with which he had loved her. And Amnon said to her, "Get up! Go!"
>
> But she said to him, "No, my brother, for this wrong in sending me away is greater than the other that you did to me." But he would not listen to her. He called the young man who served him and said, "Put this woman out of my presence and bolt the door after her."
> **2 Sam 13:12-17**

Amnon was so tormented that he made himself ill.

Seeking God to give me/us PURE Hearts!

O God, please come and cleanse, purify, sanctify, and root out of all aspects/areas/parts of my being anything that is impure, anything that "misses the mark" of Your callings on my life, anything that agrees with the enemy in any way!

O how I need deeper and deeper purity in my life, in my choices, in my actions, motives, words, meditations, and thoughts, in my whole being!

Come and step by step lead me into the purity You desire for me.

Increase deep Godly sorrow for every impurity that I allow to work in me in any way! O how I need You in this.

One of the ways to overcome in this is to allow Time for Seeking You to give me this PURITY!!

Thank You for the treasure of Purity, and give me deeper and deeper thirsts, hungers, desires, longings, yearnings, and Desperation for Your Purity flowing in my life!!

O I must have this! Grow me today in this! Grow the hungers and desires in me today!! O I Must Have This!!
                                                            -Pastor Daniel Martin, 3/3/17

The story of Amnon and Tamar is a tragic one. Amnon was filled with desire, passion, and fantasy toward his half-sister, Tamar. He was so consumed with his desire that it made him ill. Tamar was a virgin and virtuous, so virtuous that she offered to marry Amnon in order to save her virtue. But Amnon did not relent.

When Amnon saw Tamar's beauty, he pined for her. Fantasy can operate as a great source of emotional comfort. Fantasy and imagination can provide an alternate reality that temporarily soothes self loathing, low esteem, or even depression. Fantasy can also generate excitement that pleases the will. Fantasy and mental images play a significant role in inordinate attachments. Alternate reality, like in video games, can be addictive.

The truth is Amnon's "love" for Tamar was only a fantasy. When Tamar offered him marriage that would require love in reality, Amnon rejected her offer. Marriage did not fit into his fantasy.

After he violated her, Amnon hated her with a hatred that was greater than the "love with which he loved her." Amnon's fantasy had very little to do with the virtuous Tamar and very much to do with himself. Nothing in reality justified his hatred for her. He was focused on his feelings about himself after he violated her, and his self loathing became hatred for her.

Meditation: Consider the extent to which you engage in fantasy, imagination, or mental imaging. Discern the reasons why you engage in them. To what extent is the Lord the source of the fantasy, imagination, or mental imaging? Journal about it.

Next, seek the Lord about surrender of your imagination to Him. Ask Him to what extent you need to empty yourself of your imaginations in order to seek Him.

☫ ☫ ☫ ☫ ☫ ☫ ☫

Meet faithfully with your mentor (or devotional partner) to discuss your devotions and your journal. A trusted guide can help you understand the sources of your comfort and can share wisdom in how to deal with them.

NOTES:_____

_____

_____

_____

_____

_____

_____

_____

_____

_____

_____

_____

_____

_____

_____

_____

_____

_____

_____

_____

_____

The word of the LORD came to me:

"Son of man, behold, I am about to take the delight of your eyes away from you at a stroke; yet you shall not mourn or weep, nor shall your tears run down. Sigh, but not aloud; make no mourning for the dead. Bind on your turban, and put your shoes on your feet; do not cover your lips, nor eat the bread of men."

So I spoke to the people in the morning, and at evening my wife died. And on the next morning I did as I was commanded. And the people said to me, "Will you not tell us what these things mean for us, that you are acting thus?"

Then I said to them, "The word of the LORD came to me:

'Say to the house of Israel, Thus says the Lord GOD: Behold, I will profane my sanctuary, the pride of your power, the delight of your eyes, and the yearning of your soul, and your sons and your daughters whom you left behind shall fall by the sword. And you shall do as I have done; you shall not cover your lips, nor eat the bread of men. Your turbans shall be on your heads and your shoes on your feet; you shall not mourn or weep, but you shall rot away in your iniquities and groan to one another. Thus shall Ezekiel be to you a sign; according to all that he has done you shall do. When this comes, then you will know that I am the Lord GOD.'

"As for you, son of man, surely on the day when I take from them their stronghold, their joy and glory, the delight of their eyes and their soul's desire, and also their sons and daughters, on that day a fugitive will come to you to report to you the news. On that day your mouth will be opened to the fugitive, and you shall speak and be no longer mute. So you will be a sign to them, and they will know that I am the LORD." **Eze 24:15-27**

Son of man...I am about to take the delight of your eyes.

What Amazing Grace!!

O the Glory Of Your Presence!

Your presence has been so real to us these last 5 days. Five days that from human perspective should have been the most traumatic, the most devastating, fear-filled, grief-laden, emotionally draining days of our lives.

And yet, they have been just the opposite for both of us!

They have been days filled with JOY, filled with a deep abiding sense of Your Presence, of Your love, of Your goodness!

They have been filled with Light, not darkness at all!

They have been filled with Great Hope, regardless of what the next days ahead hold in the natural realm. For the believer, there really is GLORY—JUST AHEAD!!

Days filled with deeper appreciation, excitement, treasuring, and loving each other more than ever before in our marriage - wholesomeness, delight, glory, and fulfillment and hope - greater than we have ever known.

Much of this has come out of daily communion (for several weeks now), remembering Jesus on the cross and all that this means for us now and for all the days ahead and into eternity where there are no days!!!

For me to be able to say that these last 5 days have been the most glorious ones of my life is beyond human reason, but not beyond the grace, power, and love of my God! How great and awesome You are, O my God!!!   -Pastor Daniel Martin, 7/8/16[38]

The title "son of man" has a special place in the scriptures. Jesus refers to Himself as the "son of man" in the Gospels about 80 times. Otherwise, the title is almost unique to Ezekiel. God calls Ezekiel the "son of man" over 90 times. (Daniel is called the "son of man" once (Dan 8:17)).

"Son of man" must refer to humanity and human frailty as it speaks of human origin. For Jesus, we know that it also refers to exaltation, for the Son of Man will come in His glory (Matt 26:64). Maybe for Ezekiel, "son of man" is a title of intimacy and affection from God for one who was willing to surrender his relationship with his wife - the delight of his eyes, in order to do the will of the One Who sent him.

Meditation: As you read this passage of scripture, what were you thinking? What were you feeling? Write down your thoughts and feelings in your journal.

Spend time with God. Ask Him to show you attachments that you have to people. Ask Him to show you the nature of those attachments, and whether those attachments impact the relationship of love between you and Him.

---

‡   ‡   ‡   ‡   ‡   ‡   ‡

---

[38] This devotion was written by Pastor Martin five days after his beloved wife received a diagnosis of terminal cancer. She passed away the following month with peace of mind and love in her heart.

> Peter began to say to him, "See, we have left everything and followed you."
>
> Jesus said, "Truly, I say to you, there is no one who has left house or brothers or sisters or mother or father or children or lands, for my sake and for the gospel, who will not receive a hundredfold now in this time, houses and brothers and sisters and mothers and children and lands, with persecutions, and in the age to come eternal life.
>
> But many who are first will be last, and the last first." **Mark 10:28-31**

We have left everything and followed You.

This morning I was convicted at Men's Fraternity that I "come to myself" often, but never rise and leave the pig pens because the journey is too great, the reception might not be what I need/want at the Father's house, maybe I should stay just another day.

Lord, help me!! Help me to arise and be all that You are calling me to be as husband, father, grandfather, pastor, citizen, member of Your body, fellow pastor, neighbor, etc. I need You on every front in my life.

Give me the desire and will to rise and to risk all for You. Help me to lead, and not to just lead where it is welcome and asked for, but where You call me to lead.

Lord, I need You so much here!!   –Pastor Daniel Martin, 1/27/11

This exchange follows the story of the rich, young ruler in the Gospel of Mark – the story of the wealthy, religious man who was not willing to surrender his riches in order to follow Jesus. After witnessing that event, Peter eagerly reminds Jesus of the sacrifice that he and the other disciples made. *"See, we have left everything and followed You."* The sacrifice was not just one of surrender, but one of action.

Peter probably expected personal commendation or endorsement – what we sometimes jokingly refer to as the "gold star on his chart." In response, Jesus states powerful principles of the kingdom of God – principles that involve both surrender and action. These principles apply to Peter, and they apply to you and to me.

Meditation: Meditate on Jesus' words above. Consider the extent to which you have acted and left house, brothers, sisters, mother, father, children, or lands for Jesus' sake and for the sake of the gospel.

What do you think it means to receive "a hundredfold now in this time...with persecutions"?

NOTES:_____

_____

_____

_____

_____

_____

_____

_____

_____

_____

_____

_____

_____

_____

_____

_____

_____

_____

_____

_____

> Put no trust in a neighbor; have no confidence in a friend; guard the doors of your mouth from her who lies in your arms; for the son treats the father with contempt, the daughter rises up against her mother, the daughter-in-law against her mother-in-law; a man's enemies are the men of his own house.
>
> But as for me, I will look to the LORD; I will wait for the God of my salvation; my God will hear me. Rejoice not over me, O my enemy; when I fall, I shall rise; when I sit in darkness, the LORD will be a light to me. **Mic 7:5-8**

When I sit in darkness, the Lord will be a light to me.

My son, if you rest your peace on any person, because of your own feelings and because you live with him, you shall be unstable and entangled. But if you have recourse to the ever-living and abiding Truth, the desertion or death of a friend will not grieve you...

You ought to be so dead to such affections toward beloved men, that (so far as you are concerned) you would choose to be without all human sympathy. The nearer man draws to God, the farther he retires from all earthly comfort...

When you look to the creature, the countenance of the Creator is withdrawn. Learn in all things to overcome yourself for the sake of your Creator; then you shall have power to attain to divine knowledge. How little is anything, if it is inordinately loved and regarded, if it keeps you away from the Highest, and corrupts the soul.[39]

Relationships in general can be a source of great security for us. Our circle of friends, our relatives, our posse – all can give us comfort. But the question needs to be asked: Do they provide a substitute for comfort from the Lord?

Meditation: Meditate on the quote above and determine whether you agree with it.

        ╬   ╬   ╬   ╬   ╬   ╬   ╬

> Take your time with your devotions. Slow movement can be good. Allow time for the work of the Holy Spirit in your life.

---
[39] *The Imitation of Christ*, pp. 172-173.

> "How can you believe, when you receive glory from one another and do not seek the glory that comes from the only God?" **John 5:44**

How can you believe when...?

Come and take over in this sheep today. Grace me with correction and exposing to me when my actions are ones that could seem to be setting You before me, but my motives are robbing me of it.

Show me where it looks like I am setting You first, but in reality, through desiring glory from men, I am putting myself in front of You. How ugly, damaging, diminishing, and self-glorifying (actually self-destructing) this is.

You and You alone are worthy of all the glory!! Come and let me live giving You glory all day, glorifying You with all I do and say!

Thank You for this morning—it has been great!!   –Pastor Daniel Martin, 5/7/14

The manner in which we interact with God and the manner in which we interact with people show our faith. Jesus asks the religious leaders a rhetorical question here. How can you believe when you are attached to the glory you receive from men and you don't even seek the glory that comes from God? What kind of faith does that show?

My third core confession – my third lifeline from my illness was this: "I glorify you, O Lord, above all other beings."

I shared this lifeline with a friend. "I glorify you, O Lord, above all other beings." My friend paused thoughtfully and then said, "I am not sure that I can say that."

Now my friend was a Godly man who spent years in full time ministry. He wasn't being rebellious or resistant. He was just comparing the close and intimate relationships that he had and the reality of those attachments in light of his spiritual walk.

> **Meditation:** "I glorify you, O Lord, above all other beings." Repeat this statement slowly three times. Then think of its implications in your life. Ask the Holy Spirit to reveal your attachments to people. Consider what it means to surrender those relationships fully to the Lord. Write down your reactions to this lifeline.

Lifelines:

I believe in You, O Lord, Maker of the heavens and the earth.

I trust You, O my God, at all times and in all places.

I glorify you, O Lord, above all other beings.

Review the notes from your journal over the last two weeks.

Meditation: Sometimes, I just want to say "HELP! Help me, Lord!"

Today, seek comfort from the Lord. Present to the Lord areas in which you desire comfort. Maybe your meditations over the last two weeks revealed things or people in which you unduly seek comfort.

Expose your feelings to the Lord. Tell Him the needs or desires that you feel. Ask the Lord to be the God of all comfort to you.

✝   ✝   ✝   ✝   ✝   ✝   ✝

NOTES:_____

_____

_____

_____

_____

_____

_____

_____

_____

_____

_____

_____

II.Week Ten, Day 1 (Date:)   **TRUTH – INNER BEING**

> Buy truth, and do not sell it; buy wisdom, instruction, and understanding. **Pro 23:23**

Buy truth and do not sell it.

Truth always does destroy lies as long as I insist on the truth, living it, speaking it in my heart, and not allowing the lie any room in me! Help me to not allow lies to infest, infect, or impact my life. I want to live by the truth, insist on the truth—no matter the cost! Truth does cost me—but lies are far more costly.

Prov. 23:23 "Buy the truth and sell it not." (KJV)

Help me to pay the price for the truth to be armoring me. Help me to see that lies are always costlier in the negative sense than the truth (is costly), no matter how expensive to my flesh the present needed truth is!

I want my life to be guided, led by, and decided by truth! The fruit of truth has so much glory and life in it. The fruit of lies is pain, destruction, corruption, rottenness, defeat, emptiness, and loss! I want the truth.

O God this child/sheep Needs You!!   -Pastor Daniel Martin, 12/11/14

Part of surrender is the willingness to perceive ourselves as we really are. That is an element of devotion to Christ. We desire truth because we want to worship in Spirit and in truth. Truth includes seeing ourselves simply and clearly. A beautiful image, a glorified self perception, or an influential identity can be sources of great comfort. In fact, they can be idols. But truth implies that we want the Lord to reveal our true identity in Him.

The serpent deceived Eve by appealing to desires that she had. When Eve told the serpent that God had warned not to eat the fruit lest she die, the serpent said *"You will not surely die"* (Gen. 3:3-4).This statement appealed to a desire for life.

Then he told her that God knew her eyes would be opened and she would be like God, knowing good and evil (Gen. 3:5). This subversive statement appealed to a creature that was made in the image of God.

Then Eve saw that the tree was good for food (lust of the flesh), a delight to the eyes (lust of the eyes), and to be desired to make one wise (pride of life) (Gen. 3:6). So Eve succumbed to the deception and partook of the fruit of the tree.

Eve lost her identity and was deceived into believing that the fruit would make her some one that she was not intended to be.

240

Meditation: This week look at your own self perceptions. These perceptions are shaped both by how you perceive yourself and how you think (or want) other people to perceive you.

Consider who you are in different contexts of your life – such as family, work, friends, church, and ministry. How do you perceive yourself in those areas? Write down these perceptions in your journal.

How do your perceptions match the true identity that you have in Christ?

Behold, I was brought forth in iniquity, and in sin did my mother conceive me.

Behold, you delight in truth in the inward being, and you teach me wisdom in the secret heart. **Psa 51:5-6**

✠   ✠   ✠   ✠   ✠   ✠   ✠

NOTES:_____

_____

_____

_____

_____

_____

_____

_____

_____

_____

_____

> Now in all Israel there was no one so much to be praised for his handsome appearance as Absalom. From the sole of his foot to the crown of his head there was no blemish in him. And when he cut the hair of his head (for at the end of every year he used to cut it; when it was heavy on him, he cut it), he weighed the hair of his head, two hundred shekels by the king's weight. **2 Sam 14:25-26**

There was no one so much to be praised for his handsome appearance.

So I was riding in the car driven by my beloved Aunt Juliet. Aunt Juliet was young and beautiful and she maximized it – cosmetics, eyelashes, wig, manicure...the works. But Aunt Juliet had come to the Lord in a meaningful way not too long before and she was determined to pour into the life of me, her nephew, when I was a young teenager.

All of sudden, Aunt Juliet shouted, "David, I've had it!" I jerked a little bit as Aunt Juliet started biting her fingers.

"I've had it! I've had it! No more of this!" As I glanced over, I realized she wasn't actually biting her fingers, but she was peeling off her false finger nails one by one with her teeth. I secretly hoped she was keeping her eyes on the road.

"This isn't who I am and I'm not going to do it anymore!" Aunt Juliet proclaimed. "God has set me FREE! I don't need these things in my life!" The false finger nails came off and the makeup got hand scrubbed in the rearview mirror.

"I'm free, I'm free, thank God I am free!" In my shock, I don't recall that I said anything. But Aunt Juliet had an epiphany about her identity and decided to be true to herself.

Do you weigh the hair of your head after you cut it? Well, Absalom did – every time that he cut it.

In the story of Absalom, his appearance was very important to him. He presented himself well to people around him. In the next chapter, we read that Absalom obtained a chariot and horses, and hired 50 men to run before him. In his mind, his royal presence required an entourage.

How other people perceived Absalom was important to him. Absalom was the heir apparent to David. But the title of prince was not good enough for him. Absalom saw himself as king. And he took steps to insure that the people of Israel perceived him as regal.

False identity is a source of comfort. The thought of being more beautiful, more important, or more powerful than our reality is comforting. The thought that other people perceive you that way is doubly comforting. So we wear masks (sometimes in the form of cosmetics or clothes) and present ourselves as the way we dream to be rather than the way we are.

One more thing: In Absalom's case, his beautiful locks of hair probably led to his demise (2 Sam. 18:9).

Meditation: Spend time considering how you perceive yourself. Who and what do you think you are? How do you feel as you answer these questions?

To what extent is your identity real? To what extent is your "public persona" – your public image - an illusion? To what extent is your established identity an illusion?

Ask the Holy Spirit to reveal these things to you.

The heart is deceitful above all things, and desperately sick; who can understand it?

"I the LORD search the heart and test the mind, to give every man according to his ways, according to the fruit of his deeds." **Jer 17:9-10**

╬   ╬   ╬   ╬   ╬   ╬   ╬

NOTES:_____

_____

_____

_____

_____

_____

_____

Please feel free to spend more than one day on a devotion if you feel you need it. These devotions are designed to inquire, to probe, and to dig. Prioritize depth as opposed to numbers. Engage deeply.

David said to the messenger, "Thus shall you say to Joab, 'Do not let this matter displease you, for the sword devours now one and now another. Strengthen your attack against the city and overthrow it.' And encourage him."

When the wife of Uriah heard that Uriah her husband was dead, she lamented over her husband.

And when the mourning was over, David sent and brought her to his house, and she became his wife and bore him a son. But the thing that David had done displeased the LORD.   **2 Sam 11:25-26**

But the thing that David had done displeased the Lord.

O God, help me to have and seek for Truth in the Innermost being.

I long to be totally what You want me to be! I want to Walk in truth, Know truth, Live truth, Proclaim truth, have a life that is aligned perfectly with truth! O, give me Truth, on the outside, on the inside, and all through my whole being—every part being controlled, led, and directed by Truth!

Forgive me for where I have caved in to lies for whatever reasons. Remove from me the lies and tendencies toward them. Help me to so embrace Truth at every turn, that I Tend toward it, and away from all lies. O give me Deep yearnings for Truth to take over in me.

Show me today as I go through this day what I need to see about living by the TRUTH!
-Pastor Daniel Martin, 10/9/14

These are the final verses of the sin of David with Bathsheba. (If you have time, read all of 2 Sam 11.) The human capacity for justification of actions that appeal to fleshly desires is immense. One act of depravity leads to a larger one, but we use mental gymnastics to justify it. It is a slippery slope that, if we are not careful, will land us at the bottom of the pit.

The principle is that the mind follows the heart. Our will and heart crave a desire or an appetite. Then our mind complies by concocting justification for it. We think we are being "rational" when in fact our will is leading our mind around on a leash. It is a common form of self deception.

David's lust for Bathsheba became adultery. Adultery led to pregnancy which David tried to hide by enticing her husband, Uriah. But Uriah was one of David's "mighty men" and, in his righteousness, refused to be enticed. So David crafted a more pernicious plan. He manipulated his army so that Uriah was killed.

In short order, David had committed lust; then adultery; then deception; and then murder, and somehow he had justified them in his mind.

Meditation: Today is a day of quiet before the Lord. Eliminate all distractions and try to keep your mind from wandering. Spend time in quiet before the Lord.

Open up your heart to the Lord. See if the Holy Spirit reveals anything to you.

Woe to those who call evil good and good evil, who put darkness for light and light for darkness, who put bitter for sweet and sweet for bitter!

Woe to those who are wise in their own eyes, and shrewd in their own sight! **Isa 5:20-21**

╬ ╬ ╬ ╬ ╬ ╬ ╬

NOTES:

And the LORD sent Nathan to David. He came to him and said to him, "There were two men in a certain city, the one rich and the other poor. The rich man had very many flocks and herds, but the poor man had nothing but one little ewe lamb, which he had bought. And he brought it up, and it grew up with him and with his children. It used to eat of his morsel and drink from his cup and lie in his arms, and it was like a daughter to him.

"Now there came a traveler to the rich man, and he was unwilling to take one of his own flock or herd to prepare for the guest who had come to him, but he took the poor man's lamb and prepared it for the man who had come to him."

Then David's anger was greatly kindled against the man, and he said to Nathan, "As the LORD lives, the man who has done this deserves to die, and he shall restore the lamb fourfold, because he did this thing, and because he had no pity."

Nathan said to David, "You are the man!" 2 Sam 12:1-7a

"You are the man!"

I have an affliction. I have had it since childhood. It is not so much a physical affliction as it is an emotional one. I call it "narrative bias."

I realized one day that when I tell a story about my life, I tend to put myself in the absolute best light. I emphasize my successes and underscore my strengths. I de-emphasize my failures and ignore my weaknesses. Unless, of course, I want to promote my own humility in which case I confess my most innocent failings in order to give an appearance of humility. "Narrative bias" colors all of my speech.

Narrative bias is a great means of self promotion. When my narrative bias impresses a crowd, I gain comfort from the admiration of others. That admiration bolsters my own inflated self-perception which in turn gives me added comfort.

My observation is that narrative bias is a common disease. In fact, the "legends" in history such as Daniel Boone, Davy Crockett, and Wyatt Earp were pretty good storytellers. They called those stories "tall tales" which aptly describes some of my most eloquent autobiographical sketches.

My narrative bias paints me as pretty much an all around good guy. I guess it is just one of those identity things.

After David's sin with Bathsheba, Nathan the prophet confronted David about it. (If you have time, read the whole aftermath in 2 Sam 12:1-25). The manner that Nathan confronted David is interesting. Nathan could have approached David with "guns blazing" – exposing David's sin and his horrible actions.

But Nathan did not do that. David was a man caught in a web of deception and self justification. So Nathan first told David an objective story that did not involve David, so David could pronounce judgment. An objective approach helped David see the terrible injustice of actions that turned out to be his own.

A significant factor in truthful self perception is an ability to practice objectivity. Objectivity is the ability to step outside of yourself – to distance yourself from your desires, your emotions, and even your needs. Objectivity helps you to see the situation from outside of yourself.

Objectivity is a rare trait. It requires immense humility and self awareness to possess it. How God sees you must be more important to you than how you see yourself. How people with whom you practice accountability see you must be just as important to you as how you see yourself. Trusted and truthful friends can help you be objective.

Objectivity is a powerful tool for truth in the inner being. Objectivity can help to heal narrative bias.

Meditation: Today ask a trusted friend to tell you how that friend sees you. Ask the friend to be truthful and honest about how the friend perceives you – brutally honest if necessary. Whether good or bad, thank the friend.

Write down what your friend says and also record your feelings as you listened to him. Then spend time with the Lord seeking Him about the report.

Who shall ascend the hill of the LORD? And who shall stand in his holy place?

He who has clean hands and a pure heart, who does not lift up his soul to what is false and does not swear deceitfully.

He will receive blessing from the LORD and righteousness from the God of his salvation.

Such is the generation of those who seek him, who seek the face of the God of Jacob. Selah. **Psa 24:3-6**

╬   ╬   ╬   ╬   ╬   ╬   ╬

Receive grace during these devotions. If you sense a conviction, then repent and receive forgiveness. But don't tolerate condemnation. God offers abundant grace!

NOTES:_____

_____

_____

_____

_____

_____

_____

_____

_____

_____

_____

_____

_____

_____

_____

_____

_____

_____

> Therefore put away all filthiness and rampant wickedness and receive with meekness the implanted word, which is able to save your souls. But be doers of the word, and not hearers only, deceiving yourselves.
>
> For if anyone is a hearer of the word and not a doer, he is like a man who looks intently at his natural face in a mirror. For he looks at himself and goes away and at once forgets what he was like.
>
> But the one who looks into the perfect law, the law of liberty, and perseveres, being no hearer who forgets but a doer who acts, he will be blessed in his doing.
>
> If anyone thinks he is religious and does not bridle his tongue but deceives his heart, this person's religion is worthless. Religion that is pure and undefiled before God, the Father, is this: to visit orphans and widows in their affliction, and to keep oneself unstained from the world. **James 1:21-27**

A man who looks intently at his natural face in a mirror.

O help me to increasingly see that Your Word is full of Worth.

<u>**Through Your word show me the worthlessness of worthless things.**</u>

As I have lived my life seeing worth in worthless things, as this has been imbedded in me in powerful, strong ways, help me to now be changed, renewed and come alive, really alive with the power of Your Word, seeing worth and value in Your Word and Ways!   -Pastor Daniel Martin, 1/7/14

The word of God is like a mirror. We look into it and we see at least two things. First, we see ourselves as we actually are. We may have justified our desires and we may have been deceived about our actions, but the word tells us what is true and what is right. Application of the word to our lives corrects our deceptions.

Second, the word of God shows us what we should be. Through the word, we see righteousness, justice, purity, and truth. The word is how we should be – which is why we not only read it mentally, but we desire to make it a part of us through penetration of the heart.

So how do we respond to the word? Are we like a man who sees himself in a true light but then goes away and immediately forgets it? Or are we like a man who perseveres in the word and actually does it?

That is the astounding part of the aftermath of David and Bathsheba. When confronted with a prophet like Nathan, many kings would have beheaded him on the spot. But even when deceived, David's heart was oriented toward the Lord. Nathan delivered the word of the Lord to David and David immediately received the word. He confessed his sin and repented. *"I have sinned against the Lord"* (2 Sam. 12:13). David then sought the Lord about the consequences of his sin and submitted himself to them.

David's desire for the Lord and his desire for integrity of heart were remarkable.

> **Meditation:** Read all of Psalm 51. This Psalm was written by David after his sin with Bathsheba. As you read Psalm 51, note the desires of David's heart. How important to David were the condition of his own inner being and of the Presence of the Lord?

✝   ✝   ✝   ✝   ✝   ✝   ✝

NOTES:_____

_____

_____

_____

_____

_____

_____

_____

_____

_____

_____

_____

> Preach the Word, be instant in season and out of season, reprove, rebuke, exhort with all long-suffering and doctrine.
>
> For a time will be when they will not endure sound doctrine, but they will heap up teachers to themselves according to their own lusts, tickling the ear. And they will turn away their ears from the truth and will be turned to myths.
>
> But you watch in all things, endure afflictions, do the work of an evangelist, fully carry out your ministry. **2 Tim 4:2-5 (MKJV)**

If anyone thinks he is religious and does not bridle his tongue but deceives his heart, this person's religion is worthless (From yesterday's scripture).

Our words reveal our heart. If we do not bridle our tongue, we deceive our heart.

Tickling the ear can be a source of comfort. One way to tickle the ear is gossip. Telling something bad about someone can comfort low self esteem. Belittling others can make one feel better about oneself and maybe even superior to others. Gossip feeds a false identity.

When gossip is shared, it creates a false bond. Being "in the know" can feed a sense of mutual self importance. Once when I admonished a person who was sharing a malicious story with me, the response was "Well, if he didn't want it told, he shouldn't have done it!"

But tickling the ear has a spiritual dimension as well. "Spiritual insights" or "words of mystery" can cause an emotional thrill. Remember Brother Lawrence said human will loves excitement. Although prophecy is an inspired spiritual gift, some Christian "prophetic activity" occurs because it gives the flesh an emotional tingle. Flesh loves the excitement. Tickling the ear can deceptively feed a false identity as a bearer of hidden truth.

Meditation: Review your words and how they relate to your own self perception. How do your words reflect what is in your heart? How do you use words to create, to bolster, or to fulfill your identity? Record your meditations in your journal.

Is this from You, God? Are You trying to graphically tell me that I still don't have a clue as to who I really am in many ways, that I need to be more oriented to You? It is true that most people are totally "disoriented" because their orientations have them as the axis, the center of their lives.

The reality is that we are not oriented to truth and have no clue what the truth IS until our lives are oriented with You as the center, the axis—with You and Your ways being what our lives revolve around!

O God, reorient my life! Let my GPS system be recalculated by connecting to YOU and Your ways which are out there so far above my ways.
–Pastor Daniel Martin, 12/10/12

Review your notes over the past week. What has the Lord been showing you about your own self image? What has He shown you about your identity in Him?

Meditation: Today use artistic expression to express your identity in the Lord. You can draw, paint, compose, or create. You can use an art medium or use physical movement or expression.

Submit what you do to the Lord. Ask Him to guide you as you express to Him your identity. Ask Him to guide, teach, and purify your heart as you explore and express your identity in Him.

☩   ☩   ☩   ☩   ☩   ☩   ☩

NOTES:_____

_____

_____

_____

_____

_____

In the sixth month the angel Gabriel was sent from God to a city of Galilee named Nazareth, to a virgin betrothed to a man whose name was Joseph, of the house of David. And the virgin's name was Mary. And he came to her and said, "Greetings, O favored one, the Lord is with you!"

But she was greatly troubled at the saying, and tried to discern what sort of greeting this might be. And the angel said to her, "Do not be afraid, Mary, for you have found favor with God. And behold, you will conceive in your womb and bear a son, and you shall call his name Jesus. He will be great and will be called the Son of the Most High. And the Lord God will give to him the throne of his father David, and he will reign over the house of Jacob forever, and of his kingdom there will be no end."

And Mary said to the angel, "How will this be, since I am a virgin?"

And the angel answered her, "The Holy Spirit will come upon you, and the power of the Most High will overshadow you; therefore the child to be born will be called holy—the Son of God. And behold, your relative Elizabeth in her old age has also conceived a son, and this is the sixth month with her who was called barren. For nothing will be impossible with God."

And Mary said, "Behold, I am the servant of the Lord; let it be to me according to your word." And the angel departed from her.
Luke 1:26-38

Let it be done to me according to your word.

This story is a story of complete surrender. God sent his angel, Gabriel, to call Mary, the mother of our Lord. Surrender is an important part of the call of God. In the Bible, a person often needed to come to a place of surrender to receive the call of God. Then, that person lived out that surrender in order to fulfill the call of God.

Gabriel's words impacted Mary. Think of her reputation. Mary was a pure and chaste virgin. What would other people say when a young lady who was considered devout and holy became pregnant?

And what about Joseph? Mary was betrothed to him. What would Joseph think when his beloved became pregnant? We know the answer to that question. Joseph was going to put her away (Matt. 1:18). But Mary's devotion was such that attachment to her beloved Joseph did not hinder her response.

Mary is the foremost example in scripture of immediate surrender to the will of God. For many saints, a call came from God but then a period of preparation or of seasoning occurred before God empowered them to fulfill their call. But Mary did not need time to come to the place of surrender. Her submission was complete and God acted immediately to fulfill His will for Mary and for all of mankind.

"Behold, I am the servant of the Lord; let it be done to me according to your word." These words encapsulate the response of the soul that the Lord desires.

Meditation: Think of words that describe Mary's response to the call of the Lord. Write them down. As you review the words, how do they relate to surrender to the Lord in your life?

☦ ☦ ☦ ☦ ☦ ☦ ☦

NOTES:_____

_____

_____

_____

_____

_____

_____

_____

_____

_____

> They said to one another, "Here comes this dreamer. Come now, let us kill him and throw him into one of the pits. Then we will say that a fierce animal has devoured him, and we will see what will become of his dreams." **Gen 37:19-20**

Here comes this dreamer.

Joseph's life was defined by dreams – both his dreams and the dreams of others. As a young man, he had dreams in which he was exalted and had authority. In two dreams, his family bowed before him (Gen 37:5ff). God called Joseph to his destiny through his dreams.

But for much of Joseph's life, those dreams did not come true. In fact, the opposite occurred as Joseph was humiliated – time after time. His brothers plotted to kill him. Then they sold him into slavery (Gen 37:28).

As a slave, Joseph could have despaired. Despair is often an excuse to seek worldly comfort. But Joseph did not allow despair to cause him to succumb to the continual sexual overtures of his master's wife (Gen 39:7-10). Yet Joseph's reward for his moral purity was worse humiliation - imprisonment (Gen 39:20).

Joseph languished in prison for years. While in prison, Joseph rightfully interpreted the dreams of Pharaoh's chief baker and cupbearer. He requested that the cupbearer remember him when the cupbearer was restored. But the cupbearer forgot him (Gen 40:23).

Joseph's dreams seemed meaningless for many years. But scripture does not indicate that Joseph doubted, despaired, or denied. Joseph lived in surrender of his hopes and dreams until the time that God exalted him and brought his dreams to fruition.

Meditation: Consider the dreams that God has placed in your heart. Think about roles, ministries, or functions to which He has called you and your hopes for them. Write down your dreams in your journal.

Now surrender your hopes and dreams to the Lord. Ask Him to bring them to pass in His time and by His design. Be willing to wait on Him fully submitted to His will.

---

*"Joseph is a fruitful bough, a fruitful bough by a spring; his branches run over the wall. **The archers bitterly attacked him, shot at him, and harassed him severely, yet his bow remained unmoved**; his arms were made agile by the hands of the Mighty One of Jacob (from there is the Shepherd, the Stone of Israel), by the God of your father who will help you, by the Almighty who will bless you with blessings of heaven above, blessings of the deep that crouches beneath, blessings of the breasts and of the womb."* (From the Blessing of Jacob) **Gen 49:22-25**

✠   ✠   ✠   ✠   ✠   ✠   ✠

NOTES:_____

_____

_____

_____

_____

_____

_____

_____

_____

_____

_____

_____

_____

_____

Now the LORD said to Abram, "Go from your country and your kindred and your father's house to the land that I will show you. And I will make of you a great nation, and I will bless you and make your name great, so that you will be a blessing. I will bless those who bless you, and him who dishonors you I will curse, and in you all the families of the earth shall be blessed."

So Abram went, as the LORD had told him, and Lot went with him. Abram was seventy-five years old when he departed from Haran. **Gen 12:1-4**

Go from your country and your kindred and your father's house.

Abraham is commended in scripture for his great faith. God told Abraham to "Go!" God is a sending God. So in order to fulfill his spiritual destiny, Abraham had to leave everything he knew – his home, his country, his family, and his heritage. And Abraham did so with only a promise to assure him.

If Abraham thought that the Lord would quickly multiply his family in droves, he was sadly mistaken. The man destined to become a great nation did not have any offspring for many years. His wife was barren.

But Abraham obeyed nonetheless. He surrendered his heritage and he surrendered his reality in order to trust God's promise. Abraham must have understood the greatness of God.

Mediation: Have you left anything in order to pursue God's call on your life? Consider whether you have abandoned anything or sacrificed it in order to pursue your spiritual destiny. Write those things down in your journal.

What promises of God did you have when you abandoned or sacrificed those things?

⚜ ⚜ ⚜ ⚜ ⚜ ⚜ ⚜

If a meditation is not really applicable to you, that is okay. Spend the time with the Lord receiving from Him and allow Him to work in His perfect time and in His special way.

NOTES:_____

_____

_____

_____

_____

_____

_____

_____

_____

_____

_____

_____

_____

_____

_____

_____

_____

_____

> By faith Moses, when he was grown up, refused to be called the son of Pharaoh's daughter, choosing rather to be mistreated with the people of God than to enjoy the fleeting pleasures of sin. He considered the reproach of Christ greater wealth than the treasures of Egypt, for he was looking to the reward.
>
> By faith he left Egypt, not being afraid of the anger of the king, for he endured as seeing him who is invisible.
>
> By faith he kept the Passover and sprinkled the blood, so that the Destroyer of the firstborn might not touch them. By faith the people crossed the Red Sea as on dry land, but the Egyptians, when they attempted to do the same, were drowned.   **Heb 11:24-29**

Choosing rather to be mistreated with the people of God

than to enjoy the fleeting pleasures of sin.

In the temptation of Jesus, Jesus rejected the offer of all the kingdoms of the world in order to fulfill the will of His Father. Moses faced a similar temptation. Because of his place in Pharaoh's household, he had a path to power and prestige. He had any pleasure which the world could offer at his fingertips. Moses only had to reach out and to grab them.

Instead Moses surrendered massive worldly power, pleasure, and wealth to the Lord. Moses pursued his destiny in the Lord. He chose the reproach of Christ and considered it greater wealth. He became rich toward God.

And the LORD came down in a pillar of cloud and stood at the entrance of the tent and called Aaron and Miriam, and they both came forward.

And he said, "Hear my words: If there is a prophet among you, I the LORD make myself known to him in a vision; I speak with him in a dream. Not so with my servant Moses. He is faithful in all my house. With him I speak mouth to mouth, clearly, and not in riddles, and he beholds the form of the LORD. Why then were you not afraid to speak against my servant Moses?" *(Num 12:5-8).*

Meditation: *"He is faithful in all my house."* Spend time with these words. Do you desire that the Lord say about you – "He is faithful in all my house"?

"With him I speak mouth to mouth, clearly, and not in riddles." Spend time with these words. Do you desire that type of relationship with the Lord?

Speak to the Lord the desire of your heart.

> "And I say to you: whoever divorces his wife, except for sexual immorality, and marries another, commits adultery."
>
> The disciples said to him, "If such is the case of a man with his wife, it is better not to marry."
>
> But he said to them, "Not everyone can receive this saying, but only those to whom it is given. For there are eunuchs who have been so from birth, and there are eunuchs who have been made eunuchs by men, and there are eunuchs who have made themselves eunuchs for the sake of the kingdom of heaven. Let the one who is able to receive this receive it." **Matt 19:9-12**

Let the one who is able to receive this receive it.

By the vow of chastity, I not only renounce the married state of life, but I also consecrate to God the free use of my internal and external acts – my affections. I cannot in conscience love a creature with the love of a woman for a man. I no longer have the right to give that affection to any other creature but only to God.

What then? Do we have to be stones, human beings without hearts? Do we simply say: "I don't care; to me all human beings are the same"? No, not at all. We have to keep ourselves as we are, but keep it all for God, to whom we have consecrated all our external and internal acts.   -Mother Teresa[40]

There are eunuchs who have made themselves eunuchs for the sake of the kingdom of heaven. This verse describes one form of surrender of sexuality. The call of the Lord to live for the sake of the kingdom is so compelling that the believer does not marry and thus refrains from sexual activity.

Paul had a deep sense of call from the Lord. In order to fulfill that call, he remained single so that he could go forth in mission without restraint. *Do we not have the right to take along a believing wife, as do the other apostles and the brothers of the Lord and Cephas?* (1 Cor 9:5).

Note that Paul did not say we have the right to engage in sexual activity. Sexual activity is not a right but a privilege that is intended in the context of marriage only. The right that Paul asserts is the right is to take a wife. But instead, Paul made himself a eunuch for the sake of the kingdom of heaven.

---

[40] *Total Surrender*, p.64.

Meditation: Today we focus on sexuality and the kingdom of heaven. Consider your sexuality and how you view it. What are your hopes and dreams for your sexuality? With regard to your sexuality, what do you consider a right, a privilege, a need, or a desire? Record your thoughts in your journal.

Now surrender your sexuality to the Lord. Seek the Lord about the proper role of your sexuality in the kingdom of God. Ask the Holy Spirit to give you a vision for the kingdom of God and to reveal the ways that your sexuality conforms to His will for your life. Write down what the Lord shows you.

✠   ✠   ✠   ✠   ✠   ✠   ✠

NOTES:_____

_____

_____

_____

_____

_____

_____

_____

_____

_____

_____

_____

_____

Then the word of the LORD came to him, "Arise, go to Zarephath, which belongs to Sidon, and dwell there. Behold, I have commanded a widow there to feed you."

So he arose and went to Zarephath. And when he came to the gate of the city, behold, a widow was there gathering sticks. And he called to her and said, "Bring me a little water in a vessel, that I may drink." And as she was going to bring it, he called to her and said, "Bring me a morsel of bread in your hand."

And she said, "As the LORD your God lives, I have nothing baked, only a handful of flour in a jar and a little oil in a jug. And now I am gathering a couple of sticks that I may go in and prepare it for myself and my son, that we may eat it and die."

And Elijah said to her, "Do not fear; go and do as you have said. But first make me a little cake of it and bring it to me, and afterward make something for yourself and your son. For thus says the LORD, the God of Israel, 'The jar of flour shall not be spent, and the jug of oil shall not be empty, until the day that the LORD sends rain upon the earth.'"

And she went and did as Elijah said. And she and he and her household ate for many days. **1Kings 17:8-15**

For myself and my son, that we may eat of it and die.

This story focuses on the great prophet, Elijah. But this story also concerns the call of the widow at Zarephath to whom Elijah was sent by the Lord.

It was hard in those days to be a widow. But it was even harder to be a widow with a son to feed in a time of severe famine. She and her son faced imminent death by starvation.

The widow lived in the pagan kingdom of Sidon. (Elijah was familiar with that pagan kingdom because his nemesis, Queen Jezebel, was the daughter of the king of Sidon.) Based on what Jesus later said about the widow at Zarephath, she was not an Israelite (Luke 4:25-26). But she knew something of the Lord as He had commanded her to feed Elijah before Elijah arrived. In obedience, she gave her last remaining provisions to the prophet and fed him. Then God provided for her, her son, and for Elijah.

But the story does not end there. The widow's son fell sick and died. In her grief, the widow chastised Elijah about her son's death. Elijah took her son's body and prayed to the Lord. He covered her son with his own body three (3) times. And the Lord raised him from the dead.

That miracle is noteworthy because until that time there had been many miracles by God. Moses parted the waters of the Red Sea, people were healed of leprosy and other illnesses, and the walls of Jericho fell before Joshua and the children of Israel.

But the raising of the widow's son is the <u>first</u> time in the Bible that anyone was raised from the dead. God was not only the God of miracles, but He was the God Who had power over life and death!

Understand that many religious people at that time (just like the Sadducees) thought that death was the end. The grave was the end of life. The widow's faith led to a foreshadowing of the resurrection of the body – a demonstration of the great power of our awesome God!

Meditation: Imagine the plight of the widow of Zarephath. What did she feel as her food supply dwindled and death seemed imminent for her and her son?

What was she thinking when Elijah asked for food from her? What surrender did that request require? What hope did she feel when the food did not run out?

Then her son dies. What is she feeling then?

What joy did she experience when God raised her son from the dead through the power and spirit of Elijah? Ask God to help you feel the joy of resurrection through His great and awesome love.

The call of the Lord is important in our life as it connects us to our role in His kingdom and to our destiny in Him. Don't have an expectation about timing. He will call you when it is time. But do seek Him often about your role and destiny in Him.

> And I am sure of this, that he who began a good work in you will bring it to completion at the day of Jesus Christ. **Phil 1:6**

Review your notes over the past week. What areas of surrender in your own life did you note?

- Mary, blessed among women, fulfilled her call to be the mother of our Lord and Savior.

- Abraham became the father of many nations and is the spiritual father of all who believe in Jesus Christ.

- Joseph became the prime minister of Egypt and saved his family.

- Moses delivered his people. Moses and Elijah both appeared with Jesus in the Transfiguration.

- Paul was the apostle to the Gentiles and expanded the kingdom of God into many hearts and souls.

- The widow of Zarephath served as the hostess of Elijah, the great prophet of God, and rejoiced in the life of her son.

Meditation: Today we focus on the goodness of God. God has a good plan for your life. Spend time in gratitude and joy for the good plans that God has for you. Exercise faith that He will complete the good work that He began within you.

Be assured!

☩   ☩   ☩   ☩   ☩   ☩   ☩

NOTES:_____

_____

_____

_____

_____

> When they had finished breakfast, Jesus said to Simon Peter, "Simon, son of John, do you love me more than these?" He said to him, "Yes, Lord; you know that I love you." He said to him, "Feed my lambs."
> **John 21:15**

"Simon, son of John, do you love Me more than these?"

Desire can be a good thing. Not every desire finds its source in human depravity. God has placed desires within us that are holy, pure, and godly – the foremost of which is a desire for Him. God has placed desires within us that arise from the gifts and character that He has given us so that we can fulfill our call in Him. But even good desires – godly desires – can be misinterpreted or misapplied.

The days following Jesus' death and crucifixion were confusing to Jesus' disciples. Their expectations of an earthly rule did not materialize. It slowly dawned upon them what the kingdom of God meant. Peter was no doubt shaken – both by the crucifixion and by his betrayal of Jesus. So Peter went back to what Peter knew and loved. He fell back on a basic desire that he had. Peter went fishing with his fellow disciples.

As Peter was fishing, Jesus appeared on the shore. After another miraculous catch of fish, Peter realized it was Jesus and swam to Him from the boat. Following a breakfast that Jesus prepared, Jesus asks Peter the question *"Simon, son of John, do you love me more than these?"*

Many people think Jesus was asking if Peter loved Him more than the other disciples. But other people think Jesus was asking Peter if he loved Him more than the fish, the nets, and the fishing gear that had been pulled to shore. The translation from the Greek is not clear.

What is clear is that this interaction is a second call from Jesus to Peter that parallels Peter's first call. Both times Peter was fishing. Both times there was a miraculous catch. And both times Jesus calls Peter to Himself.

At the first call, Jesus told Peter and his fellow fishermen *"Follow me, and I will make you fishers of men"* (Matt 4:19b). This second time, Jesus is calling Peter again. It is as if He is saying "You know you love to fish. But that desire has godly purpose. Use that desire to draw people into the kingdom of God."

Perhaps more importantly, Jesus asks Peter if he loves Him. Jesus is restoring Peter and is reminding him of the love which they share. Jesus is calling Peter back to Himself.

The foundation for the proper (ordered) application of Peter's desire to fish is Peter's love for Jesus. The loving relationship with the Lord is primary and it guides the proper application of the desires He has given us.

Unbeknownst to Peter, within a short period of time, under the power of the Holy Spirit, Peter would cast his spiritual net and draw 3000 souls into the kingdom of God (Acts 2:41).

Meditation: Identify three desires of your heart that are good and godly. Write them down. Ask the Holy Spirit to reveal to you the reasons that these desires exist.

What has the Lord shown you about the application and fulfillment of those godly desires?

✠   ✠   ✠   ✠   ✠   ✠   ✠

NOTES:_____

_____

_____

_____

_____

_____

_____

_____

_____

_____

_____

And there came a man of God to Eli and said to him, "Thus says the LORD, 'Did I indeed reveal myself to the house of your father when they were in Egypt subject to the house of Pharaoh? Did I choose him out of all the tribes of Israel to be my priest, to go up to my altar, to burn incense, to wear an ephod before me? I gave to the house of your father all my offerings by fire from the people of Israel. Why then do you scorn my sacrifices and my offerings that I commanded for my dwelling, and honor your sons above me by fattening yourselves on the choicest parts of every offering of my people Israel?'

Therefore the LORD, the God of Israel, declares: 'I promised that your house and the house of your father should go in and out before me forever,' but now the LORD declares: 'Far be it from me, for those who honor me I will honor, and those who despise me shall be lightly esteemed. Behold, the days are coming when I will cut off your strength and the strength of your father's house, so that there will not be an old man in your house.'" **1 Sam 2:27-31**

"Why then do you honor your sons above Me?"

Your beloved is of that nature that He will admit of no rival, but will have your heart alone, and sit on His throne as King. If you could empty yourself perfectly from all creatures, Jesus would willingly dwell with you.[41]

This story concerns Eli. We have already described the sins of Eli's sons, Hophni and Phinehas, and their contempt for the Lord and for His offering. [II.Week Eight, Day 5]. But in this story, the Lord rebukes their father, Eli.

God gives many people a godly desire for family and children. Even more, He often grants a desire for heritage to the family so that the children follow in the steps of their parents. God's intention was to grant both family and priestly heritage to Eli.

But Eli not only had an inordinate attachment to food. He had an inordinate desire for his children that became disordered. He allowed his sons to misbehave and to abuse the priestly authority they had. Eli's desire for his sons grew larger than Eli's desire for the Lord. *"Why then do you honor your sons above Me?"* Eli worshipped his children.

---

[41] *The Imitation of Christ*, p. 74.

Children worship is a significant problem in our culture. Parents in the last few generations have tended to worship their children. The parents give everything for the child thinking that they are blessing the child. In fact, children worship is often a form of surrogate narcissism by the parent. And the result is a self indulged child who unrealistically expects worship (or at least deference) from the rest of the world. Parents should love their children wholly and healthily, but children worship is not conducive to training and godliness.

Godly desires can be misinterpreted and misapplied. This disorder occurs when we allow the desire we feel to surpass our desire for the Lord.

Meditation: Write down desires that you believe God has put into your heart. Take your time and explore things that motivate you and things that excite you.

Now, using your list, consider how you have interpreted these desires and how you have applied them. Are there any instances in which these desires have become disordered?

Now submit these desires to God. Seek God about how He intends the desires to be fulfilled.

---

‡   ‡   ‡   ‡   ‡   ‡   ‡

NOTES:_____

_____

_____

_____

_____

_____

_____

_____

> I do not write these things to make you ashamed, but to admonish you as my beloved children. For though you have countless guides in Christ, you do not have many fathers. For I became your father in Christ Jesus through the gospel.
>
> I urge you, then, be imitators of me. That is why I sent you Timothy, my beloved and faithful child in the Lord, to remind you of my ways in Christ, as I teach them everywhere in every church. 1 Cor 4:14-17

For though you have countless guides in Christ, you do not have many fathers.

My grandparents, Papa and Meme, had nine children and as if that wasn't enough, they adopted a Down's Syndrome child, Jimmy. One day, they had a visitor from church who came to see them. The visitor and Papa sat down on the front porch to play a game of checkers and talk. As they were playing, children started walking by and going in and out - first one child, and then another.

The visitor watched all these children for a while and then asked, "Where do all these children come from?"

Papa said, "They're my children."

The visitor was a little surprised. "All of them?"

Papa said, "Yes. All of them."

The visitor pondered for a minute. Then he asked, "Why did you have all these children, Tom?"

Papa chuckled and then said, "Well, you know the Bible says to be fruitful and multiply, and to replenish the earth."

The visitor paused and said, "Well, you're right. The Bible does say that. But it doesn't say that you're supposed to do it all by yourself!"[42]

Paul is exhorting the Corinthian church. In this passage, Paul labels the Corinthians and Timothy as his children. Paul is their father. God put the desire for parenthood into Paul's heart in order to fulfill His call.

God puts the desire for reproduction and for parenthood into many hearts. The natural desire parallels a kingdom principle. Multiple times God commanded man: *"Be fruitful and multiply"* (Gen 1:28; 9:1; 35:11).

---

[42] Quoted from *Dod Knows* (by the author).

"Be fruitful and multiply!" is a command for labor in the kingdom of God. Reproductive passions can be godly desires. But godly desires for reproduction can be misapplied. Reproductive desires can lead to lust, pornography, and sexual immorality as the flesh, the world, and the devil twist them and abuse them.

We have already discussed Paul and his sacrifice of sexuality for the sake of the kingdom of God. [II.Week Eleven, Day 5]. As the scripture for today shows, Paul correctly interpreted his desire for fatherhood and its function within his call.

Another manner in which a desire for parenthood can be wrongly applied is in the role of authority and rule in the household. Children can be viewed as subjects of the parent's kingdom – mere vassals. It is an abuse of authority. The children exist for the pleasure and whim of the parent.

But Paul also did not apply his desire this way. He served the churches that he fathered and did not lord his status over them for selfish ends.

Meditation: Today is a day of quiet listening. Eliminate all distractions and try to settle your mind.

Spend time listening to the nudge or movement of the Holy Spirit. Write down any words you sense. Note any movement of your feelings.

✝ ✝ ✝ ✝ ✝ ✝ ✝

NOTES:_____

_____

_____

_____

_____

_____

_____

Rehoboam went to Shechem, for all Israel had come to Shechem to make him king. And as soon as Jeroboam the son of Nebat heard of it (for he was still in Egypt, where he had fled from King Solomon), then Jeroboam returned from Egypt. And they sent and called him, and Jeroboam and all the assembly of Israel came and said to Rehoboam, "Your father made our yoke heavy. Now therefore lighten the hard service of your father and his heavy yoke on us, and we will serve you."

He said to them, "Go away for three days, then come again to me." So the people went away.

Then King Rehoboam took counsel with the old men, who had stood before Solomon his father while he was yet alive, saying, "How do you advise me to answer this people?" And they said to him, "If you will be a servant to this people today and serve them, and speak good words to them when you answer them, then they will be your servants forever."

But he abandoned the counsel that the old men gave him and took counsel with the young men who had grown up with him and stood before him. And he said to them, "What do you advise that we answer this people who have said to me, 'Lighten the yoke that your father put on us'?" And the young men who had grown up with him said to him, "Thus shall you speak to this people who said to you, 'Your father made our yoke heavy, but you lighten it for us,' thus shall you say to them, 'My little finger is thicker than my father's thighs. And now, whereas my father laid on you a heavy yoke, I will add to your yoke. My father disciplined you with whips, but I will discipline you with scorpions.'" So Jeroboam and all the people came to Rehoboam the third day, as the king said, "Come to me again the third day."

And the king answered the people harshly, and forsaking the counsel that the old men had given him, he spoke to them according to the counsel of the young men, saying, "My father made your yoke heavy, but I will add to your yoke. My father disciplined you with whips, but I will discipline you with scorpions."

1 Kings 12:1-14

"My little finger is thicker than my father's thighs."

O God, I need YOU to show me every Offensive way in my life, in my thoughts, in my choices, in my words! Help me to seek You to reveal them to me, because I don't know them all.

<u>Sin has a way of being very crafty and hiding in my flesh that likes to get its own way while hiding behind a cover of looking like it is being Godly and submissive to You!</u> O come and expose to me every place that this is happening.

Self-righteousness is a powerful cloak of evil, offensiveness, wickedness, Self-ishness, resulting in my embracing the offensive, evil, etc. while thinking I am being very good! Come and try/test me and show me—show me in ways that I cannot refute the truth— that I need to change and be delivered from that missing the mark!
–Pastor Daniel Martin, 5/26/13

The kingdom of Israel reached the height of its earthly glory and power under King Solomon. Rehoboam was Solomon's son and the heir to his throne. Israel came to Rehoboam to make him their king as he had been chosen.

The Lord places many people in positions of authority and rule – in government, in courts, in schools, in homes, and even in churches. But the purpose of authority from the Lord is to serve the people subject to that authority – a purpose that Rehoboam's older advisers seemed (in appearance at least) to understand.

But Rehoboam did not correctly interpret or apply his desire for rule. His passion catered to fleshly appetites for control, domination, and self glory. When he let his passions be known, his disordered desire cost him the greater part of his kingdom. Any person who exercises authority out of self interest or a disordered desire abuses the people around him, and will lose their affection if not their allegiance.

Any kingdom authority that is used for self interest or self glory is an abomination to the Lord.

Meditation: Identify areas of authority that the Lord has given you or for which you have a desire. Write them down in your journal. Ask the Lord to purify your desires in the areas of authority and rule so that they are used only for His glory and His kingdom, and not for your own fleshly desires or weaknesses.

╬   ╬   ╬   ╬   ╬   ╬   ╬

Stay in touch with your feelings during these devotions. If you feel an emotion rising with you, then note it and take time to explore the reasons why it exists.

> And with great power the apostles were giving their testimony to the resurrection of the Lord Jesus, and great grace was upon them all. There was not a needy person among them, for as many as were owners of lands or houses sold them and brought the proceeds of what was sold and laid it at the apostles' feet, and it was distributed to each as any had need.
>
> Thus Joseph, who was also called by the apostles Barnabas (which means son of encouragement), a Levite, a native of Cyprus, sold a field that belonged to him and brought the money and laid it at the apostles' feet. **Acts 4:33-37**

Which means "son of encouragement."

Nicknames often reflect a person's character and passion. From this account, we know what fueled Joseph. He had such a heart for people and he encouraged the saints so much that they called him Barnabas – the "son of encouragement." The nickname fit him so well he was called Barnabas through the rest of scripture.

I personally have known a brother who has this passion for encouragement and he edifies many people. Barnabas had such a heart for people that he sold his land and surrendered the proceeds to the apostles to use for saints in need. Later, he would play a vital role in the encouragement and development of Paul (Acts 9 and 11).

But after the first missionary journey together, Barnabas and Paul had a "sharp disagreement" (Acts 15:39). Paul did not want to take Mark again because Mark had turned back in the first trip. Barnabas had godly desire to encourage and to develop young leaders. This desire led Barnabas to promote Mark and not to drop him despite his earlier failure. Barnabas and Paul disagreed so strongly that they parted ways. So did Barnabas misapply the desire that God put in his heart?

Scripture isn't clear. He could have. So how do we distinguish between ordered desires and disordered desires in our own lives? How do we determine when a godly desire is being misinterpreted or misapplied?

David Benner says:

One of the ways I have found helpful to distinguish between ordered and disordered desires is the particular, though sometimes subtle, effect each has on me. Ordered – or purified – desires expand me and connect me to others and the world in life-enhancing ways. Disordered desires suck me into myself and rather than adding vitality to life, leach it away. This is because ordered desires spring from willingness and surrender, while disordered ones are my willful attempt to arrange for my own happiness and fulfillment.[43]

Ordered desires lead to life while disordered desires lead to death.

Meditation: Look back at Day 2 of this week and review the godly desires of your heart that you identified. Add any other desires that you have discovered since them.

Then consider how you apply those desires in your own life. Reread the quote above, and discern if these desires are being applied in ways that are ordered, ways that are disordered, or both.

Ask the Lord to help you use these desires in the ways that God intended as you walk on your journey.

✝   ✝   ✝   ✝   ✝   ✝   ✝

NOTES:_____

_____

_____

_____

_____

_____

_____

_____

---

[43] *Desiring God's Will*, pp. 81-82.

When they had finished breakfast, Jesus said to Simon Peter, "Simon, son of John, do you love me more than these?" He said to him, "Yes, Lord; you know that I love you." He said to him, "Feed my lambs."

He said to him a second time, "Simon, son of John, do you love me?" He said to him, "Yes, Lord; you know that I love you." He said to him, "Tend my sheep."

He said to him the third time, "Simon, son of John, do you love me?" Peter was grieved because he said to him the third time, "Do you love me?" and he said to him, "Lord, you know everything; you know that I love you." Jesus said to him, "Feed my sheep. Truly, truly, I say to you, when you were young, you used to dress yourself and walk wherever you wanted, but when you are old, you will stretch out your hands, and another will dress you and carry you where you do not want to go." (This he said to show by what kind of death he was to glorify God.) And after saying this he said to him, "Follow me." **John 21:15-19**

Tend My sheep.

This story continues Jesus' restoration of relationship with Peter, and His second call to him. Jesus tenderly restores Peter's relationship of love with Him. Then He calls Peter again.

But when Jesus calls Peter again, He does not just remind Peter of the first call to be a "fisher of men." Jesus goes deeper into a call and desire of which Peter may not even be aware – a call to shepherd the flock of God. Jesus is calling Peter to pastoral ministry.

Often God has placed deep desires in us that we do not even realize. David Benner says: *"Most of us do not even know our deepest desires."* Then he says *"The only way to know our deepest desires is to start with our surface desires that we can access and to follow them downward to our underlying longings."*[44]

---

[44] *Desiring God's Will*, pp. 79-80.

In our story, Peter knew that he was a fisherman. He knew his heart, his talents, his training, and his instincts screamed "fisherman." But Jesus reveals a deeper desire to Peter – a desire to shepherd. The desire is connected to a call that Peter would fulfill over his life and ministry. Thus, Peter gives instructions to shepherds in his epistle and calls himself a "fellow elder" (1 Pet 5:1-5).

Meditation: Spend time seeking the Lord about the deepest desires of your heart. Ask the Holy Spirit to reveal to you any desires or passions of which you do not have awareness.

Trust God to speak to your heart in His time about the call that He has appointed.

✝ ✝ ✝ ✝ ✝ ✝ ✝

NOTES:_____

_____

_____

_____

_____

_____

_____

_____

Don't neglect your journal during your devotions. You will want to refer back to these sections on desire and call in the future.

O God, come and sanctify my desires!

Show me where they need to change, where I need to stop feeding wrong ones, and how I need to feed Yours!! Come and deliver me in this!

O correct all "disordered desires" in my life!!

Change me!!   -Pastor Daniel Martin, 1/25/13

Review your notes over the past week.

Meditation: Today is a day of repentance. It is a day to confess to the Lord desires, passions, and appetites that you have misunderstood, misapplied, or misused. It is a day to confess desires that are disordered and are not used in the ways that God intended. Repent of occasions that you have acted on your desires in ways that were selfish, self pleasing, or self glorifying.

During this time, you can use physical actions such as kneeling, crying, emoting, or humbling yourself ("sackcloth and ashes") to express your repentance to the Lord as you are led to do so.

Then ask God to help you use your godly desires in ways that He intended. Surrender your desires, passions, and appetites to Him. Tell Him that you want to use them for His glory, and to please Him and not to please yourself.

✝   ✝   ✝   ✝   ✝   ✝   ✝

NOTES:_____

_____

_____

_____

_____

_____

_____

_____

(This final week of Section II is a practicum on seeking living water – the flow of the Holy Spirit in our lives. During this time we seek the Lord for grace for His flow.)

II.Week Thirteen, Day 1 (Date:)   **PRACTICUM: DRIP, TRICKLE, FLOW**

Then he brought me back to the door of the temple, and behold, water was issuing from below the threshold of the temple toward the east (for the temple faced east). The water was flowing down from below the south end of the threshold of the temple, south of the altar. Then he brought me out by way of the north gate and led me around on the outside to the outer gate that faces toward the east; and behold, the water was trickling out on the south side.

Going on eastward with a measuring line in his hand, the man measured a thousand cubits, and then led me through the water, and it was ankle-deep. Again he measured a thousand, and led me through the water, and it was knee-deep. Again he measured a thousand, and led me through the water, and it was waist-deep.

Again he measured a thousand, and it was a river that I could not pass through, for the water had risen. It was deep enough to swim in, a river that could not be passed through. And he said to me, "Son of man, have you seen this?" Then he led me back to the bank of the river. As I went back, I saw on the bank of the river very many trees on the one side and on the other.

And he said to me, "This water flows toward the eastern region and goes down into the Arabah, and enters the sea; when the water flows into the sea, the water will become fresh. And wherever the river goes, every living creature that swarms will live, and there will be very many fish. For this water goes there, that the waters of the sea may become fresh; so everything will live where the river goes. Fishermen will stand beside the sea. From Engedi to Eneglaim it will be a place for the spreading of nets. Its fish will be of very many kinds, like the fish of the Great Sea. But its swamps and marshes will not become fresh; they are to be left for salt. And on the banks, on both sides of the river, there will grow all kinds of trees for food. Their leaves will not wither, nor their fruit fail, but they will bear fresh fruit every month, because the water for them flows from the sanctuary. Their fruit will be for food, and their leaves for healing." **Eze 47:1-12**

When the water flows into the sea, the water will become fresh.

This vision of Ezekiel, the son of man, occurs near the end of the Book of Ezekiel. Flowing from the temple and the Presence of God are life-giving streams of water.

Note the increasing flow of this stream of life as it progresses further and further. At the gate, the flow is a trickle (or a ripple). But as Ezekiel is led along the flow, it is ankle-deep; then knee-deep; then waist-deep; and then so voluminous it was deep enough to swim in. The journey of the prophet led him to deeper and deeper water.

As we walk with the Lord and our level of surrender in Him goes deeper and deeper, the anointing of His Spirit in our lives increases as well. Drip, then trickle, then flow.

Meditation: As you read the Ezekiel 47 passage slowly, close your eyes and imagine what Ezekiel is seeing and experiencing. See the water as it increases. Imagine the prophet in the flow of life – ankle-deep; knee-deep; waist-deep; and then swimming.

Now, imagine the water as it hits the sea – here, the Dead Sea (Eze 47:8). The Dead Sea is the lowest elevation on the surface of the earth. It is the DEAD Sea – a body of water so salty that fish and aquatic plants can't live in it.

But now the river of life hits the Dead Sea. But the Dead Sea doesn't bring death to the river. No, instead the river brings life to the Dead Sea. See the life – the teeming fish and the fishermen.

Finally, imagine the trees along both sides of the river. They absorb their life from the river through their roots into the trunk and into the branches. Look at the fruit which is spiritual food and feel the leaves which are healing for the nations.

What desire or longing does this vision place within you? Write about it.

✠   ✠   ✠   ✠   ✠   ✠   ✠

NOTES:_____

_____

_____

_____

_____

> Has a nation changed its gods, even though they are no gods? But my people have changed their glory for that which does not profit. Be appalled, O heavens, at this; be shocked, be utterly desolate, declares the LORD, for my people have committed two evils: they have forsaken me, the fountain of living waters, and hewed out cisterns for themselves, broken cisterns that can hold no water. **Jer 2:11-13**

They have hewed out cisterns – broken cisterns that can hold no water.

God is the fountain of living waters. He calls for his people to partake of a life giving flow. This invitation is issued throughout scripture. God tells His people "Come!"

But this passage from Jeremiah describes vessels that can hold no water. The people of God have not only forsaken Him for other gods, but they also have become broken cisterns that hold no water. These are two evils. But what if there is only one evil? What if the people of God have not forsaken Him? What if the people of God still believe in Him, but they still have made themselves broken cisterns that can hold no water?

The vessel is important. Time spent with the Lord can repair our hearts and prepare our hearts to receive the fountain of living waters.

Mediation: Spend time with these words: "appalled," "shocked," and "desolate." Why does the prophet use these words in this passage?

Next, meditate on the line: *"But My people have changed their glory for that which does not profit."* What does this line mean? What is the glory? What is that which does not profit?

What type of vessel does the prophet describe here that makes this type of exchange?

⚜   ⚜   ⚜   ⚜   ⚜   ⚜   ⚜

> Grace is something that is not earned. Here we seek a grace – a flow of the Spirit. As you seek this grace, receive His grace. It is something that God wants to give and wants His people to have. It comes from the very heart of God.

NOTES:_____

_____

_____

_____

_____

_____

_____

_____

_____

_____

_____

_____

_____

_____

_____

_____

_____

_____

> O God, you are my God; earnestly I seek you; my soul thirsts for you; my flesh faints for you, as in a dry and weary land where there is no water. **Psa 63:1** A Psalm of David, when he was in the wilderness of Judah.

My soul thirsts for you.

O God, I have tasted Your goodness, and it has both satisfied me and made me thirsty for more. I am painfully conscious of my need of further grace.

I am ashamed of my lack of desire.

O God, I want to want You; I long to be filled with longing;

I thirst to be made more thirsty still.

Show me Your glory, I pray, so I may know You indeed.

Begin in mercy a new work of love within me.

Say to my soul, "Rise up, my love, my fair one, and come away."

Then give me grace to rise and follow You

up from this misty lowland

where I have wandered so long.[45]

O God, how this child needs You! Needs You restoring him in so many ways—memory, energy, healing, rejuvenating, energizing. Also needing Deeper and Deeper Longings, Yearnings, Desires, and Devotion, Commitment to You.   –Pastor Daniel Martin, 8/1/19

David is in the wilderness where water is scarce. He and his men must be thirsty. But David realizes that it is really his soul that thirsts.

A desert, an illness, loneliness, or desolation is a difficult place. But they can be a blessing to the child of God if those difficult places cause a thirst in the child's heart.

I recall the first time that I was actually thirsty for God – a time when I really desired Him. I was nineteen years old. My older sister, Rebecca, worked for the telephone company on a late shift, but I stayed up many times until she got home.

One evening, she didn't come home. I waited and waited, but she didn't come in. We didn't have cell phones back then, so I got in my car and went out along her route to find her. My search took me almost to Montgomery but I didn't see anything. On the way back, I stopped at a gas station to call home to see if somehow I had missed her.

---

[45] Quoted by Pastor Martin from A. W. Tozer, *The Pursuit of God* p.12 (N/P 1948).

At the gas station, there was a highway patrolman. He was talking about a bad accident that happened that evening. The car he described matched Rebecca's car and the age of the victim matched her as well. Rebecca had been in a bad car wreck. Her vehicle had been broadsided by a speeding car that ran a stop sign.

I rushed home and woke up my parents. We rushed to the hospital. Rebecca had severe injuries. She had broken bones including broken ribs. I stayed at the hospital until early morning when the doctors got her stabilized. Then most of us went home to get some rest.

Around Noon the next day, we got a call from the hospital that things had taken a turn for the worse. The doctors found that one of the broken ribs had punctured Rebecca's liver and she had internal bleeding. They were going into emergency surgery to try to save her life.

After that call, my parents, my siblings, and I went to the living room. We fell on our knees and began crying out to God. When I say "crying out," I mean crying out! We weren't holding anything back. We were thirsty for God and desired with all our hearts that God would intervene on Rebecca's behalf.

And it wasn't for a short period of time. We spent hours praying, beseeching, crying, and interceding with God for Rebecca. We were thirsty!

I don't know how long it was, but we got a call late that afternoon that Rebecca survived the surgery. Her recovery took months, but she lived and is still alive 50 years later. But I will never forget the fervent manner in which we sought God.
      – Pastor Daniel Martin

Thirst for God is a spring of life. Emptiness results from lack of felt need for God. If we don't feel as if we need God, then we don't long for His living waters. The vessel that is filled is the vessel that thirsts and faints for the life-giving flow. This type of vessel will be filled.

> **Meditation:** Describe a time in your life when you were thirsty for God – when you desired Him so much that you cried out to Him. Write about this time in your journal.
>
> Then search your heart and its desires. What is the state of your vessel? How thirsty are you for the life-giving flow of the Spirit? Ask Him to fill you with living waters.

✝   ✝   ✝   ✝   ✝   ✝   ✝

> Don't force things as you experience the Lord. Allow Him to work and to move as He sees fit in your heart. Seek and even seek intensely. But allow movement to come from His Spirit.

> On the last day of the feast, the great day, Jesus stood up and cried out, "If anyone thirsts, let him come to me and drink. Whoever believes in me, as the Scripture has said, 'Out of his heart will flow rivers of living water.'"
>
> Now this he said about the Spirit, whom those who believed in him were to receive, for as yet the Spirit had not been given, because Jesus was not yet glorified. **John 7:37-39**

"If anyone thirsts, let him come to Me and drink."

Let this Love, Grace, and Communion flow into my life in a steady stream all day today!

This child/sheep needs more and more of these Life-giving STREAMS!! Come and quench this thirsting of my soul with them!

As I typed those words I also realized that I need DEEPER THIRST in my soul, thirst that is satisfied with the flow, but that also increases with the flow instead of thinking it has enough!

Satisfies, but at the same time creates longing for more!!

O give me this glorious thirst!   –Pastor Daniel Martin, 10/9/14

In his Gospel, John notes that it is the last day of the Feast – the "great day." Jesus stands up and publicly cries out. It isn't coincidental that Jesus chooses this occasion to cry out about living waters. By tradition during the Feast of Tabernacles, the priest drew water from the pool of Siloam and poured it out below the altar as the people sang the words of Isa 12:3 - *With joy you will draw water from the wells of salvation.*[46]

At the Feast, Jesus is offering the actual fulfillment of the Feast. Jesus is not offering water that is poured out and then stops. Jesus is offering a flow of rivers of living water.

Drip, trickle, flow is not just about increasing volume; drip, trickle, flow is also about increasing desire. Some seek the Lord and receive occasional drips. The drips taste good so there may be temporary satisfaction from a few drips. "Oh my! That tasted good! I'm okay now."

Pastor Martin says *"I need DEEPER THIRST in my soul, thirst that is satisfied with the flow, but that also increases with the flow instead of thinking it has enough!"* After a drip, some vessels go deeper and then they experience a trickle. Then Jesus offers a flow – a flow to the one who thirsts for that flow.

---

[46] Source: *Jamieson, Fausset, and Brown Commentary* on Jn. 7:37.

Mediation: Today is a day of seeking the Lord for a flow. Eliminate all distractions. Try to quiet your mind and any other interference.

Spend time with the Lord seeking His Spirit. Repeat John 7:37-39 slowly. Then pray that scripture. Seek God for a flow of rivers of living water within you.

NOTES:_____

_____

_____

_____

_____

_____

_____

_____

_____

_____

_____

_____

_____

_____

_____

Jesus answered her, "If you knew the gift of God, and who it is that is saying to you, 'Give me a drink,' you would have asked him, and he would have given you living water."

The woman said to him, "Sir, you have nothing to draw water with, and the well is deep. Where do you get that living water? Are you greater than our father Jacob? He gave us the well and drank from it himself, as did his sons and his livestock."

Jesus said to her, "Everyone who drinks of this water will be thirsty again, but whoever drinks of the water that I will give him will never be thirsty again. The water that I will give him will become in him a spring of water welling up to eternal life."

The woman said to him, "Sir, give me this water, so that I will not be thirsty or have to come here to draw water." **John 4:10-15**

Worship in truth.

O, how much Proverbs 25:26 applies to this. If the Godly give in to the wicked, it's like polluting a fountain or muddying a spring. O Father, deliver me from this!

Come and help me to so live the truth, that it doesn't matter what the cost, I am willing to go with TRUTH and not allow lies to pollute and muddy Your life-giving streams! O, I need You hourly in this thing, O God of TRUTH!

O God, for a clean heart—with no polluting or muddying allowed in it. Cleanse my heart, O God, come and do a deep and powerful cleansing in it.

Remove all sin—remove all propensities toward sin. O, deliver me from all evil on every level of my being.

Come and have Your own way in me, O precious Lamb of God! I need You so much!

Come Thou Fount of every blessing, Tune My Heart, make all needed Adjustments to it, and Align my heart with You, Your ways, and Your word!!   -Pastor Daniel Martin, 10/9/14

The woman at the well was a thirsty vessel. When she spoke with Jesus, she thought they were discussing physical water. But when Jesus saw her, he immediately saw a thirsty soul - the type of soul that had a longing for a spring of water that wells up to eternal life. So Jesus instructed her and offered her this flow.

Jesus said to her, "Woman, believe me, the hour is coming when neither on this mountain nor in Jerusalem will you worship the Father. You worship what you do not know; we worship what we know, for salvation is from the Jews. But the hour is coming, and is now here, when the true worshipers will worship the Father in spirit and truth, for the Father is seeking such people to worship him.

"God is spirit, and those who worship him must worship in spirit and truth."
John 4:21-24

True worshipers will worship in Spirit and in truth. This command concerns the state of the vessel. God desires pure vessels – conduits, if you will, so that the living water remains pure, not muddied or polluted.

But this command also hits at motivation. An interesting dynamic can occur. A person can deny the flesh and live purely in order to seek the flow of the living water. But when a touch of the Lord occurs, the touch is used to gratify the flesh – to make oneself feel good or to tingle with excitement of divine connection. Self denial and seeking can still be used to gratify fleshly longing.

Our motive should be the Spirit and the truth. Our desire and our purpose should be to experience the Lord – for His glory and for His pleasure – without regard to how it makes us feel. Maybe that is one reason that the Lord often shows up when we *don't* feel good. If He is our true desire, then He will take care of everything else.

Meditation: As you continue to seek God for the flow of living water, seek Him about cleansing your vessel. Reread Pastor Martin's devotion.

Seek God about what type of cleansing is needed. Spend some time on the words **"Align my heart with You, Your ways, and Your word!"** Make this your prayer as you discern your motivations.

Don't neglect meeting with your mentor or devotional partner to share your notes and to discuss your experience. As we approach the end of the second quarter, please set aside time to review and to process your devotional journey. A quarterly retreat is highly recommended!

Three of the thirty chief men went down to the rock to David at the cave of Adullam, when the army of Philistines was encamped in the Valley of Rephaim. David was then in the stronghold, and the garrison of the Philistines was then at Bethlehem.

And David said longingly, "Oh that someone would give me water to drink from the well of Bethlehem that is by the gate!"

Then the three mighty men broke through the camp of the Philistines and drew water out of the well of Bethlehem that was by the gate and took it and brought it to David. But David would not drink it. He poured it out to the LORD and said,

"Far be it from me before my God that I should do this. Shall I drink the lifeblood of these men? For at the risk of their lives they brought it." Therefore he would not drink it. These things did the three mighty men. **1 Chr 11:15-20**

David is thirsty for a certain type of water.

I live in Charlotte. Our water supply is drawn from the Catawba River. Before the water reaches the faucet in my home, the water is treated with all sorts of chemicals such as fluoride and chlorine. I don't know what chemicals are used but I can taste them.

My wife's family lived in a remote area in the mountains where the water came from a well. My mother-in-law once commented to my wife that I must like mountain water. She said that when I arrived to visit, one of the first things that I did was to pour a glass of water from the kitchen faucet and drink it. She was right! That water tasted good, pure, and crisp to me – like the water of home.

Bethlehem is a special place. Bethlehem was David's home. But at this moment, Bethlehem is occupied by the Philistines.

David is thirsty. But he has a specific thirst. He longs for the water of home – the water that comes from the well at Bethlehem. Water has a specific flavor.

This water that David desires had such value to David's three mighty men that they are willing to fight for it. The desire of the three mighty men for the water is so great that they risk their lives to obtain it. They have an overpowering desire and they act on it.

When they deliver the water to David, He could drink it and savor the taste of home. He could satisfy his flesh with it. But David understands the significance of the water. He knows that the water belongs to the Lord and not to him. The purpose of the water is not to satisfy his appetites. The purpose of the water is to honor the Lord and to use for the Lord's glory. So David pours the water out as an offering to the Lord.

Meditation: Can you identify with the water of home? If so, write about it in your journal.

Next, spend time with this story and what it means. As you do so, search your heart as to why you desire the living waters. What is your motivation in seeking a flow from the Lord? What use do you think that the Lord intends for the flow in your life?

NOTES:_____

_____

_____

_____

_____

_____

_____

_____

_____

_____

_____

_____

> Jesus said to them again, "Peace be with you. As the Father has sent me, even so I am sending you."
>
> And when he had said this, he breathed on them and said to them, "Receive the Holy Spirit. If you forgive the sins of any, they are forgiven them; if you withhold forgiveness from any, it is withheld."
> **John 20:21-23**

As the Father has sent Me, even so I am sending you.

O, Holy Spirit, come and flow freely through me with all the life, wisdom, knowledge, healing, power, and love You have at Your disposal.

I need You, Spirit of God.

Today I need Your Communion flowing to me, through me, and out into the darkness of the world around me!

Restore unto me, Daily, Hourly, the Deep Joy of Your salvation! Not just Your salvation in the sense of salvation from hell—but all the "salvations" that You are ready to release into my day, into my world, into the people and situations I touch each day— especially this one!

Come and show me that Jesus Saves, that You have Wells Of Salvation You are wanting me to draw from all day long today!

Come and teach me how I need to respond to Your Wells You have placed all around me, in Your Word, by Your Spirit—and then help me to Draw from those Wells and pour out Your grace, mercy, Life, Hope, and power onto the needs around me! O help me to Draw With Joy!

Help me to declare Your Word and Will with Boldness, having such a Hope within me that gives me the Boldness to do so!   -Pastor Daniel Martin, 10/9/14

Jesus told the apostles that they were being sent just as the Father had sent Jesus. Then He breathed on them and imparted the Holy Spirit. Jesus imparted the Holy Spirit with purpose.

Meditation: Today as we close this week on the flow of living water, focus on the purpose for which the Holy Spirit was given. Consider the apostles and what they did in response to the outpouring of the Holy Spirit. What does the flow of the Holy Spirit mean in your life – not just for you, but for the people and the world around you?

When the poor and needy seek water, and there is none, and their tongue is parched with thirst, I the LORD will answer them; I the God of Israel will not forsake them.

I will open rivers on the bare heights, and fountains in the midst of the valleys. I will make the wilderness a pool of water, and the dry land springs of water.

I will put in the wilderness the cedar, the acacia, the myrtle, and the olive. I will set in the desert the cypress, the plane and the pine together, that they may see and know, may consider and understand together, that the hand of the LORD has done this, the Holy One of Israel has created it.
Isa 41:17-20

✠ ✠ ✠ ✠ ✠ ✠ ✠

NOTES:_____

_____

_____

_____

_____

_____

_____

_____

_____

_____

_____

_____

_____

APPENDIX A

STEPS TO PEACE (From PSALM 37)

By Steve Parker

Sometimes we have a specific situation that appears to be troubling us constantly. We are caught up in thinking about it, worrying about it, and trying to come up with ways to change it. We spend a great deal of our days talking to others about it, sometimes to the point of becoming annoying.

Some people, it seems, are given to these types of anxieties more than others. Because anxiety is a form of fear, that is, being afraid of the results of a situation if we can't do something to change it, some of these people live a fear-based existence. They are afraid of what might happen each and every day in any given number of situations. If any part of this description applies to you, you may need to consider the Psalm 37 path to peace.

Before I go into the details on this scriptural cure for anxiety, let me give you some personal background on how I came to discover this remarkable tool. This is a story from when I was in prison. [It really is remarkable how much God did in my life when I was in prison. The whole experience was like a tailor-made discipleship school! Talk about "redeeming the time!" (Eph 5:16 NKJV)]

When first sentenced to prison, North Carolina inmates are sent to a processing center in the city of Salisbury. From there, they are supposed to be sent to a correctional facility that is close to their home. For me, that would have been near Asheville, up in the mountains of western North Carolina. But that wasn't what happened.

I was assigned to Tyrell Correctional Facility in Columbia, NC. You haven't heard of Columbia, NC? Neither had I. I was surprised to find it was a small town on the east coast of North Carolina - almost in the ocean. Not only was I not close to home, I was as far away as I could get and still be in North Carolina. This meant I wouldn't be getting visitors very often. I was disappointed about that. And it went downhill from there.

When I arrived at Tyrell, I found that it was one of the only prisons in the NC system that didn't have air conditioning. And because it was on the coast, it was hot, and I was sent there in June. I hated hot weather! And, for some reason, instead of being able to wear shorts and a t-shirt like you could at most prisons in North Carolina, we had to wear heavy jumpsuits whenever we were outdoors. I was truly miserable.

So how did I respond? I tried to fix it. I complained to whoever would listen to me. I went to my case manager. "I'm supposed to be in a prison close to my home," I said. He agreed with me, said he would see what he could do, and sent me away. I wrote letters to administrators. I called my mom and asked her to do something. She had a cousin in the State Legislature, so she asked him if he could help. He told her there wasn't really anything he could do. So, I continued to complain.

And most of all, I complained to God. Why was He letting this happen to me? After all, I had recommitted my life to Christ. I was trying to follow Him and become a better Christian. This didn't seem fair. And I told Him this. I prayed. And nothing happened. My misery deepened!

This went on for a couple months. Then, I picked up a little book in the prison library. I don't remember the name of the book or I would reference it. I do recall it had been written by a Lutheran pastor, and it was around 25 years old. It certainly didn't look like anything remarkable, but that little book was pure spiritual dynamite! Within its pages, a path was laid out that one could take to deal with anxiety-causing situations in one's life.

Based on the first eight verses of Psalm 37, here are the six steps from that book for moving from a place of worry to a place of continuing peace.

1.   *"Fret not yourself because of evildoers; be not envious of wrongdoers! For they will soon fade like the grass and wither like the green herb."* (Psalm 37:1)

Stop fretting. According to Dictionary.com, the word "fret" can be used as both a noun and a verb. As a noun, it means, "an irritated state of mind; annoyance; vexation." As a verb, to fret is "to feel or express worry, annoyance, discontent, or the like."[47] If a person is fretting, much or all of their mental energies are focused on a subject that irritates them and causes them to worry. And the sad thing about it is that, even though it requires a great deal of thought, taking up a lot of space in one's head, it doesn't really accomplish anything positive.

Indeed, another definition of "fret" as a verb is "to cause corrosion; gnaw into something." This definition isn't meant to apply to fretting as a mental process, but it does a pretty good job of describing its effects. Constantly focusing on something that leads to a state of discontent, worry, irritation, annoyance, and vexation sounds like corrosive material gnawing into our mind. And just as corrosion on the surface of metal weakens it and can cause it to break, fretting can actually weaken our ability to think clearly and, over periods of time, can even lead us into a mental breakdown!

So the first step on the path to peace with God is to stop fretting. Instead of letting your thoughts and emotions run your life, you need to use your will to choose what is occupying space in your head. This change may prove challenging at first, especially if your worries have had free rein in your mind for a while and have become a pattern or a habit. But it can be done. How? Through strength of your will power? No, that's not possible. But you can

---

[47] Source: **www.dictionary.com** (2020).

do it with the help of Christ, who pointed out to His disciples that, "with God, ALL things are possible" (Matthew 19:26, *emphasis added*).

(I have further personal experience related to the concept of not fretting that you may find useful at the end of this teaching.)

2.   *"Trust in the Lord and do good; dwell in the land and befriend faithfulness"* (Psalm 37:3).

Now that you have worked to stop fretting, it is time to turn to God with the situation that has been disturbing you. Hand it over to Him and begin to move into a place of trust. Look to Him as the one who is all powerful and loves you with a love beyond comprehension. Reflect on times in your past where He has brought you through difficulties and has shown Himself faithful. Read examples in Scripture where God has brought people through incredibly challenging situations, such as Daniel or Joseph. Meditate on Scripture verses that remind us of God's faithful character.

Meditating on this part of God's personality allows you to "dwell" there, as this Scripture suggests. Before this, you have been living in a place of anxiety. Now you are beginning to reside in a place of trust.

Something that can be very helpful during this stage is to speak God's promises out loud. In the third chapter of James, the author writes that our tongue is like the rudder on a boat or the bit in a horse's mouth. Both are small instruments but yield great power (Jam 3:4-5). Whichever way you turn the rudder, that's the direction the boat goes. Pulling on the reins connected to the bit in a horse's mouth causes the animal to go in that direction. Likewise, our tongues are very small, but have the power to turn our life in whatever direction it leads. If you speak Godly, faith-filled words, you will find you have the power to turn your life toward faith.

Therefore, you can say things like, "I will trust in the Lord with all my heart and not lean on my own understanding. In all my ways I will acknowledge Him, and He will direct my paths" (based on Proverbs 3:5-6). Or "I will put my trust in you Lord, for you never forsake those who seek you" (based on Psalm 9:10).

Taking the truth of God's word and changing it into a confession we speak over our lives and about ourselves is one of our most powerful tools. It is literally like reprogramming our mind to be sensitive to God and follow His voice. As you practice this with God's word, you will find your faith and confidence in God growing and becoming real. This practice prepares you for the next step.

294

3.   *"Delight yourself in the Lord, and he will give you the desires of your heart"* (Psalm 37:4).

Now that you have worked against fretting and moved into a place of trust, you are positioned to begin praising the Lord. Worship is a powerful force. Indeed, we are told that God dwells in the praises of His people! (Psalm 22:3) When we are honoring God, focusing on how wonderful He is, singing to Him, speaking highly of Him, our words are actually vessels carrying the power of God into the situation we face. This is a great place to practice gratitude. No matter how awful a situation may be, you can always find things for which to be thankful. There is so much to be thankful for. This is one path to expressing delight in the Lord!

Another way to delight yourself in God is to reflect upon the goodness of God. This is a great place, again, to find Scriptures that speak to the subject and reflect on them and speak them out loud. This could include scriptures like:

•   *The Lord, the Lord God, merciful and gracious, longsuffering, and abounding in goodness and truth* (Exodus 34:6).

•   *Oh, give thanks to the Lord, for He is good! For His mercy endures forever* (1 Chronicles 16:34).

•   *Good and upright is the Lord* (Psalm 25:8).

•   *Surely goodness and mercy shall follow me all the days of my life; and I will dwell in the house of the Lord forever* (Psalm 23:6).

As you delight in the Lord, His presence becomes more real in your life and you are further empowered to put away fretting (Step 1) and move into trust (Step 2). Then you are ready to move into the next step on the path to peace.

(I have some personal notes on gratitude at the end of this teaching)

4.   *"Commit your way to the Lord, trust in Him and he will act"* (Psalm 37:5).

This verse also has the word "trust" in it (see Step 2), and it's not surprising because the two are closely related. In this step, you take the situation that you have been fretting about and you not only hand it over to God, but you release all of your expectations and desires about how you want it to work out. You give God permission to do whatever He wants to do in this situation. You are releasing control of the situation to God. You turn it over to Him.

This release of control may sound really hard, but if you have prepared your heart in the other three steps, it should fall naturally into place. Because you are no longer worried and are, instead, trusting God and delighting in God, you now find yourself in a place where you can completely let go of the matter. A good verse to reflect on here is one that is known by most Christians: *"And we know that for those who love God all things work together for good, for those who are called according to his purpose"* (Romans 8:28). This is a huge step that leads us to the place we are created to be, the place we long to be.

5.   *"Be still before the Lord, and wait patiently for Him…"* (Psalm 37:7a)

The NASB translates this verse as "Rest in the Lord…" These are both good translations, but "rest" seems to speak more clearly about our inner state. You are not just still in body; you are still in your mind and emotions. You are "at rest." This has been the Lord's goal for us throughout this process. He desires to take you into an experience where you are totally at peace in Him. No situation or circumstance can disturb you. This place is where you can really get to know the Lord more deeply because you are quiet before Him. The "static" in your thoughts and feelings to which you have grown accustomed are no longer there. You are now perfectly positioned to sense His presence and hear His voice. And then, having completed the cycle, you move back to Step 1.

6.   *"Fret not yourself…"* (Psalm 37:7b).

You have now come full circle. You have deepened your experience with the Lord, and you have a path to follow whenever the anxious thoughts you have dismissed try to come back, or new ones try to intrude. You simply start the cycle over again. You repeat the cycle again and again. Put off fretting. Move into trust. Spend time rejoicing. Commit every element of your situation to God. And remain in the state of rest and peace. Begin consciously practicing this series of steps on a regular basis and you will soon find that anxiety, worry, and fear are fading away and being replaced with a deep abiding sense of peace and calm. This is the state that we were created to experience throughout life. It is the place where we are free to encounter God and learn more of Him and of His ways. It is the place where we begin to experience the Lord's promise of "abundant life" (John 10:10).

When I read through the Psalm 37 book in prison, I felt as if God was speaking directly to me. This was what He wanted me to do with my need to be transferred out of Tyrell. He wanted me to lay my cares down and embrace this as a way to walk in peace with Him. And that's exactly what I did. Step by step, I walked through the Psalm 37 path. And when I was done, I had a peace I had never known. I knew that, if I needed to, I could stay at Tyrell the entire time I was incarcerated, and that I could do so peacefully.

That was a remarkable shift in my view of the situation, and further evidence at the time that God was really doing a major work of transformation in my life. But what happened next was truly amazing and has had a dramatic impact on how I understand God's workings in our lives.

I read the book and offered up my anxiety to God on a Friday. Three days later, on the following Monday, I was talking to my Mom on the phone and she was very excited. She said that her cousin in the state legislature had called her back and said he had talked with the North Carolina Bureau of Prisons and they had agreed to move me.

So deep had been the work that God had done in my life through Psalm 37, I didn't respond emotionally. In fact, I suspected that it would take a good bit of time to move me, if it happened at all. And I was totally okay with that!

But as my mother and I talked, I heard an announcement come over the loudspeaker. Because I was on the phone, I didn't hear it clearly. But I thought it sounded like they were calling my name to come to the office. I dismissed the notion and kept talking. But a few minutes later, the speaker came on again and I clearly heard, "Steve Parker, report to the central office." I wrapped up my talk with Mom and went to the office.

When I got there, I received unexpected good news: "You're being transferred to Haywood County tomorrow. Get your belongings packed and be ready to go in the morning." I was stunned and elated all at the same time! Had God really moved this quickly?

He had indeed! The next day I made the trip across the state into the mountains of Western North Carolina. Haywood Correctional was the opposite of Tyrell. It was a small facility with air conditioning and good-natured guards. It was still prison, but my life became much better at this point.

A couple observations came to me during this season. The first was that inner transformation precedes a change in circumstances. The peace I was now experiencing in Haywood County was merely the outer manifestation of what had happened in my interior world. I had made room for the Kingdom of God in my inner life, and, like leaven, it had expanded into my outer world (Matthew 13:33).

Secondly, I came to see that the difficult seasons in life are necessary, but God allows them to be there for a purpose. Once the purpose is accomplished, He removes the difficulty. Just as a good parent wouldn't inflict discipline beyond the needed correction, God has no desire to see His children suffer, UNLESS it is working something positive in our life. Find out what that is, work with God to accomplish it, and the length and severity of challenging times can be diminished.

<u>Personal notes on "not fretting"</u>: For me, stopping to fret about finding a way out of Tyrell County came easily, but only because God had already been working in my life to help take control of my thoughts. In Romans 12:2, we are told to *"be transformed by the renewing of your mind."* Soon after recommitting my life to Christ in prison, I had found that my mind really needed to be renewed. It needed to be renewed A LOT! My memory was filled with sinful images and experiences that could pop up at any time. For me, that was one of the biggest challenges I had faced in beginning to live a pure life for Christ.

What I had found to be helpful was to first of all recognize that I couldn't accomplish this in my own power. The images and memories in my mind were too powerful and plentiful to get rid of in my own strength. In fact, I think this is one of the reasons that many people give up on trying to live for Christ. They are trying to "be good" by sheer will power. That approach is often not very helpful!

A scripture verse that God made very real to me during this time was James 4:6 - *"God opposes the proud, but gives grace to the humble."* Whenever I tried to rely on my own strength to change my life, I was actually being proud, elevating myself and my ability to achieve. Rather than help me accomplish my goal, this attitude actually pushed God away.

However, by being humble, by acknowledging my powerlessness before God and crying out to Him for help, I was actually drawing His presence to me and enabling grace. I pictured the experience like that of two magnets. When you face magnets toward each other with similar poles facing each other, they push each other apart. This was what happened when I tried to take charge of my thoughts with my own power. My strength faced God's strength and we were pushed apart. But when I humbled myself and reached out to God for His help, it was as if the magnet had been flipped and now the opposite poles drew each other near! My weakness drew His strength to me.

So what does it look like to turn to God for help in controlling your thoughts? I found out that timing was very important. As soon as I realized that I was thinking about something that didn't belong in my head, I would cry out to the Lord. Sometimes this was an actual physical cry, something like "Jesus, help me!" And I found that, when I did that, I was able to easily turn my thoughts to something else that was not offensive to God. Often, this might be a prayer, or a scripture I had recently memorized. Or it might just be a thought about something pleasant going on in my life. In any event, the troublesome thought was gone.

However, if I didn't turn to God for help right away, and I took time to reflect upon the thought or memory, it was as if it had time to dig into my mind and take root.   This often led to more offensive thoughts and, sometimes, offensive words and actions. But rather than get down on myself when this happened, I simply confessed it to God and asked for help to do the right thing the next time I had challenges in my mind.

The more I practiced this crying out to God, the easier it became. Soon, I didn't have to cry out so vehemently. Instead of a desperate plea for help, it became more like a gentle handoff. I simply passed the destructive thought to God and calmly shifting to something more productive.

This is the system I applied to my anxiety about leaving Tyrell Prison. I simply started calling out to God when I began worrying about the issue, and then handed the thought off to him. Fortunately, I had developed this into a pretty useful skill by this point, so it didn't take too much time to getting rid of my fretful, worrisome, anxiety-ridden thinking.

Personal notes on gratitude: To cultivate an attitude of thanksgiving in my prison situation, instead of focusing on the things I hated, I began to look at how blessed I was. I was in prison, yes, but I had a roof over my head, food to eat, and clothes to wear. I was better off than a good number of people around the world.   Further, I had access to a Bible, books to read, and Christian brothers to fellowship with. I had family members who loved me and sent me money. I was growing in my relationship with Christ! By focusing on my blessings rather than what I hated, I was able to experience much greater gratitude in my heart.

[Steve Parker is the President and Founder of FOCHUS Ministries (**www.fochus.org**). He can be contacted at steve.parker@fochus.org.]

APPENDIX B

FULL INDEX OF DEVOTIONS

Week Four: Faith – Pleasing God

Day 1: *Love is our destination. Faith is the fuel to get us there.*

Day 2: *Faith during our journey is God's work.*

Day 3: *Faith during our journey is God's work.*

Day 4: *Without faith, it is impossible to please Him.*

Day 5: *"I always do the things that are pleasing to Him."*

Day 6: *You are accepted by God.*

Day 7: *Review – Faith – Pleasing God*

Week Five: Faith – Endurance

Day 1: *It is a marathon, not a sprint.*

Day 2: *I trust You, O my God, at all times and in all places.*

Day 3: *What happened to Job, the servant of the Lord?*

Day 4: *What does it mean to be sifted like wheat?*

Day 5: *Was Judas Iscariot braver than Peter?*

Day 6: *Examine yourselves!*

Day 7: *Review – Faith - Endurance*

Week Six: Faith and Hope – Rebirth

Day 1: *Faith is the assurance of things that we hope for.*

Day 2: *In hope, he believed against hope.*

Day 3: *Hope that is seen is not hope.*

Day 4: *"No, my lord, I am a woman troubled in spirit."*

Day 5: *"My heart exults in the Lord; my horn is exalted in the Lord."*

Day 6: *He looked on me, to take away my reproach among people.*

Day 7: *Review – Faith and Hope - Rebirth*

Week Seven: Hope Builders

Day 1: *A sure and steadfast anchor of the soul.*

Day 2: *"That...through the encouragement of scriptures, we might have hope."*

Day 3: *So they [the next generation] should set their hope in God.*

Day 4: *God acts with righteousness.*

Day 5: *God is the God of the future.*

Day 6: *Glory just ahead!*

Day 7: *Review – Hope Builders*

Week Eight: Love and Hope

Day 1: *Dare to hope.*

Day 2: *"But this I call to mind and therefore I have hope."*

Day 3: *He loved us first.*

Day 4: *"Son, I love you!"*

Day 5: *When he saw him and felt compassion, he ran and embraced him and kissed him.*

Day 6: *Rejoice with me for I have found my sheep that was lost.*

Day 7: *Review – Love and Hope*

Week Nine: Demonstrations of God's Love

Day 1: *God demonstrates His love for us.*

Day 2: *"Because the great love with which He loved us."*

Day 3: *Compassion.*

Day 4: *Why does God love His enemies?*

Day 5: *Mercy to a sinner.*

Day 6: *No condemnation.*

Day 7: *Review – Demonstrations of God's Love*

Week Ten: Receiving Love – Hindrances

Day 1: *How are you at receiving God's love?*

Day 2: *Our self sufficiency is a myth.*

Day 3: *Our performance does not earn the love of God.*

Day 4: *And he inflicted cruelties upon some of the people.*

Day 5: *Love is not arrogant.*

Day 6: *Love rejoices with the truth.*

Day 7: *Review – Receiving Love - Hindrances*

Week Eleven: Journey – Faith, Hope, and Love

Day 1: *Work of faith; labor of love; steadfastness of hope.*

Day 2: *The interworkings of faith, hope, and love.*

Day 3: *Hope is a bridge between faith and love.*

Day 4: *Encouragement provides a bridge of hope.*

Day 5: *Love to hope to faith. The reverse can also occur.*

Day 6: *The God of endurance and encouragement.*

Day 7: *Review – Journey – Faith, Hope, and Love*

Week Twelve: Overcoming With Joy

Day 1: *Love and faith empower us to overcome.*

Day 2: *That you may abound in hope.*

Day 3: *There is joy in the process.*

Day 4: *Gushing springs of joy.*

Day 5: *We are more than conquerors through Him who loved us.*

Day 6: *He will exult over you with loud singing.*

Day 7: *Review - He will quiet you by His love.*

Week Thirteen: Practicum - Loving God

Day 1: *The disciple whom Jesus loved.*

Day 2: *Devote yourself to the right master.*

Day 3: *Receiving love at the worst moments.*

Day 4: *Holding fast to Him in love.*

Day 5: *"It is the Lord!"*

Day 6: *"With all of their heart."*

Day 7: *Review – Practicum – Loving God*

SECTION II - SURRENDER

Week One: Surrender – Discipleship

Day 1: *I bow my knees before the Father.*

Day 2: *The conditions of discipleship.*

Day 3: *What does it mean to take up my cross?*

Day 4: *Thy kingdom come; Thy Will be done.*

Day 5: *And there followed Him a great multitude of people.*

Day 6: *Poor recruitment methods.*

Day 7: *Review – Surrender - Discipleship*

Week Two: Surrender – The Temptation

Day 1: *Spirit led.*

Day 2: *He was hungry.*

Day 3: *Sources of temptation.*

Day 4: *The pride of life.*

Day 5: *The means of sinful nature.*

Day 6: *Apples of gold in a setting of silver.*

Day 7: *Review - Today is a day of simplicity and rest.*

Week Three: Desire and Destiny

Day 1: *Called according to His purpose.*

Day 2: *He supposed that his brothers would understand that God was giving them salvation by his hand.*

Day 3: *Jesus emptied Himself.*

Day 4: *Jesus has a destiny.*

Day 5: *He will give you the desires of your heart.*

Day 6: *After all, He desires good things for us.*

Day 7: *Review – Desire and Destiny*

Week Four: Deny Yourself

Day 1: *Passions and desires.*

Day 2: *The desires of the flesh are against the Spirit.*

Day 3: *God gave them up to a debased mind.*

Day 4: *They worshiped and served the creature rather than the Creator.*

Day 5: *Worship in spirit and in truth.*

Day 6: *That which is born of the spirit is spirit.*

Day 7: *Review – Deny Yourself*

Week Five: Torment

Day 1: *The passions of the flesh wage war against your soul.*

Day 2: *His soul was vexed to death.*

Day 3: *A mess of pottage.*

Day 4: *Vexed and sullen.*

Day 5: *Consumed.*

Day 6: *Who will deliver me from this body of death?*

Day 7: *Review - Torment*

Week Six: Brokenness

Day 1: *But when he came to himself...*

Day 2: *Full dependence.*

Day 3: *Why is the heart of the Lord so close to the poor?*

Day 4: *Brokenness has value when the will is surrendered.*

Day 5: *Now which of them will love him more?*

Day 6: *Whatever is exciting pleases the will.*

Day 7: *Review – The Beatitudes*

Week Seven: Indifference

Day 1: *He has nothing in Me.*

Day 2: *The role of created things.*

Day 3: *Let Him do to me what seems good to Him.*

Day 4: *Shall we receive good from God, and shall we not receive evil?*

Day 5: *She out of her poverty put in all she had to live on.*

Day 6: *Life cut short.*

Day 7: *Review - Indifference*

Week Eight: Comfort – Things

Day 1: *They stagger...they reel...they stumble.*

Day 2: *Disheartened by the saying, he went away sorrowful, for he had great possessions.*

Day 3: *Soul, you have ample goods laid up for many years.*

Day 4: *We behaved in the world with simplicity and sincerity.*

Day 5: *Now the sons of Eli were worthless men.*

Day 6: *Delight yourselves in rich food!*

Day 7: *Review – Comfort - Things*

Week Nine: Comfort – People

Day 1: *Now Solomon clung to these in love.*

Day 2: *Amnon was so tormented that he made himself ill.*

Day 3: *Son of man…I am about to take the delight of your eyes.*

Day 4: *We have left everything and followed You.*

Day 5: *When I sit in darkness, the Lord will be a light to me.*

Day 6: *How can you believe when…?*

Day 7: *Review – Comfort - People*

Week Ten: Truth – Inner Being

Day 1: *Buy truth and do not sell it.*

Day 2: *There was no one so much to be praised for his handsome appearance.*

Day 3: *But the thing that David had done displeased the Lord.*

Day 4: *"You are the man!"*

Day 5: *A man who looks intently at his natural face in a mirror.*

Day 6: *If anyone thinks he is religious and does not bridle his tongue but deceives his heart, this person's religion is worthless.*

Day 7: *Review – Truth – Inner Being*

Week Eleven: Surrender and Call

Day 1: *Let it be done to me according to your word.*

Day 2: *Here comes this dreamer.*

Day 3: *Go from your country and your kindred and your father's house.*

Day 4: *Choosing rather to be mistreated with the people of God than to enjoy the fleeting pleasures of sin.*

Day 5: *Let the one who is able to receive this receive it.*

Day 6: *For myself and my son, that we may eat of it and die.*

Day 7: *Review – Surrender and Call*

Week Twelve: Disordered Desires

Day 1: *"Simon, son of John, do you love Me more than these?"*

Day 2: *"Why then do you honor your sons above Me?"*

Day 3: *For though you have countless guides in Christ, you do not have many fathers.*

Day 4: *"My little finger is thicker than my father's thighs."*

Day 5: *Which means "son of encouragement."*

Day 6: *Tend My sheep.*

Day 7: *Review – Disordered Desires*

Week Thirteen: Practicum - Drip, Trickle, Flow

Day 1: *When the water flows into the sea, the water will become fresh.*

Day 2: *They have hewed out cisterns – broken cisterns that can hold no water.*

Day 3: *My soul thirsts for you.*

Day 4: *"If anyone thirsts, let him come to Me and drink."*

Day 5: *Worship in truth.*

Day 6: *David is thirsty for a certain type of water.*

Day 7: *As the Father has sent Me, even so I am sending you.*

APPENDIX C
INDEX OF SCRIPTURE PASSAGES
(Listed by book of the Bible with devotional page number)

OTHER BOOKS BY THE AUTHOR

(Available on Amazon.com and other online booksellers)

THE CALL series will help you identify God's call in your life and equip you to fulfill that call. God calls His people to live under His kingship and to participate in His work. God's call is His imprint on you and on your life. You need to understand God's special purpose for your life.

Formatted as work books for use in ministry training programs, THE CALL series is written in a progression. This first book, *THE CALL (Book One – Functional)*, describes a discipleship progression designed for maximum impact. In Book One, you will learn how to:
- ✓ Create a model for exponential spiritual reproduction
- ✓ Operate ministry with lasting results
- ✓ Share truth in a manner that hits home
- ✓ Equip others for ministry through shared experience
- ✓ Help other disciples realize and fulfill their call

Endorsements of THE CALL series:

"THE CALL series is steeped in powerful Biblical truth, profound insights derived from decades of personal ministry experiences, and is directly applicable in your personal life and ministry environments. David's brilliant mind, heart for making disciples, and intimacy with God are earthed in these pages. We at Missionary Athletes International have utilized this great work for years as a cornerstone for our curriculum in our one-year Residency Training Program. THE CALL is essential to our success and will catalyze yours as well."
DAVID SANFORD
US Director, Missionary Athletes International

"THE CALL books have been very influential for myself and our staff with I AM 24/7. After personally going through David's books a number of years back, I remember having the thought that if I ever was responsible for leading a church or ministry that I would use them as a part of training staff and include the revelatory teachings on the "Cycle of Discipleship" as part of our core values for training up Godly leaders. When my wife and I co-founded an urban ministry in Charlotte, NC, David was one of my first calls. We took our young staff through the books and David met with them weekly during a summer Residency program during our first 2 years of operation. THE CALL books and his teachings helped solidify a solid foundation of Biblical understanding on effective discipleship ministry, operating under authority, understanding spiritual gifts, and defining individual call for each of the young men in our program. Ephesians 4:12 declares the duty of the church is to "equip the saints for works of ministry." In light of the lack of equipping of disciples of Christ in the American church today, I pray that the Lord would continue to use THE CALL books as a voice in the desert, calling the body of Christ to a new level of power and influence one disciple at a time. I am forever grateful for my good friend, David Thurman, and his humble devotion to his own call and the role his example and legacy left in the pages of these books has played in my personal walk with the Lord and the ministry I serve."
BEN PAGE
President and Co-founder, I AM 24/7 Ministries

"THE CALL series provides experience-based practices and Christ-centered teaching to equip the urban missionary who seeks to advance the Kingdom of God in their unique setting. I have personally partnered with the author, David Thurman, in applying this material while working within the refugee community of Charlotte, NC. It is effective and life-changing."
STEVE PARKER
President and Founder, FOCHUS Ministries

OTHER BOOKS BY THE AUTHOR

(Available on Amazon.com and other online booksellers)

THE CALL series is written in a progression. The first book, *THE CALL (Book One – Functional)*, described important discipleship principles. This second book, *THE CALL (Book Two – Foundational)*, shows how the fivefold gifts operate in a progression to train, equip and mature the Body of Christ. In Book Two, you will learn how to:

- ✓ Apply key principles of God's authority to your life and ministry
- ✓ Identify God's call on your life
- ✓ Function in the context of the fivefold gifts in the way that God intended
- ✓ Discern and replicate the Cycle of Discipleship to maturity
- ✓ Operate effectively in a body context to maximize the potential of its members

OTHER BOOKS BY THE AUTHOR

(Available on Amazon.com and other online booksellers)

THE CALL series is written to train workers in the kingdom. The second book, *THE CALL (Book Two – Foundational)*, showed how the fivefold gifts operate within the Cycle of Discipleship to train, equip and mature the Body of Christ. This third book, *THE CALL (Book Three – Fruitful)*, explores God's call in a corporate context. In Book Three, you will learn how to:

- ✓ Discern the heart of God for the world around you
- ✓ Survey your community for needs and resources
- ✓ Change the culture of the people around you
- ✓ Cast a vision to your church or ministry for transformational action
- ✓ Implement a plan to bring the kingdom of God to your area

OTHER BOOKS BY THE AUTHOR

(Available on Amazon.com and other online booksellers)

DOD KNOWS chronicles the story of Jimmy Stuckey, an undisciplined five year old boy with Down's Syndrome, who was taken into the Martin home because no one else wanted him. What started as temporary foster care for a few days turned into fifty years of fun, laughter, and unpredictability.

DOD KNOWS details the trials and challenges of raising a strong willed but tenderhearted Down's Syndrome child in a large family, and the joys and misadventures of a fun-seeking and oh so competitive young man. Jimmy was raised as the author's uncle and as the brother of Pastor Daniel Martin. What the family did not realize is the huge impact and the marvelous blessing that Jimmy would bring to the Martin family and to every other person that came into contact with him!

"DOD KNOWS" was one of Jimmy's many sayings. When something happened that Jimmy did not understand or that confused him, Jimmy simply held up his hands, shrugged his shoulders, and said "Dod knows" (God knows). And, as in many things, Jimmy was right!

For more information on these books, go to: **www.surrenderandtrust.net** (Note: .net).

Made in the USA
Columbia, SC
22 December 2021

50473084R00187